Social Semantics

SEMANTIC WEB AND BEYOND
Computing for Human Experience

Series Editors:

Ramesh Jain
University of California, Irvine
http://ngs.ics.uci.edu/

Amit P. Sheth
Wright State University
http://knoesis.wright.edu/amit/

As computing becomes ubiquitous and pervasive, computing is increasingly becoming an extension of human, modifying or enhancing human experience. Todays car reacts to human perception of danger with a series of computers participating in how to handle the vehicle for human command and environmental conditions. Proliferating sensors help with observations, decision making as well as sensory modifications. The emergent semantic web will lead to machine understanding of data and help exploit heterogeneous, multi-source digital media. Emerging applications in situation monitoring and entertainment applications are resulting in development of experiential environments.

SEMANTIC WEB AND BEYOND
Computing for Human Experience
addresses the following goals:

➢ brings together forward looking research and technology that will shape our world more intimately than ever before as computing becomes an extension of human experience;
➢ covers all aspects of computing that is very closely tied to human perception, understanding and experience;
➢ brings together computing that deal with semantics, perception and experience;
➢ serves as the platform for exchange of both practical technologies and far reaching research.

For further volumes:
www.springer.com/series/7056

Harry Halpin

Social Semantics

The Search for Meaning on the Web

Foreword by Henry S. Thompson

 Springer

Harry Halpin
Computer Science and W3C/CSAIL
 Laboratory
Massachusetts Institute of Technology
Cambridge, MA, USA

ISSN 1559-7474
ISBN 978-1-4899-8946-8   ISBN 978-1-4614-1885-6 (eBook)
DOI 10.1007/978-1-4614-1885-6
Springer New York Heidelberg Dordrecht London

Printed on acid-free paper

Springer is part of Springer Science+Business Media (www.springer.com)

I dedicate this thesis to my father and mother, Harry Halpin Sr. and Rebecca Halpin. One must always remember that our parents knew us before we even knew ourselves.

Foreword

The World Wide Web demands our attention, not only in terms of its role as a major contributor to the increasing centrality of technology in society, but also in purely scientific terms.

To say that the Web is ubiquitous, at least in the so-called developed world, is commonplace to the point of vacuity. But ubiquity alone doesn't require scientific exploration. After all, paved roads are ubiquitous (and socially important) too, but they don't engender a lot of scientific interest. What makes the scientific study of the Web attractive is the unique nature of the thing that binds the Web together, that actually makes it a Web: the Uniform Resource Identifier, or URI. What makes this study urgently *necessary* is the huge economic and social pressure behind innovation on the Web, and the resulting stresses on its foundational technologies.

If we don't have clear and explanatory theories of these technologies, we are at real risk of breaking the Web by accident. Different sectors of Web usage are pushing the technology in different directions, and without care there is no guarantee that the result will remain coherent, not only intellectually, but literally. Interoperability is the *sine qua non* for a distributed architecture – if we lose that, we lose everything.

All of this makes the work reported here, and the unique combination of philosophical and experimental perspectives that it adopts, of very special value. As things stand today, theory and practice differ about the nature of URIs. By bringing multiple novel sources of insight to bear on the problem, this work offers real hope of progress towards bridging that gap, and giving us a sound basis for the future growth of the Web.

Edinburgh, UK   Henry S. Thompson

Preface

There may seem to be no more abstract and theoretical pursuit that the study of *meaning* itself. There's even no a priori reason why individual 'minds' should be capable of understanding how meaning somehow exists in a world that is - at least according to the more mature science of physics – ultimately atomic in nature. Yet far from feeling alone in a world devoid of meaning, I take it for granted that we strive in a rich social world that is overflowing with undiscovered facets. The Web is the universal method of intertwingling and sharing these facets with each other. Representations are the texture of our life on the Web. Even if the task is impossible, the calling is worthwhile. Across the Mediterranean, I find the courage of Egypt contagious as I follow their digital photos and text in my Web browser.

A friend once said that the world is not composed of atoms, it is composed of stories. So this book can be considered the trace of my particular story. The story I am telling in this book is not exactly the story I had hoped to tell as a graduate student. This book is to a large extent a reworked and highly edited version of my thesis, and as such suffers from the problems that any thesis has, namely that the studies it comprises were done as small shots in the dark in order to reveal some aspect of a much more sophisticated question. There is much to be done, like formalizing a computational theory of sense and evaluating such a theory. At the time of writing these studies I did not have access to the Web-scale data-sets or processing power needed to formulate a testable theory of social semantics, and as I sit here in Yahoo! Research, I cannot but be amazed by the fact that I have an entire copy of the Web accessible from my desktop. Looking back, the idea of social semantics came upon me in a visit to Amsterdam when I first arrived in Europe: meaning is not something we possess alone, but something we create together. To this day, I still cannot think of a better way to phrase the hypothesis of social semantics.

Barcelona, Spain   Harry Halpin

Acknowledgements

The majority of this book was written as my thesis *Sense and Reference on the Web* at the University of Edinburgh, so this book would not have been possible without the support of my community of friends and colleagues across the globe and in Edinburgh. In particular, this thesis would not have been possible had it not been for the unwavering support of my advisor, Henry S. Thompson, who encouraged me to pursue considering Web architecture a first-rate citizen of inquiry, a brave act few advisors would have been willing to do. I would also like to thank Andy Clark for philosophical inspiration and Victor Lavrenko for his invaluable help on the empirical evaluation. Conversations and support from other colleagues at Edinburgh have been important. However, even more support has come from the global community of Web hackers and Semantic Web researchers. I have been particularly privileged to have had numerous discussions with Pat Hayes and Tim Berners-Lee on these subjects, and I hope I have accurately given an exegesis of their debate. My time at Duke, where I was fortunate enough to study under Fredric Jameson and Michael Hardt, has had a decisive if subterranean influence on this book. Various friends and co-authors deserve my gratitude. In particular, I would like to single out Rob Didham, Kavita Thomas, Dan Connolly, Brandon Jourdan, Jochen Leidner, Maciej Zurawski, Priya Reddy, Malamo Korbetis, Claire Grover, Richard Tobin, Peter Buneman, Phil Wadler, Valentin Robu, Jonathan Oppenheimer, Michael Wheeler, Laura Gomez, Dirk Bollen, Hana Shepard, Dan Brickley, Orit Halpern, Paolo Bouquet, Nicholas and Rita Tishuk, Ras Al-Majnuun, Alexandre Monnin, Arturo Escobar, and everyone in Bilston, the Forest Cafe, and Carrboro. Particular acknowledgments must be given to Brian and Mooness Davarian, both of whom masterfully proofread the entire book. Others shall not be named to protect the innocent. Lastly, I have found intellectually invaluable my time at the Santa Fe Institute, the Oxford Internet Institute, the Island seminar with Brian Cantwell Smith, and the Interface Seminar at Duke University – and more recently, my time with Peter Mika at Yahoo! Research Barcelona. Special gratitude must go to the late Karen Spärck Jones, who called me out of the blue and encouraged this strangely philosophical approach to information retrieval and semantics when I was first beginning.

Contents

Chapter 1
Introduction

> You have abandoned the old domain, the old concepts. Here you
> are in a new domain, for which new concepts will give you the
> knowledge. The sign that a real change in locus and problematic
> has occurred, and that a new adventure is beginning, the
> adventure of science in development.
>
> Louis Althusser *(1963)*

This book is an inquiry into representation. Given the almost impossibly wide
scope of possible kinds of questions pertaining to representations, we will deploy
an analysis that is simultaneously both historical and scientific by restricting our
inquiry to an investigation of representations on the World Wide Web. Yet regardless
of our careful scoping, we will nonetheless be blindly driven into the realm of
semantics, the hard question of how meaning is assigned to representation – a
question that is as hard, it seems, as that of the more popular hard problem
of consciousness (Chalmers 1995). The nature of representation is no longer
fashionable to even pursue in philosophy or even in artificial intelligence; it is
a problem whose immensity overwhelms us. As a subject matter the apparent
phenomenon of *reference*, the suspiciously mysterious – and so perhaps even non-
existent! – connection between a representation and that which it represents, verges
upon the totality of our social relationship with the world. From Plato's Theory of
Forms to the evolution of representation in artificial life (Halpin 2006), science is
littered with theories of the semantics, all of which equally purport to solve this
thorny matter in one way or another. One would be forgiven in thinking, given the
lack of clear success of any theory so far, that perhaps the question is unscientific
or simply intractable in nature, yet that compels us with only a more irresistible
attraction.

At first glance, representation and semantics seem strangely old-fashioned,
particularly given the current enthusiasm for embodiment in cognitive science,
which in its more extreme versions leads to claims of "intelligence without representation" (Brooks 1991). Yet this fetish for embodiment may be strangely disciplinary

H. Halpin, *Social Semantics: The Search for Meaning on the Web*,
Semantic Web and Beyond 13, DOI 10.1007/978-1-4614-1885-6_1,
© Springer Science+Business Media New York 2013

and – although radical on the surface – actually ends up being a reactionary fad when viewed within the context of a larger landscape outside academic philosophy and cognitive science. In particular, computer science – with the exception of the peculiarly anthropomorphic line of research of artificial intelligence (AI) – does not seem to care about embodiment. In his *One Hundred Billion Lines of C++*, computer scientist-turned-philosopher Brian Cantwell Smith notes that in artificial intelligence, debates over representation tend to frame the debate as if it were between "classical" logic-based symbolic reasoners and some "connectionist" and "embodied" alternative ranging from neural networks to epigenetic robotics (1997). Smith then goes on to aptly state that the kinds of computational systems discussed in artificial intelligence and philosophy tend to ignore the vast majority of existing systems, for "it is impossible to make an exact estimate, but there are probably something on the order of 10^{11} – one hundred billion lines of C++, in the world. And we are barely started. In sum: symbolic AI systems constitute approximately 0.01% of written software" (1997). What Smith fails to mention is that the same small fraction likely holds true of "non-symbolic AI" computational systems such as robots, artificial life, and old-fashioned connectionist networks (an exception may soon be made for the machine-learning that runs phenomena such as advertising and search on the Web). As raw statistics of deployed systems by themselves hold little intellectual weight, no doubt a philosopher could argue that the vast majority of computational systems may have no impact on our understanding of representation and intelligence. In other words, what the vast majority of the planet is doing with computation and representation – which is increasingly focused on the World Wide Web – is simply intellectually uninteresting. In this book we argue otherwise.

Although one can easily deny that anything resembling digital representations exists 'inside the brain,' it is much harder to argue that there are no digital representations on the Web. As one clicks from web-page to web-page, it seems that the Web is nothing but a vast network of digital representations. The thesis of this book is that the wide class of computational systems outside of those traditionally considered by artificial intelligence or philosophy presents what Cantwell Smith calls a "middle distance" where questions of representation (and perhaps even intelligence) come to the forefront in a peculiarly obvious manner and are likely more tractable than they are for humans, given the relative complexity of computers and humans (Smith 1996). At the present moment, with all the totalizing attraction of a black hole, computational systems the world over are becoming part and parcel of the World Wide Web, described by Tim Berners-Lee – the person widely acclaimed to be the 'inventor' of the Web – as "a universal information space" (1992). We further argue that not only may the Web reveal general insights about the nature of representation, but its unique historical status as the first *actual* universal information space may prompt an entire re-thinking of semantics. When asked to consider this hypothesis, Michael Wheeler – a philosopher who is well-known for his Heideggerian defense of embodiment – surmises that "the power of the Web as a technological innovation is now beyond doubt" but "what is less well appreciated is the potential power of the Web to have a conceptual impact on cognitive science" and so the Web may provide a new "fourth way" in addition to the "three kinds of cognitive science or artificial intelligence: classical, connectionist, and (something like) embodied-embedded" (2008). While countless papers have been produced on the technical aspects of the Web, very little has been done explicitly on the Web *qua* Web as a subject matter of interest to philosophy. This does not mean there has not been interest, although the interest has come in particular more from the side of those engineers working on developing the Web rather than those already entrenched in philosophy, linguistics, and artificial intelligence (Halpin et al. 2006; Bouquet et al. 2007 2008). In this spirit, what we will undertake in this thesis as a whole is to apply many well-known philosophical theories of reference and representation to the phenomenon of the Web, and see which theory survives – and finally, if the Web points a way to a *new* theory of semantics, which we surmise may be a social semantics.

1.1 Scope

The World Wide Web is without a doubt one of the most significant computational phenomena to date. Yet there are some questions that cannot be answered without a *theoretical* understanding of the Web. Although the Web is impressive as a practical success story, there has been little in the way of developing a theoretical framework to understand what – if anything – is different about the Web from the standpoint of long-standing questions of representation and semantics in philosophy. While this situation may have been tolerable so far, serving as no real barrier to the further growth of the Web, with the development of the Semantic Web, a next generation of the Web "in which information is given well-defined meaning, better enabling computers and people to work in cooperation," these philosophical questions come to the forefront, and only a practical solution to them can help the Semantic Web repeat the success of the hypertext Web (Berners-Lee et al. 2001). At this moment, there is little doubt that the Semantic Web faces gloomy prospects – and perhaps for good reason. On first inspection, the Semantic Web appears to be a close cousin to another intellectual project, known politely as 'classical artificial intelligence' (also known as 'Good-Old Fashioned AI') an ambitious project whose progress has been relatively glacial and whose assumptions have been found to be cognitively questionable (Clark 1997). The initial bet of the Semantic Web was that somehow the *Web* part of the Semantic Web would somehow overcome whatever problems the Semantic Web inherited from classical artificial intelligence, in particular, its reliance on logic and inference as the basis of meaning (Halpin 2004).

This thesis is explicitly limited in scope, concentrating only on the terminology necessary to phrase a single, if broad, question: How can we determine the meaning of a Uniform Resource Identifier (a URI, such as http://www.example.org) on the Web? Although the thesis is interdisciplinary, as it involves elements as diverse as the philosophy of language and machine-learning, these elements are only harnessed insofar as they are necessary to phrase our central thesis and present a possible solution. Due to constraining ourselves to the scope of the Web and the topic of representation, this thesis is not an attempt to develop a philosophy of computation (Smith 2002), or a philosophy of information (Floridi 2004), or even a comprehensive "philosophy of the Web" (Halpin 2008b). These are much larger projects than can fit within the scope of a single book or even a single individual's life-long calling. However, in combination with more fully-formed work in philosophy, we hope that at least this book provides a starting point for future work in these areas. So we use notions from philosophy selectively, and then define the terms in lieu of our goal of articulating the principles of Web architecture and the Semantic Web, rather than attempting to articulate or define the terms of a systematic philosophy or with reference to the many arguments over these terms in analytic philosophy. Many of the terms in this thesis could be explored much further, but by virtue of our scoping are not explored, as to constrain the book to a reasonable size. Unlike a philosophical work, in this book counter-arguments and arguments are generally not given for terminological definitions, but instead references are given to the key works that explicate these terms further.

This thesis does not inspect every single possible answer to the question of *What is the meaning of a URI?*, but only three distinct positions. An inspection of every possible theory of meaning and reference is beyond the scope of the thesis, as is an inspection of the tremendous secondary literature that has accrued over the years. Instead, we will focus only on theories of meaning and representation that have been brought up explicitly in the various arguments over this question by the primary architects of the Web and the Semantic Web. Our proposed solution of social semantics rests on a theory of meaning, a neo-Wittgensteinian theory, that is one of the most infamously dense and infuriatingly obscure theories of meaning.

Finally, while the experimental component of this book has done its best to be realistic, it is in no way complete. Pains have been taken to ensure that experiments, unlike much work in the Semantic Web, at least uses real data and users, and are properly evaluated over a range of algorithms and parameters. Our work on tagging systems takes its data from a real system, *del.icio.us*, as well. While various parts of the experiments could no doubt be optimized and scaled up still further, these experiments should be sufficient to motivate our movement towards social semantics, although a full formalization of such a theory and testing of it would require access to the data of a large-scale search engine such as Google, which for the time being is outside of scope. For future work, we would like to pursue the formalization and large-scale testing of social semantics.

1.2   Summary

The thesis of this book must be stated in a twofold fashion: first to analyze the problem, and then to propose a solution. To analyze the problem of representation on the Web, one must ask the question: **What is the meaning of a URI?** First, we will clarify the problem that the Web is a kind of new language that can be defined by its engineering conformance to the principles of Web architecture, but nonetheless inherits problems regarding sense and reference from the philosophy of natural language. So there is no easy way out of the hard question of representation. Our proposed answer is then that only a theory of representation and semantics that takes into account the socially grounded use of a multiplicity of representations is sufficient to provide the meaning of a representation on the Web, from which the meaning of a peculiar URI can be derived. In essence, we turn the question on its head; instead of saying that a URI can have its meaning only by virtue of what representations can be accessed from it, we instead say that the network of representations and their use provides the meaning of a URI. Thanks must be given to co-authors for letting me expand upon our earlier findings and re-use our earlier words. The term 'we' is deployed in order to acknowledge their contributions. Note that all previously published versions of work in this book have been edited, amended, and otherwise expanded.

In order to orient the reader to the Web, we give an extended introduction to its history and its architecture in Chap. 2, while introducing the philosophical terminology in concert with examples from the Web. In Chap. 3 we propose that the Semantic Web, as embodied by the Resource Description Framework (RDF), is a kind of URI-based knowledge representation language for data integration and illustrate it by providing the elements of Web architecture in terms of a formal Semantic Web ontology. The ontology in particular is joint work with Valentina Presutti, whose latest version is published as *The identity of resources on the Web: An ontology for Web architecture* in the journal *Applied Ontology* Halpin and Presutti (2011). These works have in earlier forms been published as *An Ontology of Resources: Solving the Identity Crisis* (Halpin and Presutti 2009) with Valentina Presutti and my early essay *The Semantic Web: The Origins of Artificial Intelligence Redux* (Halpin 2004).

In Chap. 4 we illustrate the crisis of the Semantic Web: There is no answer to the aforementioned question of how to assign meaning to a URI. There are at least two distinct positions to this question on the Semantic Web, each corresponding to a distinct philosophical theory of semantics. The first response is the ***logicist position***, which states that *the meaning of a URI is determined by whatever model(s) satisfy the formal semantics of the Semantic Web* (Hayes 2004). This answer is identified with both the formal semantics of the Semantic Web itself and the traditional Russellian theory of names and its descriptivist descendants (Russell 1905). While this answer may be sufficient for automated inference engines, this answer is insufficient for humans, as it often crucially under-determines what kind of things the URI identifies. As the prevailing position in early Semantic Web research, this position has borne little fruit. Another response is the ***direct reference position*** for the Web, which states that *the meaning of a URI is whatever was intended by the owner.* This answer is identified with the intuitive understanding of many of the original Web architects like Berners-Lee and a special case of Putnam's 'natural kind' theory of meaning. This position is also a near relative to Kripke's famous response to Russell (Kripke 1972; Putnam 1975). Further positions that have been marginal to the debate on the Web, such as that of semiotics, are not explored.

A much shorter version of this work has been previously published as *Sense and Reference on the Web* in the journal *Minds and Machines* (Halpin 2011).

Then we dive from the heights of theory to the depths of experimental work. In Chap. 5 we begin the exploration of an alternative form of discovering the meaning of a representation, namely that of 'bottom-up' collaborative tagging systems, where users simply 'tag' a resource with a term they find useful or descriptive and so define the 'sense' of a URI as a set of terms. We commit a number of experiments to determine if these tags converge over time and over a diversity of resources. Then in Chap. 6 we extend this exploration to search engines, considering the 'bag-of-words' produced by a document to be equivalent to a set of tags, and therefore the sense of the URI. In particular, we explore this using documents from both the Semantic Web and the hypertext Web, and use relevance models to combine them. The study of tagging was previously published as *The Complex Dynamics of Collaborative Tagging* in *ACM Transactions on the Web* co-authored with Valentin Robu and Hana Shepard (Halpin et al. 2007; Robu et al. 2009), while the user study was co-authored with Dirk Bollen as *An Experimental Analysis of Suggestions in Collaborative Tagging* (Bollen and Halpin 2009). A few elements of the study of search engines and relevance feedback was previously published as *Relevance Feedback between Web Search and the Semantic Web* with Victor Lavrenko, who co-wrote some of the text and the equations (Halpin and Lavrenko 2011b) with a longer version published as a journal article entitled *Relevance feedback between hypertext and Semantic Web search: Frameworks and Evaluation* in the *Journal of Web Semantics* (Halpin and Lavrenko 2011a).

We finally turn to formulate a third position in Chap. 7, **social semantics**, which states that since the Web *is a form of language, and as language exists as a public mechanism among multiple agents, then the meaning of a URI is determined by the socially-grounded use of networks of representations on the Web by ordinary users*. As vague as this position seems at first glance, we argue this analysis of meaning and representation is the best fit to how natural language works, and it supersedes and even subsumes the two other positions. Furthermore, it goes beyond a certain quietism about natural language attributed to Wittgenstein as well as a certain belief in the occult powers of some 'mental' lexicon. Ideas in this version were previously published with Andy Clark and Michael Wheeler as *Towards a Philosophy of the Web: Representation, Enaction, Collective Intelligence* (Halpin et al. 2010). The entire Ph.D. thesis was submitted and approved to University of Edinburgh, with Yorick Wilks being the external examiner, as *Sense and Reference on the Web* (Halpin 2009b), with the precis being published with Henry S. Thompson as *Social Meaning on the Web: From Wittgenstein to Search Engines* in *IEEE Intelligent Systems* (Halpin and Thompson 2009).

As Wittgenstein would say, one must remember that every "language game" comes with a "form of life" (Wittgenstein 1953), and the Web is a new form of life that goes beyond the philosophy of natural language, and leads us straight into a new philosophy of dynamic machinic and human assemblages, a philosophy-to-come of collective intelligence.

1.3 Notational Conventions

In order to aid the reader, this book employs a number of notational conventions. In particular, we only use "double" quotes to quote a particular author or other work. When a new word is introduced and used in an unusual manner to be clarified later, we use 'single' quotes. The use of 'single' quotes is also used when a word is supposed to be understood as the word *qua* word, a mention of the word, rather than a use of the word. When a term is defined, the word is first labeled using ***bold and italic*** fonts, and either immediately followed or preceded by the definition given in *italics*. Mathematical or formal terms are *italicized*, as is the use of *emphasis* in any sentence. Finally, the names of books and other works are often italicized. In general, technical terms like HyperText Transport Protocol (HTTP) are often abbreviated by their capitalized initials. The World Wide Web is usually referred to as the Web. One of the largest problems is that this whole area historically has had a rather ad-hoc use of terms, so we hope this fairly rigorous notational convention helps separate the use, mention, definition, and direct quotations of terms.

Chapter 2
Architecture of the World Wide Web

> *All the important revolutions that leap into view must be*
> *preceded in the spirit of the era by a secret revolution that is not*
> *visible to everyone, and still less observable by contemporaries,*
> *and that is as difficult to express in words as it is to understand.*
>
> G.W.F. Hegel *(1959)*

In order to establish the relative autonomy of the Web as a subject matter, we recount its origins and so its relationship to other projects, both intellectual such as Engelbart's Human Augmentation Project, as well as more purely technical projects such as the Internet (1962). It may seem odd to begin this book, which involves very specific questions about representation and meaning on the Web, with a historical analysis of the Web. To understand these questions we must first have an understanding of the boundaries of the Web and the normative documents that define the Web. The Web is a fuzzy and ill-defined subject matter – often considered a ill-defined 'hack' by both academic philosophers and computer scientists – whose precise boundaries and even definition are unclear. Unlike some subject matters like chemistry, the subject matter of the Web is not necessarily very stable, like a 'natural kind,' as it is a technical artifact subject to constant change. So we will take the advice of the philosopher of technology Gilbert Simondon, "Instead of starting from the individuality of the technical object, or even from its specificity, which is very unstable, and trying to define the laws of its genesis in the framework of this individuality or specificity, it is better to invert the problem: it is from the criterion of the genesis that we can define the individuality and the specificity of the technical object: the technical object is not this or that thing, given *hic et nunc*, but that which is generated" (1958). In other words, we must first trace the creation of the Web before attempting to define it, imposing on the Web what Fredric Jameson calls "the one absolute and we may even say 'transhistorical' imperative, that is: Always historicize!" (1981). Only once we understand the history and significance of the Web, will we then proceed to dissect its components one-by-one, and attempt to align them with certain still-subterranean notions from philosophy.

H. Halpin, *Social Semantics: The Search for Meaning on the Web*,
Semantic Web and Beyond 13, DOI 10.1007/978-1-4614-1885-6_2,
© Springer Science+Business Media New York 2013

2.1   The History of the Web

What is the Web, and what is its significance? At first, it appears to be a relative upstart upon the historical scene, with little connection to anything before it, an historical and unprincipled 'hack' that came unto the world unforeseen and with dubious academic credentials. The intellectual trajectory of the Web is a fascinating, if unknown, revolution whose impact has yet to be historically comprehended, perhaps even by its creators. Although it is well-known that the Web bears some striking similarity to Vannevar Bush's 'Memex' idea from 1945, the Web is itself usually thought of more as a technological innovation rather than an intellectually rich subject matter such as artificial intelligence or cognitive science (1945). However, the Web's heritage is just as rich as artificial intelligence and cognitive science, and can be traced back to the selfsame root, namely the 'Man-Machine Symbiosis' project of Licklider (1960).

2.1.1   The Man-Machine Symbiosis Project

The first precursor to the Web was glimpsed, although never implemented, by Vannevar Bush, chief architect of the military-industrial complex of the United States of America. For Bush, the primary barrier to increased productivity was the lack of an ability to easily recall and create records, and Bush saw in microfiche the basic element needed to create what he termed the "Memex," a system that lets any information be stored, recalled, and annotated through a series of "associative trails" (1945). The Memex would lead to "wholly new forms of encyclopedias with a mesh of associative trails," a feature that became the inspiration for links in hypertext (Bush 1945). However, Bush could not implement his vision on the analogue computers of his day.

The Web had to wait for the invention of digital computers and the Internet, the latter of which bears no small manner of debt to the work of J.C.R. Licklider, a disciple of Norbert Wiener (Licklider 1960). Wiener thought of feedback as an overarching principle of organization in any science, one that was equally universal amongst humans and machines (1948). Licklider expanded this notion of feedback loops to that of feedback between humans and digital computers. This vision of 'Man-Machine Symbiosis' is distinct and prior to cognitive science and artificial intelligence, both of which were very infantile disciplines at the time of Licklider, and both of which are conjoined at the hip by hypothesizing that the human mind can be construed as either computational itself or even implemented on a computer. Licklider was not a true believer in the computational mind, but held that while the human mind itself might not be computational (Licklider cleverly remained agnostic on that particular gambit), the human mind was definitely *complemented* by computers. As Licklider himself put it, "The fig tree is pollinated only by the insect Blastophaga grossorun. The larva of the insect lives in the ovary of the fig tree, and there it gets its food. The tree and the insect are thus heavily interdependent: the tree cannot reproduce without the insect; the insect cannot eat without the tree; together, they constitute not only a viable but a productive and thriving partnership. This cooperative 'living together in intimate association, or even close union, of two dissimilar organisms' is called symbiosis. The hope is that, in not too many years, human brains and computing machines will be coupled together very tightly, and that the resulting partnership will think as no human brain has ever thought and ·process data in a way not approached by the information-handling machines we know today" (1960). The goal of 'Man-Machine Symbiosis' is then the enabling of reliable coupling between the humans and their 'external' information as given in digital computers. To obtain this coupling, the barriers of time and space needed to be overcome so that the symbiosis could operate as a single process. This required the invention of ever decreasing low latency feedback loops between humans and their machines.

In pursuit of that goal, the 'Man-Machine Symbiosis' project was not merely a hypothetical theoretical project, but a concrete engineering project. In order to provide the funding needed to assemble what Licklider termed his "galactic network" of researchers to implement the first step of the project, Licklider became the institutional architect of the Information Processing Techniques Office at the Advanced Research Projects Agency (ARPA) (Waldrop 2001). Licklider first tackled the barrier of time. Early computers had large time lags in between the input of a program to a computer on a medium such as punch-cards and the reception of the program's output. This lag could then be overcome via the use of time-sharing, taking advantage of the fact that the computer, despite its centralized single processor, could run multiple programs in a non-linear fashion. Instead of idling while waiting for the next program or human interaction, in moments nearly imperceptible to the human eye, a computer would share its time among multiple humans (McCarthy 1992).

In further pursuit of its goal of human-machine symbiosis, in which some over-enthusiastic science-fiction fans or academics with a penchant for the literal might see the idea of a cyborg, the 'Man-Machine Symbiosis' project gave funding to two streams of research: artificial intelligence and another lesser-known strand, the work on 'human augmentation' exemplified by the Human Augmentation Project of Engelbart (1962). Human augmentation, instead of hoping to replicate human intelligence as artificial intelligence did, only thought to enhance it. At the same time Licklider was beginning his 'Man-Machine Symbiosis' project, Douglas Engelbart had independently generated a proposal for a 'Human Augmentation Framework' that shared the same goal as the 'Man-Machine Symbiosis' idea of Licklider, although it differed by placing the human at the centre of the system, focusing on the ability of the machine to extend to the human user. In contrast, Licklider imagined a more egalitarian partnership between humans and digital computers, more akin to having a somewhat intelligent machine as a conversational partner for the human (1962). This focus on human factors led Engelbart to the realization that the primary reason for the high latency between the human and the machine was the interface of the human user to the machine itself, as a keyboard was at best a limited channel even compared to punchcards. After extensive testing of what devices enabled the lowest latency between humans and machines, Engelbart invented the mouse and other, less successful interfaces, like the one-handed 'chord' keyboard (Waldrop 2001). By employing these interfaces, the temporal latency between humans and computers was decreased even further. Strangely enough, we have not – despite all the hyperbole around tactile or haptic interfaces from various media-labs – gone far beyond keyboards, mice, and touch-screens in 50 years.

2.1.2   The Internet

The second barrier to be overcome was space, so that any computer should be accessible regardless of its physical location. The Internet "came out of our frustration that there were only a limited number of large, powerful research computers in the country, and that many research investigators who should have access to them were geographically separated from them" (Leiner et al. 2003). Licklider's lieutenant Bob Taylor and his successor Larry Roberts contracted out Bolt, Beranek, and Newman (BBN) to create the Interface Message Processor, the hardware needed to connect the various time-sharing computers of Licklider's "galactic network" that evolved into the ARPANet (Waldrop 2001). While BBN provided the hardware for the ARPANet, the software was left undetermined, so an informal group of graduate students constituted the Internet Engineering Task Force (IETF) to create software to run the Internet (Waldrop 2001).

The IETF has historically been the main standardization body that creates the protocols that run the Internet. It still maintains the informal nature of its foundation, with no formal structure such as a board of directors, although it is officially overseen by the Internet Society. The IETF informally credits as their main organizing principle the credo "We reject kings, presidents, and voting. We believe in rough consensus and running code" (Hafner and Lyons 1996). Decisions do not have to be ratified by consensus or even majority voting, but require only a rough measure of agreement on an idea. The most important product of these list-serv discussions and meetings are IETF RFCs (Request for Comments) which differ in their degree of reliability, from the unstable 'Experimental' to the most stable 'Standards Track.' The RFCs define Internet standards such as URIs and HTTP (Berners-Lee et al. 1996 2005). RFCs, while not strictly academic publications, have a de facto normative force on the Internet and therefore on the Web, and so they will be referenced considerably throughout this book.

Before the Internet, networks were assumed to be static and closed systems, so one either communicated with a network or not. However, early network researchers determined that there could be an "open architecture networking" where a meta-level "internetworking architecture" would allow diverse networks to connect to each other, so that "they required that one be used as a component of the other, rather than acting as a peer of the other in offering end-to-end service"

(Leiner et al. 2003). In the IETF, Robert Kahn and Vint Cerf devised a protocol that took into account, among others, four key factors, as cited below (Leiner et al. 2003):

1. Each distinct network would have to stand on its own and no internal changes could be required to any such network to connect it to the Internet.
2. Communications would be on a best effort basis. If a packet didn't make it to the final destination, it would shortly be retransmitted from the source.
3. Black boxes would be used to connect the networks; these would later be called gateways and routers. There would be no information retained by the gateways about the individual flows of packets passing through them, thereby keeping them simple and avoiding complicated adaptation and recovery from various failure modes.
4. There would be no global control at the operations level.

In this protocol, data is subdivided into 'packets' that are all treated independently by the network. Data is first divided into relatively equal sized packets by TCP (Transmission Control Protocol), which then sends the packets over the network using IP (Internet Protocol). Together, these two protocols form a single protocol, TCP/IP (Cerf and Kahn 1974). Each computer is named by an Internet Number, a 4 byte destination address such as *152.2.210.122*, and IP routes the system through various black-boxes, like gateways and routers, that do not try to reconstruct the original data from the packet. At the recipients end, TCP collects the incoming packets and then reconstructs the data.

The Internet connects computers over space, and so provides the physical layer over which the universal information space of the Web is implemented. However, it was a number of decades before the latency of space and time became low enough for something like the Web to become not only universalizing in theory, but universalizing in practice, and so actually come into being rather than being merely a glimpse in a researcher's eye. An historical example of attempting a Web-like system before the latency was acceptable would be the NLS (oNLine System) of Engelbart (1962). The NLS was literally built as the second node of the Internet, the Network Information Centre, the ancestor of the domain name system. The NLS allowed any text to be hierarchically organized in a series of outlines, with summaries, giving the user freedom to move through various levels of information and link information together. The most innovative feature of the NLS was a journal for users to publish information in and a journal for others to *link* and comment upon, a precursor of blogs and wikis (Waldrop 2001). However, Engelbart's vision could not be realized on the slow computers of his day. Although time-sharing computers reduced temporal latency on single machines, too many users sharing a single machine made the latency unacceptably high, especially when using an application like NLS. Furthermore, his zeal for reducing latency made the NLS far too difficult to use, as it depended on obscure commands that were far too complex for the average user to master within a reasonable amount of time. It was only after the failure of the NLS that researchers at Xerox PARC developed the personal computer, which by providing each user their own computer reduced the temporal latency to an acceptable amount (Waldrop 2001). When these computers were connected with the Internet and given easy-to-use interfaces as developed at Xerox PARC, both temporal and spatial latencies were made low enough for ordinary users to access the Internet. This convergence of technologies, the personal computer and the Internet, is what allowed the Web to be implemented successfully and enabled its wildfire growth, while previous attempts like NLS were doomed to failure as they were conceived before the technological infrastructure to support them had matured.

2.1.3   The Modern World Wide Web

Perhaps due to its own anarchic nature, the IETF had produced a multitude of incompatible protocols such as FTP (File Transfer Protocol) and Gopher (Postel and Reynolds 1985; Anklesaria et al. 1993). While protocols could each communicate with other computers over the Internet, there was no universal format to identify information regardless of protocol. One IETF participant, Tim Berners-Lee, had the concept of a "universal information space" which he dubbed the "World Wide Web" (1992). His original proposal to his employer CERN brings his belief in universality to the forefront, "We should work towards a universal linked information system, in which generality and portability are more important than fancy graphics and complex extra facilities" (Berners-Lee 1989). The practical reason for Berners-Lee's proposal was to connect the tremendous amounts of data generated by physicists at CERN together. Later as he developed his ideas he came into direct contact with Engelbart, who encouraged him to continue his work despite his work being rejected at conferences like ACM Hypertext 1991.[1]

In the IETF, Berners-Lee, Fielding, Connolly, Masinter, and others spear-headed the development of URIs (Universal Resource Identifiers), HTML (HyperText Markup Language) and HTTP (HyperText Transfer Protocol). Since by being able to reference anything with equal ease due to URIs, a web of information would form based on "the few basic, common rules of 'protocol' that would allow one computer to talk to another, in such a way that when all computers everywhere did it, the system would thrive, not break down" (Berners-Lee 2000). The Web is a *virtual space for naming information* built on top of the physical infrastructure of the Internet that could move bits around, and it was built through specifications that could be implemented by anyone: "What was often difficult for people to understand about the design was that there was nothing else beyond URIs, HTTP, and HTML. There was no central computer 'controlling' the Web, no single network on which these protocols worked, not even an organization anywhere that 'ran' the Web. The Web was not a physical 'thing' that existed in a certain 'place.' It was a 'space' in which information could exist" (Berners-Lee 2000).

The very idea of a *universal* information space seemed at least ambitious, if not de facto impossible, to many. The IETF rejected Berners-Lee's idea that any

---

[1]Personal communication with Berners-Lee.

identification scheme could be universal. In order to get the initiative of the Web off the ground, Berners-Lee surrendered to the IETF and renamed URIs from *Universal Resource Identifiers* (URIs) to *Uniform Resource Locators* (URLs) (Berners-Lee 2000). The Web begin growing at a prodigious rate once the employer of Berners-Lee, CERN, released any intellectual property rights they had to the Web and after Mosaic, the first graphical browser, was released. However, browser vendors started adding supposed 'new features' that soon led to a 'lock-in' where certain sites could only be viewed by one particular corporate browser. These 'browser wars' began to fracture the rapidly growing Web into incompatible information spaces, thus nearly defeating the proposed universality of the Web (Berners-Lee 2000).

Berners-Lee in particular realized it was in the long-term interest of the Web to have a new form of standards body that would preserve its universality by allowing corporations and others to have a more structured contribution than possible with the IETF. With the informal position of merit Berners-Lee had as the supposed inventor of the Web (although he freely admits that the invention of the Web was a collective endeavour), he and others constituted the World Wide Web Consortium (W3C), a non-profit dedicated to "leading the Web to its full potential by developing protocols and guidelines that ensure long-term growth for the Web" (Jacobs 1999). In the W3C, membership was open to any organization, commercial or non-profit. Unlike the IETF, W3C membership came at a considerable membership fee. The W3C is organized as a strict representative democracy, with each member organization sending one member to the Advisory Committee of the W3C, although decisions technically are always made by the Director, Berners-Lee himself. By opening up a "vendor neutral" space, companies who previously were interested primarily in advancing the technology for their own benefit could be brought to the table. The primary product of the World Wide Web Consortium is a W3C Recommendation, a standard for the Web that is explicitly voted on and endorsed by the W3C membership. W3C Recommendations are thought to be similar to IETF RFCs, with normative force due to the degree of formal verification given via voting by the W3C Membership and a set number of implementations to prove interoperability. A number of W3C Recommendations have become very well known technologies, ranging from the vendor-neutral later versions of HTML (Raggett et al. 1999), which stopped the fracture of the universal information space, to XML, which has become a prominent transfer syntax for many types of data (Bray et al. 1998).

This book will cite W3C Recommendations when appropriate, as these are one of the main normative documents that define the Web. With IETF RFCs, these normative standards collectively define the foundations of the Web. It is by agreement on these standards that the Web functions as a whole. However, the rough-and-ready process of the IETF and the more bureaucratic process of the W3C has led to a terminological confusion that must be sorted in order to grasp the nature of representations on the Web, causing even the most well-meaning of souls to fall into a conceptual swamp of undefined and fuzzy terms. This is true in spades when encountering the hotly-contested term 'representation.'

2.2   The Terminology of the Web

Can the various technologies that go under the rubric of the World Wide Web be
found to have common principles and terminology? This question would at first
seem to be shallow, for one could say that any technology that is described by its
creators, or even the public at large, can be considered trivially 'part of the Web.'
To further complicate the matter, the terms the 'Web' and the 'Internet' are elided
together in common parlance, and so are often deployed as synonyms. In a single
broad stroke, we can distinguish the Web and the Internet. The Internet is a type of
packet-switching network as defined by its use of the TCP/IP protocol. The purpose
of the Internet is to get bits from one computer to another. In contrast, the Web is
a space of names defined by its usage of URIs. So, the purpose of the Web is the
use of URIs for accessing and referring to information. The Web and the Internet
are then strictly separable, for the Web, as a space of URIs, could be realized on
top of other types of networks that move bits around, much as the same virtual
machine can be realized on top of differing physical computers. For example, one
could imagine the Web being built on top of a network built on principles different
from TCP/IP, such as OSI, an early competitor to the TCP/IP stack of networking
protocols (Zimmerman 1980). Likewise, before the Web, there were a number of
different protocols with their own naming schemes built upon the Internet like
Gopher (Anklesaria et al. 1993).

Is it not presumptuous of us to hope that such an unruly phenomenon such as
the Web even has guiding principles? Again we must appeal to the fact that unlike
natural language or chemistry, the Web is like other engineered artifacts, created
by particular individuals with a purpose, and designed with this purpose in mind.
Unlike the case of the proper function of natural language, where natural selection
itself will forever remain silent to our questions, the principal designers of the
Web are still alive to be questioned in person, and their design rationale is overtly
written down on various notes, often scribbled on some of the earliest web-pages
of the Web itself. It is generally thought of that the core of the Web consists of the
following standards, given in their earliest incarnation: HTTP (Berners-Lee et al.
1996), URI (Berners-Lee 1994a), and HTML (Berners-Lee and Connolly 1993). So
the basic protocols and data formats that proved to be successful were the creations
of a fairly small number of people, such as Tim Berners-Lee, Roy Fielding, and Dan
Connolly.

The primary source for our terminology and principles of Web architecture is
a document entitled *The Architecture of the World Wide Web* (AWWW), a W3C
Recommendation edited by Ian Jacobs and Norm Walsh to "describe the properties
we desire of the Web and the design choices that have been made to achieve
them" (Jacobs and Walsh 2004). The AWWW is an attempt to systematize the
thinking that went into the design of the Web by some of its primary architects,

and as such is both close to our project and an inspiration.[2] In particular, AWWW is an exegesis of Tim Berners-Lee's notes on "Design Issues: Architectural and philosophical points"[3] and Roy Fielding's dissertation "Architectural Styles and the Design of Network-based Software Architectures" (Fielding 2010), often abbreviated as REST. The rationale for the creation of such a document of principles developed organically over the existence of the W3C, as new proposed technologies were sometimes considered to be either informally compliant or non-compliant with Web architecture. When the proponents of some technology were told that their particular technology was not compliant with Web architecture, they would often demand that somewhere there be a description of this elusive Web architecture. The W3C in response set up the Technical Architecture Group (TAG) to "document and build consensus" upon "the underlying principles that should be adhered to by all Web components, whether developed inside or outside W3C," as stated in its charter.[4] The TAG also maintains a numbered list of problems (although the numbers are in no way sequential) that attempts to resolve issues in Web architecture by consensus, with the results released as notes called 'W3C TAG findings,' which are also referred to in this discussion. The TAG's only Recommendation at the time of writing is the aforementioned *Architecture of the Web: Volume 1* but it is reasonable to assume that more volumes of *Architecture of the Web* may be produced after enough findings have been accumulated. The W3C TAG's AWWW is a blend of common-sense and sometimes surprising conclusions about Web architecture that attempts to unify diverse web technologies with a finite set of core design principles, constraints, and good practices (Jacobs and Walsh 2004). However, the terminology of AWWW is often thought to be too informal and ungrounded to use by many, and we attempt to remedy this in the next few chapters by fusing the terminology of Web architecture with our own peculiar brand of philosophical terminology.

To begin our reconstruction of Web architecture, the first task is the definition of terms, as otherwise the technical terminology of the Web can lead to as much misunderstanding as understanding. To cite an extreme example, people coming from communities like the artificial intelligence community use terms like 'representation' in a way that is different from those involved in Web architecture. We begin with the terms commonly associated with a typical exemplary Web interaction. For an agent to learn about the *resource* known as the Eiffel Tower in Paris, a person can access its *representation* using its *Uniform Resource Identifier (URI)* http://www.tour-eiffel.fr/ and retrieve a web-page in the HTML *encoding* whose *content* is the Eiffel Tower using the HTTP *protocol*.

---

[2]Although to what extent the Web as it actually exists follows these design choices is still a matter for debate, and it is very clear some of the more important parts of the Web such as the ubiquity of scripting languages, and thus HTML as mobile code, are left unmentioned.

[3]These unordered personal notes are at: http://www.w3.org/DesignIssues/, which we also refer directly to in the course of this chapter.

[4]Quoted from their charter, available on the Web at: http://www.w3.org/2001/07/19-tag (last accessed April 20th, 2007).

2.2.1   Protocols

A **protocol** is *a convention for transmitting information between two or more agents*, a broad definition that encompasses everything from computer protocols like TCP/IP to conventions in natural language like those employed in diplomacy. A protocol often specifies more than just the particular encoding, but also may attempt to specify the interpretation of this encoding and the meaningful behaviour that the sense of the information should engender in an agent. An **agent** is *any thing capable of interacting via a protocol*. These are often called a 'user agent' on the Web, and the term covers both web-browsers, humans, web spiders, and even combinations such as humans operating web-browsers. A **payload** is *the information transmitted by a protocol*. Galloway notes that protocols are "the principle of organization native to computers in distributed networks" and that agreement on protocols are necessary for any sort of network to succeed in the acts of communication (2004).[5] The paradigmatic case of a protocol is TCP/IP, where the payload transmitted is just bits in the body of the message, with the header being used by TCP to ensure the lossless delivery of said bits. TCP/IP transmits strictly an encoding of data as bits and does not force any particular interpretation on the bits; the payload could be a picture of the Eiffel Tower, web-pages about the Eiffel Tower, or just meaningless random bits. All TCP/IP does is move some particular bits from one individual computer to another, and any language that is built on top of the bit-level are strictly outside the bounds of TCP/IP. Since these bits are usually communication with some purpose, the payload of the protocol is almost always an encoding on a level of abstraction above and beyond that of the raw bits themselves.

The Web is based on a **client-server architecture**, meaning that *protocols take the form of a request for information and a response with information*. The **client** is defined as *the agent that is requesting information* and the **server** is defined as *the agent that is responding to the request*. In a protocol, an **endpoint** is *any process that either requests or responds to a protocol*, and so includes both client and servers. The client is often called a **user-agent** since it is the user of the Web. A user-agent may be anything from a web-browser to some sort of automated reasoning engine that is working on behalf of another agent, often the specifically human user. The main protocol in this exposition will be the **HyperText Transfer Protocol** (HTTP), as most recently defined by IETF RFC 2616 (Fielding et al. 1999). HTTP is a protocol originally intended for the transfer of hypertext documents, although its now ubiquitous nature often lets it be used for the transfer of almost any encoding over the Web, such as its use to transfer XML-based SOAP (originally the *Simple Object Access Protocol*) messages in Web Services (Box et al. 2000). HTTP consists of sending a **method**, *a request for a certain type of response from a user-agent to the server*, including information that may change the state of the server.

---

[5] Although unlike Galloway, who descends into a sort of postmodern paranoia of protocols, we recognize them as the very conditions of collectivity.

Fig. 2.1 An HTTP request
from a client

```
GET /index.html HTTP/1.0
User-Agent: Mozilla/5.0
Accept: */*
Host: www.example.org
Connection: Keep-Alive
```

These methods have a list of **headers** that *specify some information that may be used by the server to determine the response*. The **request** is *the method used by the agent and the headers, along with a blank line and an optional message body*.

The methods in HTTP are HEAD, GET, POST, PUT, DELETE, TRACE, OPTIONS, and CONNECT. We will only be concerned with the most frequently used HTTP method, GET. GET is informally considered 'commitment-free,' which means that the method has no side effects for either the user-agent or the server, besides the receiving of the response (Berners-Lee et al. 1996). So a GET method should not be used to change the state of a user-agent, such as charging someone for buying a plane ticket to Paris. To change the state of the information on the server or the user-agent, either PUT (for uploading data directly to the server) or POST (for transferring data to the server that will require additional processing, such as when one fills in a HTML form) should be used. A sample request to http:///www.example.org from a Web browser user-agent is given in Fig. 2.1.

The first part of an HTTP response from the server then consists of an HTTP **status code** which is *one of a finite number of codes which gives the user-agent information about the server's HTTP response itself*. The two most known status codes are HTTP 200, which means that the request was successful, or 404, which means the user-agent asked for data that was not found on the server. The first digit of the status code indicates what general class of response it is. For example, the 200 series (2xx) response codes mean a successful request, although 206 means partial success. The 4xx codes indicate that the user-agent asked for a request that the server could not fulfill, while 1xx is informational, 3xx is redirectional, and 5xx means server error. After the status codes there is an **HTTP entity** which is *"the information transferred as the payload of a request or response"* (Fielding et al. 1999). This technical use of the word 'entity' should be distinguished from our earlier use of the term 'entity' like the Eiffel Tower which can only be realized by the thing itself, not in another realization. In order to do so, we will take care to preface the protocol name 'HTTP' before any 'HTTP entity,' while the term 'entity' by itself refers to the philosophical notion of an entity. An HTTP entity consists of "entity-header fields and. . . an entity-body" (Fielding et al. 1999) An **HTTP response** consists of *the combination of the status code and the HTTP entity*. These responses from the server can include an additional header, which specifies the date and last modified date as well as optional information that can determine if the desired representation is in the cache and the content-type of the representation. A sample HTTP response to the previous example request, excluding the HTTP entity-body, is given in Fig. 2.2.

In the HTTP response, an HTTP entity body is returned. The encoding of the HTTP entity body is given by the HTTP entity header fields that specify its

Fig. 2.2 An HTTP response
from a server

```
HTTP/1.1 200 OK
Date: Wed, 16 Apr 2008 14:12:09 GMT
Server: Apache/2.2.4 (Fedora)
Accept-Ranges: bytes
Connection: close
Content-Type: text/html; charset=ISO-8859-1
Content-Language: fr
```

Content-type and Content-language. These are both considered different languages, as a single web-page can be composed in multiple languages, such as the text being given in English with various formatting given in HTML. Every HTTP entity body should have its particular encoding specified by the Content-type. *The formal languages that can be explicitly given in a response or request in HTTP* are called ***content types***. In the example response, based on the header that the content type is text/html a user-agent can interpret ('display as a web-page') the encoding of the HTTP entity body as HTML. Since the same encoding can theoretically represent many different languages besides HTML, a user-agent can only know definitely how to process a message through the content type. If no content type is provided, the agent can guess the content type through various heuristics including looking at the bytes themselves, a process informally called *sniffing*. A user-agent can specify what media types they (can) prefer, so that a web-server that can only present JPEG images can specify this by also asking for the content type image/jpeg in the request.

Content-types in HTTP were later generalized as 'Internet Media Types' so they could be applied with any Internet protocol, not just HTTP and MIME (*Multimedia Internet Message Extensions*, an e-mail protocol) (Postel 1994). A ***media type*** consists of *a two-part scheme that separates the type and a subtype of an encoding*, with a slash indicating the distinction. Internet media types are centrally registered with IANA,[6] although certain 'experimental' media types (those beginning with 'x-') can be created in a decentralized manner (Postel 1994). A central registry of media types guarantees the interoperability of the Web, although increasingly new media-types are dependent on extensions to specific applications (plug-ins) in order to run. Support for everything from new markup languages to programming languages such as Javascript can be declared via support of its media type.

To move from concrete bits to abstract definitions, a protocol can be defined and implemented in many different types of way. In the early ARPANet, the first wide-area network and foundation of the Internet, the protocol was 'hard-wired' in the hardware of the Interface Message Processor (IMP), a separate machine attached to computers in order to interface them with ARPANet (Hafner and Lyons 1996). As more and more networks multiplied, these heterogeneous networks began using different protocols. While the invention of TCP/IP let these heterogeneous networks communicate, TCP/IP does not interpret messages beyond bits. Further

---

[6] At http://www.iana.org/assignments/media-types/.

protocols are built on top of TCP/IP, such as FTP (File Transfer Protocol) for the retrieval of files (Postel and Reynolds 1985), Gopher for the retrieval of documents (Anklesaria et al. 1993), and SMTP (Simple Mail Transfer Protocol) for the transfer of mail (Postel 1982). Since one computer might hold many different kinds of information, IP addresses were not enough as they only identified where a particular device was on the network. Thus each protocol created its own naming scheme to allow it to identify and access things on a more fine-grained level than IP addresses. Furthermore, each of these protocols was often associated (via registration with a governing body like IANA, the *Internet Assigned Numbers Authority*) with particular ports, such that port 25 was used by SMTP and port 70 by Gopher. With this explosion of protocols and naming schemes, each Internet application was its own 'walled garden.' Names created using a particular protocol were incapable of being used outside the original protocol, until the advent of the naming scheme of the Web (Berners-Lee 2000).

2.2.2 Information Encoding and Content

There is a relationship between a server sending a message – such as a web-page about the Eiffel Tower – to a client in response to an HTTP request and certain notions from information theory, however hazy and qualitative. To phrase informally, *information* is *whatever regularities held in common between a source and a receiver* (Shannon and Weaver 1963). Note that the source and receiver do not have to be spatially separate, but can also be temporally separate, and thus the notion of a self-contained 'message' resembling a postcard being sent between sender and receiver is incomplete if not incorrect.[7] To have something in common means to share the same regularities, e.g. parcels of time and space that cannot be distinguished at a given level of abstraction. This definition correlates with information being the inverse of the amount of 'noise' or randomness in a system, and the amount of information being equivalent to a reduction in uncertainty. It is precisely this preservation or failure to preserve information that can be thought of the as sending of a *message* between the source and the receiver over a channel, where the channel is over time, space, and – most likely – both. *Whether or not the information is preserved over time or space is due to the properties of a physical substrate* known as the *channel*. So in our example, the channel is the fiber-optic or copper wires that must accurately carry the voltages which the bits consist of. The *message* is *the physical thing that realizes the regularities of the information due to its local characteristics*, which in this case would be particular patterns of bits being preserved over multiple channels as they are popped from an electro-magnetic hard-disk on a server to fibre-optic then over the air via wireless and finally back to the

---

[7]Imagine that your eye color not changing is a message from yourself at 10 years old to yourself at 70!

electric charges stored in memory chips in a client device, such as a web browser on a mobile phone. These messages are often called the *realization* of some abstract informational content.

Already, information reveals itself to be not just a singular thing, but something that exists at multiple levels: How do the bits become a message in HTTP? In particular, we are interested in the distinction in information between content and encoding. Here our vague analogy with Shannon's information theory fails, as Shannon's theory deals with finding the optimal encoding and size of channel so that the message can be guaranteed to get from the sender to the receiver, which in our case is taken care of by the clever behavior of the TCP/IP protocol operating over a variety of computational devices (Shannon and Weaver 1963). Yet, how can an encoding be distinguished from the content of information itself in a particular HTTP message? Let's go back to bits by leaning on aesthetic theory of all things; art critic and philosopher Nelson Goodman defines a *mark* as a *physical characteristic* ranging from marks on paper one can use to discern alphabetic characters to ranges of voltage that can be thought of as bits (1968). To be reliable in conveying information, an encoding should be physically 'differentiable' and thus maintain what Goodman calls 'character indifference' so that (at least within some context) each character (as in 'characteristic') can not be mistaken for another character. One cannot reconstruct a message in bits if one cannot tell apart 1 and 0, much as one cannot reconstruct a HTML web-page if one cannot tell the various characters in text apart. So, an *encoding* is *a set of precise regularities that can be realized by the message*. Thus, one can think of multiple levels of encoding, with the very basic encoding of bits being handled by the protocol TCP/IP, and then the protocol HTTP handing higher-level encodings in textual encodings such as HTML.

Unforunately, we are not out of the conceptual thicket yet; there is more to information than encoding. Shannon's theory does not explain the notion of information fully, since giving someone the number of bits that a message contains does not tell the receiver *what* information is encoded. Shannon explicitly states, "The fundamental problem of communication is that of reproducing at one point either exactly or approximately a message selected at another point. Frequently the messages have meaning; that is they refer to or are correlated according to some system with certain physical or conceptual entities. These semantic aspects of communication are irrelevant to the engineering problem" (1963). He is correct, at least for his particular engineering problem. However, Shannon's use of the term 'information' is for our purposes the same as the 'encoding' of information, but a more fully-fledged notion of information is needed. Many intuitions about the notion of information have to deal with not only how the information is encoded or how to encode it, but what a particular message is about, the *content* of an information-bearing message.[8] 'Content' is a term we adopt from Israel and Perry,

---

[8] An example of the distinguishment between content and encoding: Imagine Daniel sending Amy a secret message about which one of her co-employees won a trip to the Eiffel Tower. Just determining that a single employee out of 8 won the lottery requires at least a 3 bit encoding

as opposed to the more confusing term 'semantic information' as employed by Floridi and Dretske (Israel and Perry 1990; Dretske 1981; Floridi 2004). One of the first attempts to formulate a theory of informational content was due to Carnap and Bar-Hillel (1952). Their theory attempted to bind a theory of content closely to first-order predicate logic, and so while their "theory lies explicitly and wholly within semantics" they explicitly do not address "the information which the sender intended to convey by transmitting a certain message nor about the information a receiver obtained with a certain message," since they believed these notions could eventually be derived from their formal apparatus (Carnap and Bar-Hillel 1952). Their overly restrictive notion of the content of information as logic did not gain widespread traction, and neither did other attempts to develop alternative theories of information such as that of Donald McKay (1955). In contrast, Dretske's *semantic theory of information* defines the notion of content to be compatible with Shannon's information theory, and his notions have gained some traction within the philosophical community (Dretske 1981). To him, the content of a message and the amount of information – the number of bits an encoding would require – are different, for "saying 'There is a gnu in my backyard' does not have more content than the utterance 'There is a dog in my backyard' since the former is, statistically, less probable" (Dretske 1981). According to Shannon, there is more information in the former case precisely because it is less likely than the latter (Dretske 1981). So while information that is less frequent may require a larger number of bits in encoding, the content of information should be viewed as to some extent separable if compatible with Shannon's information theory, since otherwise one is led to the "absurd view that among competent speakers of language, gibberish has more meaning than semantic discourse because it is much less frequent" (Dretske 1981). Simply put, Shannon and Dretkse are talking about distinct notions that should be separated, the notions of encoding and content respectively.

Is there a way to precisely define the content of a message? Dretske defines the content of information as "a signal r carries the information that s is F when the conditional probability of s's being F, given r (and k) is 1 (but, given k alone, less than 1). k is the knowledge of the receiver" (1981). To simplify, the **content** of any

---

and does not tell Amy (the receiver) which employee in particular won the lottery. Shannon's theory only measures how many bits are needed to tell Amy precisely who won. After all, the false message that her office-mate Sandro won a trip to Paris is also 3 bits. Yet content is not independent of the encoding, for content is conveyed by virtue of a particular encoding and a particular encoding imposes constraints on what content can be sent (Shannon and Weaver 1963). Let's imagine that Daniel is using a code of bits specially designed for this problem, rather than natural language, to tell Amy who won the free plane ticket to Paris. The content of the encoding 001 could be yet another co-employee Ralph while the content of the encoding 010 could be Sandro. If there are only two possible bits of information and all eight employees need one unique encoding, Daniel cannot send a message specifying which friend got the trip since there aren't enough options in the encodings to go round. An encoding of at least 3 bits is needed to give each employee a unique encoding. If 01 has the content that 'either Sandro or Ralph won the ticket' the message has not been successfully transferred if the purpose of the message is to tell Amy *precisely* which employee won the ticket.

information-bearing message is *whatever is held in common between the source and the receiver as a result of the conveyance of a particular message.* While this is similar to our definition of information itself, it is different. The content is whatever is shared in common as a result of a *particular* message, such as the conveyance of the sentence 'The Eiffel Tower is 300 m high.' The content of a message is called the "facts" by Dretske, (F). This content is conveyed from the source (s) successfully to the receiver (r) when the content can be used by the receiver with certainty, *and* that before the receipt of the message the receiver was not certain of that particular content. Daniel can only successfully convey the content that 'Ralph won a trip to Paris' if before receiving the message Amy does not know 'Ralph won a trip to Paris' and after receiving the message Amy does know that fact. Dretkse himself notes that information "does not mean that a signal must tell us everything about a source to tell us something," it just has to tell enough so that the receiver is now certain about the content within the domain (1981). Millikan rightfully notes that Dretske states his definition too strongly, for this probability of 1 is just an approximation of a statistically "good bet" indexed to some domain where the information was learned to be recognized (2004). For example, lightening carries the content that "a thunderstorm is nearby" in rainy climes but in an arid prairie lightning can convey a dust-storm. However, often the reverse is true, as the same content is carried by messages in different encodings, like a web-page about the Eiffel Tower being encoded in either English or French. These notions of encoding and content are not strictly separable, which is why they together compose the notion of information. An updated famous maxim of Hegel could be applied: for information, there is no encoding without content, and no content without encoding (1959).

The relationship of an encoding to its content, is an **interpretation**. The interpretation 'fills' in the necessary background left out of the encoding, and maps the encoding to some content. In our previous example using binary digits as an encoding scheme, a mapping could be made between the encoding 001 to the content of the Eiffel Tower while the encoding 010 could be mapped to the content of the Washington Monument. When the word 'interpretation' is used as a noun, we mean the content given by a particular relationship between an agent and an encoding, i.e. the interpretation. Usual definitions of "interpretation" tend to conflate these issues. In formal semantics, the word "interpretation" often can be used either in the sense of "an interpretation structure, which is a 'possible world' considered as something independent of any particular vocabulary" (and so any agent) or "an interpretation mapping from a vocabulary into the structure" or as shorthand for both (Hayes 2004). The difference in use of the term seems somewhat divided by fields. For example, computational linguistics often use "interpretation" to mean what Hayes called the "interpretation structure." In contrast, we use the term 'interpretation' to mean what Hayes called the "interpretation mapping," reserving the word 'content' for the "interpretation structure" or structures selected by a particular agent in relationship to some encoding. Also, this quick aside into matters of interpretation does not explicitly take on a formal definition of interpretation as done in model theory, although our general definition has been designed to be compatible with model-theoretic and other formal approaches to interpretation.

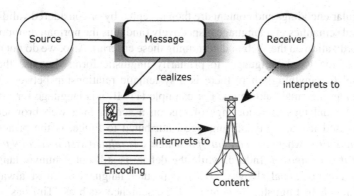

Fig. 2.3 Information, encoding, content

These terms are all illustrated in Fig. 2.3. A source is sending a receiver a message. The information-bearing message realizes some particular encoding such as a few sentences in English and a picture of the Eiffel Tower, and the content of the message can be interpreted to be about the Eiffel Tower.

The encoding and content of information do not in general come in self-contained bundles, with each encoding being interpreted to some free-standing propositional content. Instead, encodingevs and content come in entire interlocking informational systems. One feature of these systems is that encodings are layered inside of each other and content is also layered upon other content. The perfect example would be an English sentence in an e-mail message, where a series of bits are used to encode the letters of the alphabet, and the alphabet is then used to encode words. Likewise, the content of a sentence may depend on the content of the words in the sentence. When this happens, one is no longer dealing with a simple message, but some form of language. A *language* can be defined as *a system in which information is related to other information systematically*. In a language, this is a relationship between how the encoding of some information can change the interpretation of other encodings. Messages always have encodings, and usually these encodings are part of languages. To be more brief, information is *encoded in* languages. The relationships between encodings and content are usually taken to be based on some form of (not necessarily formalizable or even understood) rules. If one is referring to *a system in which the encoding of information is related to each other systematically*, then one is talking about the *syntax* of a language. If one is referring to *a system in which the content of information is related to each other systematically*, then one is referring to the *semantics* of the language. The lower-level of a language can be *terms*, *regularities in marks*, that may or may not have their own interpretation, such as the words or alphabet. *Any combination of terms that is valid according to the language's syntax* is a *sentence* (sometimes an 'expression') in the language, and *any combination of terms that has an interpretation to content according to the language's semantics* is a *statement* in the language.

Particular encodings and content are then accepted by or considered valid by the syntax and semantics of a language respectively (and thus the normative importance of standardization on the Web in determining these criteria). Also, we do not restrict our use of the word 'language' to primarily linguistic forms, but use the term 'language' for anything where there is a systematic relationship between syntax and (even an informal) semantics. For example HTML is a language for mapping a set of textual tags to renderings of bits on a screen in a web browser. One principle used in the study of languages, attributed to Frege, is the principle of *compositionality*, where *the content of a sentence is related systematically to terms in which it is composed*. Indeed, while the debate is still out if human languages are truly compositional (Dowty 2007), computer languages almost always are compositional. In English, the content of the sentence such as 'Tim has a plane ticket to Paris so he should go to the airport!' can then be composed from the more elementary content of the sub-statements, such as 'Tim has a plane ticket' which in turn has its content impacted by words such as 'Tim' and 'ticket.' The argument about whether sentences, words, or clauses are the minimal building block of content is beyond our scope. Do note one result of the distinction between encoding and content is that sentences that are accepted by the syntax (encoding) of a language, such as Chomsky's famous "Colorless green ideas sleep furiously" may have no obvious interpretation (to content) outside of the pragmatics of Chomsky's particular exposition (1957).

2.2.3   Uniform Resource Identifiers

The World Wide Web is defined by the AWWW as "an information space in which the items of interest, referred to as resources, are identified by global identifiers called Uniform Resource Identifiers (URI)" (Jacobs and Walsh 2004). This naming scheme, not any particular language like HTML, is the primary identifying characteristic of the Web. URIs arose from a need to organize the "many protocols and systems for document search and retrieval" that were in use on the Internet, especially considering that "many more protocols or refinements of existing protocols are to be expected in a field whose expansion is explosive" (Berners-Lee 1994a). Despite the "plethora of protocols and data formats," if any system was "to achieve global search and readership of documents across differing computing platforms," gateways that can "allow global access" should "remain possible" (Berners-Lee 1994a). The obvious answer was to consider all data on the Internet to be a single space of names with global scope.

URIs accomplish their universality over protocols by moving *all the information used by the protocol within the name itself*. The information needed to identify any protocol-specific information is all specified in the name itself: the name of the protocol, the port used by the protocol, any queries the protocol is responding to, and the hierarchical structure used by the protocol. The Web is then first and foremost a naming initiative "to encode the names and addresses of objects on the Internet" rather than anything to do with hypertext (Berners-Lee 1994a). The notion of a URI can be viewed as a "meta-name," a name which takes the existing protocol-specific Internet addresses and wraps them in the name itself, a process analogous to reflection in programming languages (Smith 1984). Instead of limiting itself to only existing protocols, the URI scheme also abstracts away from any particular set of protocols, so that even protocols in the future or non-Internet protocols can be given a URI; "the web is considered to include objects accessed using an extendable number of protocols, existing, invented for the web itself, or to be invented in the future" (Berners-Lee 1994a).

One could question why one would want to name information outside the context of a particular protocol. The benefit is that the use of URIs "allows different types of resource identifiers to be used in the same context, even when the mechanisms used to access those resources may differ" (Berners-Lee et al. 2005). This is an advantage precisely because it "allows the identifiers to be reused in many different contexts, thus permitting new applications or protocols to leverage a pre-existing, large, and widely used set of resource identifiers" (Berners-Lee et al. 2005). This ability to access with a single naming convention the immense amount of data on the entire Internet gives an application such as the ubiquitous Web browser a vast advantage over an application that can only consume application-specific information.

Although the full syntax in Backus-Naur form is given in IETF RFC 3986 (Berners-Lee et al. 2005), a URI can be given as the regular expression URI= [scheme ":"] [hierarchical component] * ["?" query] ? ["#" fragment] ?. First, a *scheme* is *a name of the protocol or other naming convention used in the URI*. Note that the scheme of a URI does not determine the protocol that a user-agent has to employ to use the URI. For example, a HTTP request may be used on ftp://www.example.org. The scheme of a URI merely indicates a preferred protocol for use with the URI. A *hierarchical component* is *the left to right dominant component of the URI that syntactically identifies the resource.* URIs are federated, insofar as each scheme identifies the syntax of its hierarchical component. For example, with HTTP the hierarchical component is given by [authority] [//] [":" port]? ["/" path component]*. The *authority* is *a name that is usually a domain name, naming authority, or a raw IP address, and so is often the name of the server*. However, in URI schemes like tel for telephone numbers, there is no notion of an authority in the scheme. The hierarchical component contains special reserved characters that are in HTTP characters such as the backslash for locations as in a file system. For *absolute URIs*, *there must be a single scheme and the scheme and the hierarchical component must together identify a resource* such as http://www.example.com:80/monument/ EiffelTower in HTTP, which signals port 80 of the authority www.example.com with the path component /monument/EiffelTower. The port authority is usually left out, and assumed to be 80 by HTTP-enabled clients. Interestingly enough there are also *relative URIs in some schemes like HTTP, where the path component itself is enough to identify a resource within certain contexts*, like that of a web-page. This is because the scheme and authority itself may have substituted some special characters that serve as indexical expressions, such as '.' for the current

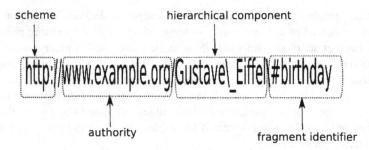

Fig. 2.4 An example URI, with components labelled

place in the path component and '..' as the previous level in the path component. So, ../EiffelTower is a perfectly acceptable relative URI. Relative URIs have a straightforward translation into absolute URIs, and it is trivial to compare absolute URIs for equality (Berners-Lee et al. 2005).

The 'hash' (#) and 'question mark' (?) are special characters at the end of a URI. The question mark denotes 'query string.' The 'query string' allows for the parameterization of the HTTP request, typically in the cases where the HTTP response is created dynamically in response to specifics in the HTTP request. The 'hash' traditionally declares a *fragment identifier*, which *identifies fragments of a hypertext document* but according to the TAG, it can also identify a "secondary resource," which is defined as "some portion or subset of the primary resource, some view on representations of the primary resource, or some other resource defined or described by those representations" where the "primary resource" is the resource identified by the URI without reference to either a hash or question mark (Jacobs and Walsh 2004). The fragment identifier (specified by a 'hash' followed by some string of characters) is stripped off for the request to the server, and handled on the client side. Often the fragment identifier causes the local client to go to a particular part of the accessed HTTP entity. If there was a web-page about Gustave Eiffel, its introductory paragraph could be identified with the URI http://www.example.com/EiffelTower#intro. Figure 2.4 examines a sample URI, http://example.org/Gustave_Eiffel#birthday:

The first feature of URIs, the most noticeable in comparison to IP addresses, is that they can be human-readable, although they do not have to be. As an idiom goes, URIs can be 'written on the side of a bus.' URIs can then have an interpretation due to their use of terms from natural language, such as http://www.whitehouse.gov referring to the White House or the entire executive branch of the United States government. Yet it is considered by the W3C TAG to be bad practice for any agent to depend on whatever information they can glean from the URI itself, since to a machine the natural language terms used by the URI have no interpretation. For an agent, all URIs are opaque, with each URI being just a string of characters that can be used to either refer to or access information, and so syntactically it can only be checked for equality with other URIs and nothing more. This is captured well by the good practice of *URI opacity*, which states that "agents making use of URIs should not attempt to infer properties of the referenced resource" (Jacobs and Walsh 2004). So, just because a URI says http://www.eiffel-tower.com does not mean it will not lead one to a web-page trying to sell one cheap trinkets and snake oil, as most users of the Web know. Second, a URI has an owner. The *owner* is *the agent that is accountable for a URI*. Interestingly enough, the domain name system that assigns control of domain names in URIs is a legally-binding techno-social system, and thus to some extent a complex notion of accountability for the name is built into URIs. Usually for URI schemes such as HTTP, where the hierarchical component begins with an authority, the owner of the URI is simply whoever controls that authority. In HTTP, since URIs can delegate their relative components to other users, the owner can also be considered the agent that has the ability to create and alter the information accessible from the URI, not just the owner of the authority. Each scheme should in theory specify what ownership of a URI means in context of the particular scheme.

2.2.4 Resources

While we have explained how a URI is formed, we have yet to define what a URI is. To inspect the acronym itself, a Uniform Resource Identifier (URI) is an identifier for a 'resource.' Yet this does not solve any terminological woes, for the term 'resource' is undefined in the earliest specification for "Universal Resource Identifiers" (Berners-Lee 1994a). Berners-Lee has remarked that one of the best things about resources is that for so long he never had to define them (Berners-Lee 2000). Eventually Berners-Lee attempted to define a resource as "anything that has an identity" (Berners-Lee et al. 1998). Other specifications were slightly more detailed, with Roy Fielding, one of the editors of HTTP, defining (apparently without the notice of Berners-Lee) a resource as "a network data object or service" (Fielding et al. 1999). However, at some later point Berners-Lee decided to generalize this notion, and in some of his later works on defining this slippery notion of 'resource,' Berners-Lee was careful not to define a resource only as information that is accessible via the Web, since not only may resources be "electronic documents" and "images" but also "not all resources are network retrievable; e.g., human beings, corporations, and bound books in a library" (Berners-Lee et al. 1998). Also, resources do not have to be singular but can be a "collection of other resources" (Berners-Lee et al. 1998).

Resources are not only concrete messages or sets of possible messages at a given temporal junction, but are a looser category that includes individuals changing over time, as "resources are further carefully defined to be information that may change over time, such as a service for today's weather report for Los Angeles" (Berners-Lee et al. 1998). Obviously, a web-page with "today's weather report" is going to change its content over time, so what is it that unites the notion of a resource over time? The URI specification defines this tentatively as a "conceptual mapping" (presumably located in the head of an individual creating the representations for the resource) such that "the resource is the conceptual mapping to an entity or set of entities, not necessarily the entity which corresponds to that mapping at any particular instance in time. Thus, a resource can remain constant even when its content – the entities to which it currently corresponds – changes over time, provided that the conceptual mapping is not changed in the process" (Berners-Lee et al. 1998). This obviously begs an important question: If resources are identified as conceptual mappings in the head of an individual(s), then how does an agent know, given a URI, what the resource is? Is it our conceptual mapping, or the conceptual mapping of the owner, or some consensus conceptual mapping? The latest version of the URI specification deletes the confusing jargon of "conceptual mappings" and instead re-iterates that URIs can also be things above and beyond concrete individuals, for "abstract concepts can be resources, such as the operators and operands of a mathematical equation" (Berners-Lee et al. 2005). After providing a few telling examples of precisely how wide the notion of a resource is, the URI specification finally ties the notion of resource directly to the act of identification given by a URI, for "this specification does not limit the scope of what might be a resource; rather, the term 'resource' is used in a general sense for whatever might be identified by a URI" (Berners-Lee et al. 2005). Although this definition seems at best tautological, the intent should be clear. A *resource* is *any thing capable of being content*, or in other words, an 'identity' in a language. Since a sense is not bound to particular encoding, in practice within certain protocols that allow access to information, *a resource is typically not a particular encoding of some content but some content that can be given by many encodings.* To rephrase in terms of sense, *the URI identifies content on a level of abstraction, not the encoding of the content.* So, a URI identifies the 'content' of the Eiffel Tower, not just a particular web-page which is subject to change. However, there is nothing to forbid someone from identifying a particular encoding of information with its own URI and resource. For example, one could also have a distinct URI for a web-page about the Eiffel Tower in English, or a web-page about the Eiffel Tower in English in HTML. In other words, a resource can be given *multiple URIs*, each corresponding to a different encoding or even different levels of abstraction. Furthermore, due to the decentralized nature of URIs, often different agents create *multiple URIs for the same content*, which are then called in Web architecture *co-referential URIs*.

We illustrate these distinctions in a typical HTTP interaction in Fig. 2.5, where an agent via a web browser wants to access some information about the Eiffel Tower via its URI. While on a level of abstraction a protocol allows a user-agent to identify some resource, what the user-agent usually accesses concretely is some realization of that resource in a particular encoding, such as a web-page in HTML or a picture in the JPEG language (Pennebaker and Mitchell 1992). In our example, the URI is resolved using the domain name system to an IP address of a concrete server, which then transmits to the user-agent some concrete bits that realizes the resource, i.e. that can be interpreted to the sense identified by the URI. In this example, all the interactions are local, since the web-page *encodes* the content of the resource. This HTTP entity can then be interpreted by a browser as a rendering on the screen of Ralph's browser. Note this is a simplified example, as some status codes like 307

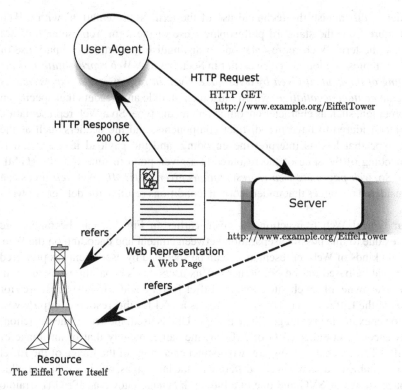

Fig. 2.5 A user agent accessing a resource

may cause a redirection to yet another URI and so another server, and so on possibly multiple times, until an HTTP entity may finally be retrieved.

One of the most confusing issues of the Web is that a URI does not necessarily retrieve a single HTTP entity, but can retrieve multiple HTTP entities. This leads to a surprising and little-known aspect of Web architecture known as content negotiation. **Content Negotiation** is *a mechanism defined in a protocol that makes it possible to respond to a request with different Web representations of the same resource depending on the preference of the user-agent.* This is because information may have multiple encodings in different languages that all encode the same sense, and thus the same resource which should have a singular URI. A 'representation' on the Web is then just "an entity that is subject to content negotiation" (Fielding et al. 1999). Historically, the term 'representation' on the Web was originally defined in HTML as "the encoding of information for interchange" (Berners-Lee and Connolly 1993). A later definition given by the W3C did not mention content negotiation explicitly, defining a representation on the Web as just "data that encodes information about resource state" (Jacobs and Walsh 2004). To descend further into a conceptual swamp, 'representation' is one of the most confusing terms in Web architecture, as the term 'representation' is used differently across philosophy.

In order to distinguish the technical use of the term 'representation' within Web architecture from the standard philosophical use of the term 'representation,' we shall use the term 'Web representation' to distinguish it from the ordinary use of the term 'representation' as given earlier in Sect. 2.2.6. A *Web representation* is *the encoding of the content given by a resource given in response to a request that is subject to content negotiation*, which must then include any headers that specify an interpretation, such as character encoding and media type. So a Web representation can be considered to have *two* distinct components, and the headers such as the media type that lets us interpret the encoding, and the payload itself, which is the encoding of the state of the resource at a given point in time (i.e. the HTML itself). So, *web-pages* are *web representations given in HTML*. Web resources can be considered resources that under 'normal' conditions result in the delivery of web-pages.

Our typical Web transaction, as given earlier in Fig. 2.5, can become more complex due to this possible separation between content and encoding on the Web. Different kinds of Web representations can be specified by user-agents as preferred or acceptable, based on the preferences of its users or its capabilities, as given in HTTP. The owner of a web-site about the Eiffel Tower decides to host a resource for images of the Eiffel Tower. The owner creates a URI for this resource, http://www.eiffeltower.example.org/image. Since a single URI is used, the sense (the depiction) that is encoded in either SVG or JPEG is the same, namely that of an image of the Eiffel Tower. That is, there are two distinct encodings of the image of the Eiffel Tower available on a server in two different iconic languages, one in a vector graphic language known as SVG and one in a bitmap language known as JPEG (Ferraiolo 2002; Pennebaker and Mitchell 1992). These encodings are rendered identically on the screen for the user. If a web-browser only accepted JPEG images and not SVG images, the browser could request a JPEG by sending a request for `Accept: image/jpeg` in the headers. Ideally, the server would then return the JPEG-encoded image with the HTTP entity header `Content-Type: image/jpeg`. Had the browser wished to accept the SVG picture as well, it could have put `Accept: image/jpeg, image/svg+xml` and received the SVG version. In Fig. 2.6, the user agent specifies its preferred media type as `image/jpeg`. So, both the SVG and JPEG images are Web representations of the same resource, an image of the Eiffel Tower, since both the SVG and JPEG information realize the same information, albeit using different languages for encoding. Since a single resource is identified by the same URI http://www.example.org/EiffelTower/image, different user-agents can get a Web representation of the resource in a language they can interpret, even if they cannot all interpret the same language. In Web architecture, content negotiation can also be deployed over not only differing computational languages such as JPG or SVG, but differing natural languages, as the same content can be encoded in different natural languages such as French and English. An agent could request the description about the Eiffel Tower from its URI and set the preferred media type to '`Accept-Language: fr`' so that they receive a French version of the web-page as opposed to an English version. Or they could set their preferred language as English but by using '`Accept-Language: en`.'

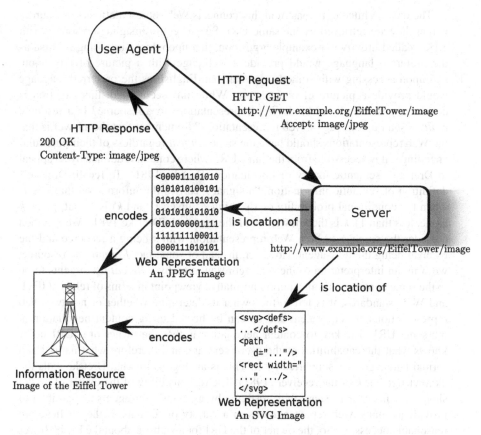

Fig. 2.6 A user agent accessing a resource using content negotiation

The preferences specified in the headers are not mandatory for the server to follow, the server may only have a French version of the resource available, and so send the agent a French version of the description, encoded in HTML or some other formal language, regardless of their preference.[9] Figure 2.6 shows that the Web representations are distinct from the resource, even if the Web representations are bound together by realizing the same information given by a resource, since accessing a resource via a single URI can return *different* Web representations depending on content negotiation.

---

[9]It is well-known there are some words in French that are difficult if not impossible to translate into English, such as 'frileusement.' Indeed, saying that one natural language encodes the same content as another natural language is akin to hubris in the general case. If this is the case, then it is perfectly reasonable to establish different resources and so URIs for the French and English language encodings of the resource, such as http://www.eiffeltower.example.org/francais and http://www.eiffeltower.example.org/english. In fact, if one believes the same image cannot be truly expressed by both SVG and JPEG image formats, one could give them distinct URIs as well.

The only architectural constraint that connects Web representations to resources is that they are retrieved by the same URI. So one could imagine a resource with a URI called http://www.example.org/Moon, that upon accessing using English as the preferred language would provide a web-page with a picture of the moon, and upon accessing with something other than English as the preferred language would provide a picture of blue cheese. While this seems odd, this situation is definitely possible. What binds Web representations to a resource? Is a resource *really* just a random bag of Web representations? Remember that the answer is that the Web representations should have the same *content* regardless of their particular encoding if it is accessible from the same URI, where content is defined by an appeal to Dretske's semantic theory of information (Dretske 1981). To recall, Dretske's definition of semantic information, "a signal r carries the information that s is F when the conditional probability of s's being F, given r (and k) is 1 (but, given k alone, less than 1). k is the knowledge of the receiver" (Dretske 1981). We can then consider the signal r to be a Web representation, with s being a resource and the receiver being the user-agent. However, instead of some fact F about the resource, we want an interpretation of the Web representation by *different* user-agents to be to the same content.[10] From a purely normative viewpoint in terms of relevant IETF and W3C standards, it is left to the owner to determine whether or not two Web representations are equivalent and so can be hosted using content negotiation at the same URI. The key to content negotiation is that the owner of a URI never knows what the capabilities of the user-agent are, and therefore what natural and formal languages are supported by it. This is analogous to what Dretske calls the "knowledge" or k of the receiver (1981). The responsibility of the owner of a URI should be, in order to share their resource by as many user-agents as possible, to provide as many Web representations in a variety of formats as they believe are reasonably necessary. So, the owner of the URI for a website about the Eiffel Tower may wish to have a number of Web representations in a wide variety of languages and formats. By failing to provide a Web representation in Spanish, they prevent speakers of only Spanish from accessing their resource. Since the maintainer of a resource cannot reasonably be expected to predict the capabilities of all possible user-agents, the maintainer of the resource should try their best to communicate their interpretation within their finite means. The reason URIs identify resources, and not individual Web representations, is that Web representations are too ephemeral to

---

[10]Of course, one cannot control the interpretations of yet unknown agents, so all sorts of absurdities are possible in theory. As the interpretation of the same encoding can differ among agents, there is a possibility that the owner of the URI http://www.example.org/Moon really thinks that for French speakers a picture of blue cheese has the same sense as a picture of the Moon for English speakers, even if users of the resource disagree. However, it should be remembered that the Web is a space of communication, and that for communication to be successful over the Web using URIs, it is in the interest of the owner of the resource to deploy Web representations that they believe the users will share their interpretation of. So content negotiation between a picture of blue cheese and a picture of the moon for a resource that depicts the Moon is, under normal circumstances, the Web equivalent of insanity at worst, or bad manners at best.

want to identify in and of themselves, being by definition the response of a server to a *particular* response and request for information. While one could imagine wanting to access a particular Web representation, in reality what is usually wanted by the user-agent is the content of the resource, which may be present in a wide variety of languages. What is important is that the sense gets transferred and interpreted by the user agent, not the individual bytes of a particular encoding in a particular language at a particular time.

2.2.5 Digitality

The Web is composed of not just representations, but digital representations. One of the defining characteristics of information on the Web is that this information is digital, bits and bytes being shipped around by various protocols. Yet there is no clear notion of what 'being' digital consists of, and a working notion of digitality is necessary to understand what can and can not be shipped around as bytes on the Web. Much like the Web itself, we can know something digital when we spot it, and we can build digital devices, but developing an encompassing notion of digitality is a difficult task, one that we only characterize briefly here.

Goodman defined marks as "*finitely differentiable*" *when it is possible to determine for any given mark whether it is identical to another mark or marks* (Goodman 1968). This can be considered equivalent to how in categorical perception, despite variation in handwriting, a person perceives hand-written letters as being from a finite alphabet. So, *equivalence classes of marks can be thought of as an application of the philosophical notion of types*. This seems close to 'digital,' so that given a number of types of content in a language, a system is digital if any mark of the encoding can be interpreted to one and only one type of content. Therefore, in between any two types of content or encoding there cannot be an infinite number of other types. Digital systems are the opposite of Bateson's famous definition of information: Being digital is simply having a difference that does not make difference (Bateson 2001). This is not to say there are characteristics of a mark which do not reflect its assignment in a type, and these are precisely the characteristics which are lost in digital systems. So in an analogue system, every difference in some mark makes a difference, since between any two types there is another type that subsumes a unique characteristic of the token. In this manner, the prototypical digital system is the discrete distribution of integers, while the continuous numbers are the analogue system par excellence, since between any real number there is another real number.

Lewis took aim at Goodman's interpretation of digitality in terms of determinism by arguing that digitality was actually a way to represent possibly continuous systems using the combinatorics of discrete digital states (1971). To take a less literal example, discrete mathematics can represent continuous subject matters. This insight caused Haugeland to point out that digital systems are always abstractions built on top of analog systems (1981). The reason we build these abstractions is because digital systems allow perfect reliability, so that once a system is in a digital type (also called a 'digital state'), it does not change unless it is explicitly made to change, allowing both flawless copying and perfect reliability. Haugeland reveals the purpose of digitality to be "a mundane engineering notion, root and branch. It only makes sense as a practical means to cope with the vagarities and vicissitudes, the noise and drift, of earthy existence" (Haugeland 1981). Yet Haugeland does not tell us what digitality actually is, although he tells us what it does, and so it is unclear why certain systems like computers have been wildly successful due to their digitality (as the success of analogue computers was not so widespread), while others like 'integer personality ratings' have not been as successful. Without a coherent definition of digitality, it is impossible to even in principle answer questions like whether or not digitality is *purely* subjective (Mueller 2008). Any information is **digital** when *the boundaries in a particular encoding can converge with a regularity in a physical realization*. This would include sentences in a language that can be realized by sound-waves or the text in an e-mail message that can be re-encoded as bits, and then this encoding realized by a series of voltages. Since the encoding of the information can be captured perfectly by a digital system, it can be copied safely and effectively, just as an e-mail message can be sent many times or a digital image reproduced countlessly.

To implement a digital system, there must be a small chance that the information realization can be considered to be in a state that is not part of the discrete types given by the encoding. The regularities that compose the physical boundary allows within a margin of error a discrete boundary decision to be made in the interpretation of the encoding. So, anything is capable of upholding digitality if that buffer created by the margin of error has an infinitesimal chance at any given time of being in a state that is not part of the encoding's discrete state. For example, the hands on a clock can be on the precise boundary between the markings on the clock, just not for very long. In a digital system, on a given level of abstraction, the margin of error does not propagate upwards to other levels of abstraction that rest on the earlier level of abstractions. Since we can create physical systems through engineering, we can create physical substrata that have low probabilities of being in states that do not map to digital at a given level of abstraction. As put by Turing, "The digital computers... may be classified amongst the 'discrete state machines,' these are the machines which move by sudden jumps or clicks from one quite definite state to another. These states are sufficiently different for the possibility of confusion between them to be ignored. Strictly speaking there are no such machines. Everything really moves continuously" (Turing 1950). **Analogue** is the rather large and heterogeneous set of *everything that is not digital*. This would include people, such as Tim Berners-Lee himself, who can be represented but not realized as a message, as well as places, like Mount Everest, whose precise boundaries are rather indeterminate. While, according to Hayles, "the world as we sense it on the human scale is basically analogue," and the Web is yet another development in a long-line of biological modifications and technological prostheses to impose digitalization on an analogue world (2005). The vast proliferation of digital technologies is possible because there are physical substrata, some more so than others, which support the realization of digital information and give us the advantages that Haugeland rightfully points out is the purpose of the digital: flawless copying and perfect reliability in a flawed and imperfect world (1981).

2.2.6 Representations

A web-page about the Eiffel Tower seems to be an obvious representation. One can sit at home on one's computer far away from Paris and access a web-page that features a clear picture of – a representation! – of the Eiffel Tower. Furthermore, others from Japan to Egypt should be able to access the exact same representation by accessing the same URI. By claiming to be a "universal space of information," the Web is asserting to be a space where any encoding can be transferred about any content (Berners-Lee et al. 1992). However, there are some distinct differences between kinds of content, for some content can be distal and other content can be local. *Things that are separated by time and space* are **distal** while *those things that are not separated by time and space are* **proximal**. As synonyms for distal and proximal, we will use **non-local** and **local**, or just **disconnected** and **connected**. Although this may seem to be an excess of adjectives to describe a simple distinction, this aforementioned distinction will underpin our notions of representation. In a message between two computers, if the content is a set of commands to 'display these bytes on the screen' then the client can translate these bytes to the screen directly without any worry about what those bytes represent to a human user. However, the content of the message may involve some distal components, such as the string "The Eiffel Tower is in Paris," which refers to many things outside of the computer. Differences between receivers allow the self-same content of a message to be both distal and local, depending on the interpreting agent. The message to 'display these bytes on the screen' could cause a rendering of a depiction of the Eiffel Tower to be displayed on the screen, so the self-same message causes not only a computer to display some bytes but also causes a human agent to receive information about what the Eiffel Tower in Paris looks like.

Any *encoding of information that has distal content* is called a **representation**, regardless of the particular encoding of the information. Representations are then a subset of information, and inherit the characteristics outlined of all information, such as having one or more possible encodings and often a purpose and the ability to evoke normative behaviour from agents. To have some relationship to a thing that one is disconnected from is to be *about* something else. Generally, *the relationship of a thing to another thing to which one is immediately causally disconnected* is a relationship of **reference** to a **referent** or **referents**, *the distal thing or things referred to by a representation*. The thing which refers to the referent(s) we call the 'representation,' and take this to be equivalent to being a *symbol*. *Linguistic expressions of a natural or formal language* are called **descriptions** while *the expressions of an iconic language* are called **depictions**. To refer to something is to *denote* something, so the content of a representation is its *denotation*. In the tradition of Bretano, the reference relation is considered *intentional* due to its apparent physical spookiness. After all, it appears there is some great looming contradiction: if the content is whatever is held in common between the source and the receiver as a result of the conveyance of a particular message, then how can the source and receiver share some information they are disconnected from?

On the surface this aspect of 'representation' seems to be what Brian Cantwell Smith calls "physically spooky," since a representation can refer to something with which it is not in physical contact (Smith 1996). This spookiness is a consequence of a violation of *common-sense* physics, since representations allow us to have some sort of what appears to be a non-physical relationship with things that are far away in time and space. This relationship of 'aboutness' or *intentionality* is often called 'reference.' While it would be premature to define 'reference,' a few examples will illustrate its usage: someone can think about the Eiffel Tower in Paris without being in Paris, or even having ever set foot in France; a human can imagine what the Eiffel Tower would look like if it were painted blue, and one can even think of a situation where the Eiffel Tower wasn't called the Eiffel Tower. Furthermore, a human can dream about the Eiffel Tower, make a plan to visit it, all while being distant from the Eiffel Tower. Reference also works temporally as well as distally, for one can talk about someone who is no longer living such as Gustave Eiffel. Despite appearances, reference is not epiphenomenal, for reference has real effects on the behaviour of agents. Specifically, one can remember what one had for dinner yesterday, and this may impact on what one wants for dinner today, and one can book a plane ticket to visit the Eiffel Tower after making a plan to visit it.

We will have to make a somewhat convoluted trek to resolve this paradox. The very idea of representation is usually left under-defined as a "standing-in" intuition, that a representation is a representation by virtue of "standing-in" for its referent (Haugeland 1991). The classic definition of a symbol from the Physical Symbol Systems Hypothesis is the genesis of this intuition regarding representations (Newell 1980): "An entity X designates an entity Y relative to a process P, if, when P takes X as input, its behaviour depends on Y." There are two subtleties to Newell's definition. Firstly, the notion of a representation is grounded in the behaviour of an agent. So, what precisely counts as a representation is never context-free, but dependent upon the agent completing some purpose with the representation. Secondly, the representation *simulates* its referent, and so the representation must be local to an agent while the referent may be non-local: "This is the symbolic aspect, that having X (the symbol) is tantamount to having Y (the thing designated) for the purposes of process P" (Newell 1980). We will call X a representation, Y the *referent* of the representation, a process P the representation-using *agent*. This definition does not seem to help us in our goal of avoiding physical spookiness, since it pre-supposes a strangely Cartesian dichotomy between the referent and its representation. To the extent that this distinction is held a priori, then it is physically spooky, as it seems to require the referent and representation to somehow magically line up in order for the representation to serve as a substitute for its missing referent.

The only way to escape this trap is to give a non-spooky theory of how representations arise from referents. Brian Cantwell Smith tackles this challenge by developing a theory of representations that explains how they arise temporally (1996). Imagine Ralph, the owner of a URI at which he wants to host a picture of the Eiffel Tower, finally gets to Paris and is trying to get to the Eiffel Tower in order to take a digital photo. In the distance, Ralph sees the Eiffel Tower. At that very moment, Ralph and the Eiffel Tower are both physically connected via light-rays. At the moment of tracking, connected as they are by light, Ralph, its light cone, and the Eiffel Tower are a system, not distinct individuals. An alien visitor might even think they were a single individual, a 'Ralph-Eiffel Tower' system. While walking towards the Eiffel Tower, when the Eiffel Tower disappears from view (such as from being too close to it and having the view blocked by other buildings), Ralph keeps staring into the horizon, focused not on the point the Eiffel Tower was at before it went out of view, but the point where he thinks the Eiffel Tower would be, given his own walking towards it. Only when parts of the physical world, Ralph and the Eiffel Tower, are now physically separated can the agent then use a representation, such as the case of Ralph using an internal "mental image" of the Eiffel Tower or the external digital photo to direct his walking towards it, even though he cannot see it. The agent is distinguished from the referent of its representation by virtue of not only disconnection but by the agent's attempt to track the referent, "a long-distance coupling against all the laws of physics" (Smith 1996). The local physical processes used to track the object by the subject are the representation, be they 'inside' a human in terms of a memory or 'outside' the agent like a photo in a digital camera.

This notion of representation is independent of the representation being either internal or external to the particular agent, regardless of how one defines these boundaries.[11] Imagine that Ralph had been to the Eiffel Tower once before. He could have marked its location on a piece of paper by scribbling a small map. Then, the marking on the map could help guide him back as the Eiffel Tower disappears behind other buildings in the distance. This characteristic of the definition of representation being capable of including 'external' representations is especially important for any definition of a representation to be suitable for the Web, since the Web is composed of information that is considered to be external to its human users.

However fuzzy the details of Smith's story about representations may be, what is clear is that instead of positing a connection between a referent and a representation a priori, they are introduced as products of a temporal process. This process is at least theoretically non-spooky since the entire process is capable of being grounded out in physics without any spooky action at a distance. To be grounded out in physics, all changes must be given in terms of connection in space and time, or in other words, via effective reach. Representations are "a way of exploiting local freedom or slop in order to establish coordination with what is beyond effective reach" (Smith 1996). In order to clarify Smith's story and improve the definition of

---

[11]The defining of "external" and "internal" boundaries is actually non-trivial, as shown in Halpin (2008a).

the Physical Symbol Systems Hypothesis, we consider Smith's theory of the "origin of objects" to be a *referential chain* with distinct stages (Halpin 2006):

- **Presentation**: Process S is connected with process O.
- **Input**: The process S is connected with R. Some local connection of S puts R in some causal relationship with process O via an encoding. This is entirely non-spooky since S and O are both connected with R. R eventually becomes the representation.
- **Separation**: Processes O and S change in such a way that the processes are disconnected.
- **Output**: Due to some local change in process S, S uses its connection with R to initiate local meaningful behaviour that is in part caused by R.[12]

In the 'input' stage, the *referent* is the cause of some characteristic(s) of the information. The relationship of *reference* is the relationship between the encoding of the information (the representation) and the referent. The relationship of interpretation becomes one of reference when the distal aspects of the content are crucial for the meaningful behaviour of the agent, as given by the 'output' stage. So we have constructed an ability to talk about representations and reference while not presupposing that behaviour depends on internal representations or that representations exist a priori at all. Representations are only needed when the relevant intelligent behaviour requires some sort of distal co-ordination with a disconnected thing.

So the interpretation of a representation – a particular kind of encoding of content – results in behavior by the user-agent that is dependent on a distal referent via the referential chain (Fig. 2.7). In this manner, the act of reference can then be defined as the interpretation of a representation. This would make our notion of representation susceptible to being labelled a *correspondence theory of truth* (Smith 1986), where a representation refers by some sort of structural correspondence to some referent. However, our notion of representation is much weaker, requiring only a causation between the referent and the representation – and not just any causal relationship, but one that is meaningful for the interpreting agent – as opposed to some tighter notion of correspondence such as some structural 'isomorphism' between a representation and its "target," the term used by Cummins to describe what we have called the "referent" of a representation (1996). So an interpretation or an act of reference should therefore not be viewed as a mapping to referents, but as a mapping to some content – where that content leads to meaningful behaviour precisely because of some referential chain. This leads to the notion of a Fregean 'objective' sense, which we turn to later.

Up until now, it has been implicitly assumed that the referent is some physical entity that is non-local to the representation, but the physical entity is still existent, such as the Eiffel Tower. However, remember that the definition of non-local includes *anything* the representation is disconnected from, and so includes physical

---

[12]In terms of Newell's earlier definition, 0 is X while S is P and R is Y.

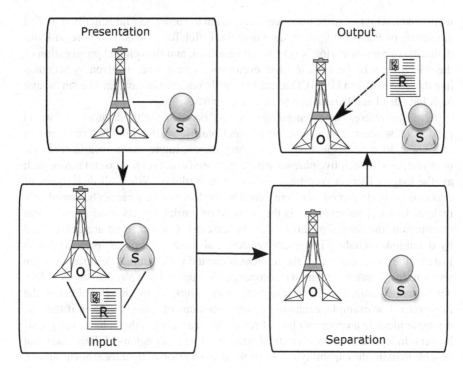

Fig. 2.7 The referential chain

entities that may exist in the past or the future. The existence of a representation does not imply the existence of the referent or the direct acquaintance of the referent by the agent using a representation – a representation only implies that some aspect of the content is non-local. However, this seems to contradict our 'input' stage in the representational cycle, which implies that part of our definition of representation is historical: for every *re*-presentation there must be a presentation, an encounter with the thing presented. By these conditions, the famous story of Putnam's example of an ant tracing a picture of Winston Churchill by sheer accident in the sand would not count as a representation (1975). If a tourist didn't know where the Eiffel Tower was, but navigated the streets of Paris and found the Eiffel Tower by reference to a tracing of a Kandinsky painting in his notebook, then the tourist would not then be engaged in any representation-dependent meaningful behaviour, since the Kandinsky painting lacks the initial presentation with the Eiffel Tower. The presentation does not have to be done by the subject that encountered the thing directly. However, the definition of a representation does not mean that the *same* agent using the representation had to be the agent with the original presentation. A representation that is created by one agent in the presence of a referent can be used by another agent as a 'stand-in' for that referent if the second agent shares the same interpretation from encoding to distal content. So, instead of relying on his own vision, a tourist buys a map and so relies on the 'second-order' representation of the map-maker, who has some historical connection to someone who actually travelled the streets of Paris and figured out where the Eiffel Tower was. In this regard, our definition of representation is very much historical, and the original presentation of the referent can be far back in time, even evolutionary time, as given by accounts like those of Millikan (1984). One can obviously refer to Gustave Eiffel even though he is long dead and buried, and so no longer exists.

Also, the referent of a representation may be what we think of as real-world patches of space and time like people and places, abstractions like the concept of a horse, to unicorns and other imaginary things, future states such as 'see you next year,' and descriptive phrases whose supposed *exact* referent is unknown, such as 'the longest hair on your head on your next birthday.' While all these types of concepts are quite diverse, they are united by the fact that they cannot be completely realized by local information, as they depend on partial aspects of an agent's local information, the future, or things that do not exist. Concepts that are constructed by definition, including imaginary referents, also have a type of 'presence,' it is just that the 'presentation' of the referent is created via the initial description of the referent. Just because a referent is a concept – as opposed to a physical entity – does not mean the content of the representation cannot have an meaningful effect on the interpreter. For example, exchanging representations of 'ghosts' – even if they do not quite identify a coherent class of referents – can govern the behavior of ghost-hunters. Indeed, it is the power and flexibility of representations of these sorts that provide humans the capability to escape the causal prison of their local environment, to plan and imagine the future.

2.3   The Principles of Web Architecture

It is now possible to show how the various Web terms are related to each other in a more systematic way. These relationships are phrased as five finite principles that serve as the normative Principles of Web architecture: The Principles of Universality, Linking, Self-Description, the Open World, and Least Power. In practice many applications violate these principles, and by virtue of their use of URIs and the HTTP protocol, many of these applications would be in some sense 'on the Web.' However, these principles are normative insofar as they define what could be considered as compliance with Web architecture, and so an application that embodies them is compliant with Web architecture.

2.3.1   *Principle of Universality*

The **Principle of Universality** can be defined as *any resource that can be identified by a URI*. The notion of both a resource and a URI was from their onset universal in its ambition, as Berners-Lee said, "a common feature of almost all the data models of past and proposed systems is something which can be mapped onto a concept of 'object' and some kind of name, address, or identifier for that object. One can therefore define a set of name spaces in which these objects can be said to exist. In order to abstract the idea of a generic object, the web needs the concepts of the universal set of objects, and of the universal set of names or addresses of objects" (1994a). The more informal notes of Berners-Lee are even more startling in their claims for universality, stating that the first 'axiom' of Web architecture is "universality" where "by 'universal' I mean that the Web is declared to be able to contain in principle every bit of information accessible by networks" (1996b). Although it appears he may be constraining himself to only talk about digital 'objects' that are accessible over the Internet in this early IETF RFCs, in later IETF RFCs the principle quickly ran amok, as users of the Web wanted to use URIs to refer to "human beings, corporations, and bound books in a library" (Berners-Lee et al. 1998).

There seems to be a certain way that web-pages are 'on the Web' in a way that human beings, corporations, unicorns, and the Eiffel Tower are not. Accessing a web-page in a browser means to receive some bits, while one cannot easily imagine what accessing the Eiffel Tower itself or the concept of a unicorn in a browser even means. This property of being 'on the Web' is a common-sense distinction that separates things like a web-page about the Eiffel Tower from things like the Eiffel Tower itself. This distinction is that between the use of URIs to *access* and *reference*, between the local and the distal. The early notes of Berners-Lee that pre-date the notion of URIs itself address this distinction between access and reference, phrasing it as a distinction between locations and names. As Berners-Lee states, "conventionally, a 'name' has tended to mean a logical way of referring to an object in some abstract name space, while the term 'address' has been used for something which specifies the physical location" (1991). So, a *location* is *a term that can be used to access the thing*, while a *name* is *a term that can be used to refer to a thing*. Unlike access, reference is the use of an identifier for a thing *to which one is immediately causally disconnected*. *Access* is *the use of an identifier to create immediately a causal connection to the thing identified* (Hayes and Halpin 2008). The difference between the use of a URI to access a hypertext web-page or other sort of information-based resource and the use of a URI to refer to some non-Web accessible entity or concept ends up being quite important, as this ability to representationally use URIs as 'stands-in' for referents forms the basis of the distinction between the hypertext Web and the Semantic Web.

Names can serve as identifiers and even representations for distal things. However, Berners-Lee immediately puts forward the hypothesis that "with wide-area distributed systems, this distinction blurs" so that "things which at first look like physical addresses... cease to give the actual location of the object. At the same time, a logical name... must contain some information which allows the name server to know where to start looking" (1991). He posits a third neutral term, "identifier" that was "generally referred to a name which was guaranteed to be unique but had little significance as regards the logical name or physical address" (Berners-Lee 1991). In other words, an *identifier* is *a term that can be used to either access or*

refer, or both access and refer to, a thing. The problem at hand for Berners-Lee was
how to provide a name for his distributed hypertext system that could get "over the
problem of documents being physically moved" (1991). Using simple IP addresses
or any scheme that was tied to a single server would be a mistake, as the thing that
was identified on the Web should be able to move from server to server without
having to change identifier.

For at least the first generation of the Web, the way to overcome this problem was
to provide a translation mechanism for the Web that could provide a methodology
for transforming "unique identifiers into addresses" (Berners-Lee 1991). Mechanisms for translating unique identifiers into addresses already existed in the form
of the domain name system that was instituted by the IETF in the early days of the
expansion of ARPANet (Mockapetris Novemeber 1983). Before the advent of the
domain name system, the ARPANet contained one large mapping of identifiers to
IP addresses that was accessed through the Network Information Centre, created
and maintained by Engelbart (Hafner and Lyons 1996). However, this centralized
table of identifier-to-address mappings became too unwieldy for a single machine as
ARPANet grew, so a decentralized version was conceived based on *domain names*,
where each domain name is *a specification for a tree structured name space, where
each component of the domain name (part of the name separated by a period) could
direct the user-agent to a more specific "domain name server" until the translation
from an identifier to an IP address was complete.*

Many participants in the IETF felt like the blurring of this distinction that
Berners-Lee made was incorrect, so URIs were bifurcated into two distinct specifications. *A scheme for locations that allowed user-agents via an Internet protocol
to access information* was called *Uniform Resource Locations* (URLs) (Berners-
Lee et al. 1994) while *a scheme whose names could refer to things outside of the
causal reach of the Internet* was called *Uniform Resource Names* (URNs) (Sollins
and Masinter 1994). Analogue things like concepts and entities naturally had to
be given URNs, and digital information that can be transmitted over the Internet,
like web-pages, were given URLs. Interestingly enough, URNs count *only* as a
naming scheme, as opposed to a protocol like HTTP, because they cannot access any
information. While one could imagine a particular Web-accessible realization, like a
web-page, disappearing from the Web, it was felt that identifiers for things that were
not accessible over the Web should "be globally unique forever, and may well be
used as a reference to a resource well beyond the lifetime of the resource it identifies
or of any naming authority involved in the assignment of its name" (Mealling and
Daniel 1999).

Precisely because of their lack of ability to access information, URNs never
gained much traction, while URLs to access web-pages became the norm. Building
on this observation about the "blurring of identifiers," the notion of URIs implodes
the distinction between identifiers used only for access (URLs) and the identifiers
used for reference (URNs). A *Uniform Resource Identifier* is *a unique identifier
whose syntax is given by its latest IETF RFC that may be used to either or both
refer to or access a resource* (Berners-Lee et al. 2005). URIs subsume both URLs
and URNs, as shown in Fig. 2.8. Berners-Lee and others were only able to push

Fig. 2.8 A Venn diagram describing the relationships between URIs, URNs, and URLs

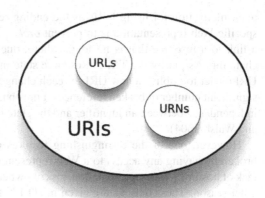

this standard through the IETF process years after the take-off of the Web. Indeed, early proposals for universal names, ranging from Raymond Lull to Engelbart's 'Every Object Addressable' principle (1990), all missed the crucial advantage of the Web; while classically names in natural language are used for reference, on the Web names can be used to access information. In a decentralized environment this is crucial for discovering the sense of a URI, as illustrated by the notions of 'linking' and 'self-description' detailed next in Sects. 2.3.2 and 2.3.3.

2.3.2 Principle of Linking

The *Principle of Linking* states that *any resource can be linked to another resource identified by a URI*. No resource is an island, and the relationships between resources are captured by linking, transforming lone resources into a Web. A *link* is *a connection between resources*. The *resource that the link is directed from* is called its *starting resource* while the *resource a link is directed to* is the *ending resource* (DeRose et al. 2001).

What are links for? Just as URIs, links may be used for either access or reference, or even both. In particular, in HTML the purpose of links is for access to additional hypertext documents, and so they are sometimes called hyperlinks. This access is often called *following* the link, a transversal from one Web representation to another, that results in access to Web representations of the ending resource. A unidirectional link that allows access of one resource from another is the predominant kind of link in hypertext. Furthermore, access by linking is transitive, for if a user-agent can access a Web representation of the ending resource from the starting resource, then it can access any links present in the Web representation, and thereby access a Web representation of an ending resource. It is precisely this ability to transitively access documents by following links that led the original Web to be a seamless Web of hypertext. While links can start in Web representations, the main motivation for using URIs as the ending resource of a link as opposed to a specific Web representation is to prevent *broken links*, where a user-agent follows a link to a resource that is no longer there, due to the Web representation itself changing. As put by the TAG, "Resource state may evolve over time. Requiring a URI owner to publish a new URI for each change in resource state would lead to a significant number of broken references. For robustness, Web architecture promotes independence between an identifier and the state of the identified resource" (Jacobs and Walsh 2004).

However, one of the distinguishing features of the Web is that links may be broken by having any access to a Web representation disappear, due to simply the lack of hosting a Web representation, loss of ownership of the domain name, or some other reason. These reasons are given in HTTP status codes, such as the infamous 404 Not Found that signals that while there is communication with a server, the server does not host the resource. Further kinds of broken links are possible, such as 301 Moved Permanently or a 5xx server error, or an inability to even connect with the server leading to a time-out error. This ability of links to be 'broken' contrasts to previous hypertext systems. Links were not invented by the Web, but by the hypertext research community. Constructs similar to links were enshrined in the earliest of pre-Web systems, such as Engelbart's *oNLine System* (NLS) (1962), and were given as part of the early hypertext work by Theodor Nelson (1965). The plethora of pre-Web hypertext systems were systematized into the Dexter Reference Model (Halasz and Schwartz 1994). According to the Dexter Reference Model, the Web would not even qualify as hypertext, but as "proto-hypertext," since the Web did not fulfill the criteria of "consistency," which requires that "in creating a link, we must ensure that all of its component specifiers resolve to existing components" (Halasz and Schwartz 1994). To ensure a link must resolve and therefore not be broken, this mechanism requires a centralized link index that could maintain the state of each resource and not allow links to be created to non-existent or non-accessible resources. Many early competitors to the Web, like HyperG, had a centralized link index (Andrews et al. 1995). As an interesting historical aside, it appears that the violation of this principle of maintaining a centralized link index was the main reason why the World Wide Web was rejected from its first academic conference, ACM Hypertext 1991, although Engelbart did encourage Berners-Lee and Connolly to pursue the Web further.[13] While a centralized link index would have the benefit of not allowing a link to be broken, the lack of a centralized link index removes a bottleneck to growth by allowing the owners of resources to link to other resources without updating any index besides their own Web representations. This was doubtless important in enabling the explosive growth of linking. The lack of any centralized link index, and index of Web representations, is also precisely what search engines like Google create post-hoc through spidering, in order to have an index of links and web-pages that enable their keyword search and page ranking algorithms. As put by Dan Connolly in response to Engelbart, "the design of the

[13]Personal communication with Tim Berners-Lee.

Web trades link consistency guarantees for global scalability" (2002). So, broken
links and 404 Not Found status codes are purposeful *features*, not defects, of
the Web.

2.3.3 Principle of Self-description

One of the goals of the Web is for resources to be 'self-describing,' currently defined
as "individual documents become self-describing, in the sense that only widely
available information is necessary for understanding them" (Mendelsohn 2006).
While it is unclear what "widely-available" means, one way for information to be
widely-available is for it to be linked to from the Web representation itself. The
Principle of Self Description states that *the information an agent needs in order
to have an interpretation of a Web Representation (resource) should be accessible
from the Web representation itself (URI)*.

How many and what sort of links are necessary to adequately describe a resource?
A resource is successfully described if an interpretation of a sense is possible. Any
representation can have links to other resources which in turn can determine valid
interpretations for the original resource. This process of following whatever data
is linked in order to determine the interpretation of a URI is informally called
'following your nose' in Web architecture.

The *Follow-Your-Nose algorithm* states that if a user-agent encounters a representation in a language that the user-agent cannot interpret, the user-agent should,
in order:

1. **Dispose of Fragment Identifiers:** As mandated (Berners-Lee et al. 2005),
   user-agents can dispose of the fragment identifier in order to retrieve whatever
   Web representations are available from the racine (the URI without fragment
   identifier). For example, in HTML the fragment identifier of the URI is stripped
   off when retrieving the webpage, and then when the browser retrieves a Web
   representation, the fragment identifier can be used to locate a particular place
   within the Web representation.
2. **Inspect the Media Type:** The media type of a Web representation provides a
   normative declaration of how to interpret a Web representation. Since the number
   of IETF media-types is finite and controlled by the IETF, a user-agent should be
   able to interpret these media types.[14]
3. **Follow any Namespace Declarations:** Many Web representations use a generic
   format like XML to in turn specify a customized dialect. In this case, a language
   or dialect is itself given a URI, called a *namespace URI*, *a URI that identifies that
   particular dialect*. A namespace URI then in turn allows access to a *namespace*

---

[14]The finite list is available at http://www.iana.org/assignments/media-types/, and a mapping from
media types to URIs has been proposed at http://www.w3.org/2001/tag/2002/01-uriMediaType-9.

document, *a Web representation that provides more information about the dialect.* In a Web representation using this dialect, a ***namespace declaration*** then *specifies the namespace URI.* In this case, the user-agent may follow these namespace declarations in order to get the extra information needed to interpret the Web representation. As a single Web representation may be encoded in multiple languages, it may have multiple namespace URIs to follow.

4. **Follow any links:** The user-agent can follow any links. There are some links in particular languages that may be preferred, such as the ending resource of a `link` header in HTML or RDF Schema links such as *rdfs:isDefinedBy* links, or links like OWL by the *owl:imports*. If links are typed in some fashion, each language may define or recommend links that have the normative status, and normative links should be preferred. However, for many kinds of links, their normative status is unclear, so the user-agent may have to follow any sort of link as a last resort.

Using this algorithm, the user-agent can begin searching for some information that allows it to interpret the Web representation. It can follow the first three guidelines and then follow the fourth, applying the above guidelines recursively. Eventually, this recursive search should bottom out either in a program that allows an interpretation of the Web representation (such as a rendering of a web-page or inferences given by a Semantic Web language) or specifications given by the IETF in plain, human-readable text, the natural bottoming point of self-description. This final fact brings up the point that the information that gets one an interpretation is not necessarily a program, but could be a human-readable specification that requires a human to make the mapping from the names to the intended sense.

2.3.4   The Open World Principle

The ***Open World Principle*** states that *the number of resources on the Web can always increase.* There can always be new acts of identification, carving out a new resource from the world and identifying it with a URI. At any given moment, a new web-page may appear on the Web, and it may or may not be linked to. This is a consequence of the relatively decentralized creation of URIs for resources given by the Principle of Universality and the decentralized creation of links by the Principle of Linking. Without any centralized link index, there is no central repository of the state of the *entire* Web. While approximations of the state of the entire Web are created by indexing and caching web-pages by search engines like Google, due to the Open World Principle, none of these alternatives will necessarily ever be guaranteed to be complete. Imagine a web-spider updating a search engine index. At any given moment, a new resource could be added to the Web that the web-spider may not have crawled. So to assume that any collection of resources of the Web can be a complete picture of the whole Web is at best impudent.

The ramifications of the Open World Principle are surprising, and most clear in terms of judging whether a statement is true or false. These repercussions transform the Open World Principle into its logical counterpart, the *Open World Assumption*, which logically states that *statements that cannot be proven to be true cannot be assumed to be false*. Intuitively, this means that the world cannot be bound. On the Web, the Open World Principle holds that since the Web can always be made larger, with any given set of statements that allow an inference, a new statement relevant to that inference may be found. So any agent's knowledge of the Web is always partial and incomplete, and thus the Open World Assumption is a safe bet for agents on the Web. The Open World Principle is one of the most influential yet challenging principles of the Web, the one that arguably separates the Web from traditional research in artificial intelligence and databases in practice. In these fields, systems tend to make the opposite of the Open World Assumption, the Closed World Assumption. The *Closed World Assumption* states that logically *statements that cannot be proven to be true can be assumed to be false*. Intuitively, this means that somehow the world can be bounded. The Closed World Assumption has been formalized on a number of different occasions, with the first formalization being due to Reiter (1978). This assumption has often been phrased as an appeal to the Law of the Excluded Middle ($\forall p.p \vee \neg p$) in classical logic (Detlefsen 1990). *Negation as failure* is an implementation of the Closed World assumption in both logic programming and databases, where failure for the program to prove a statement is true implies the statement is false (Clark 1978).

2.3.5 Principle of Least Power

The Principle of Least Power states that a *Web representation given by a resource should be described in the least powerful but adequate language*. This principle is also normative, for if there are multiple possible Web representations for a resource, the owner should chose the Web representation that is given in the 'least powerful' language. The Principle of Least Power seems odd, but it is motivated by Berners-Lee's observation that "we have to appreciate the reasons for picking not the most powerful solution but the least powerful language" (1996b). The reasons for this principle are rather subtle. The receiver of the information accessible from a URI has to be able to decode the language that the information is encoded in so the receiver can determine the sense of the encoding. Furthermore, an agent may be able to decode multiple languages, but the owner of the URI does not know what languages an agent wanting to access their URI may possess. Also, the same agent may be able to interpret multiple languages that can express the same sense. So, the question always facing any agent trying to communicate is what language to use? In closed and centralized systems, this is ordinarily not a problem, since each agent can be guaranteed to use the same language. In an open system like the Web, where one may wish to communicate a resource to an unknown number of agents, each of which may have different language capabilities, the question of which language to deploy becomes nearly insurmountable. Obviously, if an agent is trying to convey some sense, then it should minimally choose a language to encode that sense which is capable of conveying that sense. Yet as the same sense can be conveyed by different languages, what language to choose?

The Principle of Least-Power is a common-sense engineering solution to this problem of language choice. The solution is simply to build first a common core language that fulfills the minimal requirements to communicate whatever sense one wishes to communicate, and then extend this core language. Using HTML as an example, one builds first a common core of useful features such as the ability to have text be bold and have images inserted in general areas of the text, and then as the technology matures, to slowly add features such as the precise positioning of images and the ability to specify font size. The Principle of Least Power allows a straightforward story about compatibility to be built to honor the "be strict when sending and tolerant when receiving" maxim of the Internet, since it makes the design of a new version an exercise in strictly extending the previous version of the language (Carpenter 1996). A gaping hole in the middle of the Principle of Least Power is that there is no consistent definition of the concept of 'power,' and the W3C TAG seems to conflate power with the Chomsky Hierarchy. However, the problem of defining 'power' formally must be left as an open research question.

2.4 Conclusions

The Web, while to a large extent being an undisciplined and poorly-defined space, does contain a set of defining terms and principles. While previously these terms and principles have been scattered throughout various informal notes, IETF RFCs, and W3C Recommendations, in this chapter we have systematized both the terminology and the principles in a way that reveals how they internally build off each other. In general, when we are referring to the *hypertext Web*, we are referring *to the use of URIs and links to access hypertext web-pages using HTTP*. Yet there is more to the Web than hypertext. The next question is how can these principles be applied to domains outside the hypertext Web, and this will be the topic of Chap. 3 as we apply these principles to the Semantic Web, a knowledge representation language for the Web.

Chapter 3
The Semantic Web

> *The task of classifying all the words of language, or what's the*
> *same thing, all the ideas that seek expression, is the most*
> *stupendous of logical tasks. Anybody but the most accomplished*
> *logician must break down in it utterly; and even for the*
> *strongest man, it is the severest possible tax on the logical*
> *equipment and faculty.*
>
> Charles Sanders Peirce, *letter to editor B. E. Smith of the*
> *Century Dictionary*

The Web is a universal information space, but so far it has been one composed entirely of hypertext documents. As said by Berners-Lee at the World Wide Web conference in 1994, "to a computer, then, the web is a flat, boring world devoid of meaning...this is a pity, as in fact documents on the web describe real objects and imaginary concepts, and give particular relationships between them" (1994b). The heart of this particular insight is the realization that it is the content of the information, not its encoding in hypertext, that is of central importance to the Web. The purpose of the architecture of the Web is to connect information of any kind in a decentralized manner, and this architecture can be applied beyond the hypertext documents of its initial incarnation.

The next step in Berners-Lee's program to expand the Web beyond hypertext is called the *Semantic Web*, a term first used by Foucault in *The Order of Things* (Foucault 1970). The most cited definition of the Semantic Web is given by Berners-Lee et al. as "the Semantic Web is not a separate Web but an extension of the current one, in which information is given well-defined meaning, better enabling computers and people to work in cooperation" (2001). How can information be added to the Web without encoding it in hypertext? The answer is to find a language capable of representing the information about the aforementioned real objects and imaginary concepts. This requires a **knowledge representation language**, *a language whose primary purpose is the representation of non-digital content in a digital encoding.* So instead of the Eiffel Tower, we will have a number of facts about the Eiffel Tower

H. Halpin, *Social Semantics: The Search for Meaning on the Web*,
Semantic Web and Beyond 13, DOI 10.1007/978-1-4614-1885-6_3,
© Springer Science+Business Media New York 2013

on the Semantic Web, ranging from pictures to its height, encoded in a knowledge representation language available via a URI for the Eiffel Tower.

As the previous exposition of Web architecture explained in detail, resources on the Web are given by a URI that identifies the same content on the Web across different encodings. What drives the Semantic Web is the realization that at least some of the information on the Web is representational, i.e. information about distal content. Then instead of HTML, which is mainly concerned with the presentation and linking of natural language for humans, the Web needs a knowledge representation language which describes the represented content as fully as possible without regard to presentation for humans. The mixture of content and encodings for presentation forces web-spiders to "scrape" valuable content out of hypertext. In theory, encoding information directly in a knowledge representation language gives a spider more reliable and direct access to the information. As Berners-Lee puts it, "most information on the Web is designed for human consumption, and even if it was derived from a database with well defined meanings (in at least some terms) for its columns... the structure of the data is not evident to a robot browsing the Web" (1998b). This has led him to consider the Semantic Web to be a Web "for expressing information in a machine processable form" and so making the Web "machine-understandable" (Berners-Lee 1998b). This leads to the contrast between the Semantic Web as a 'web of data' as opposed to the hypertext 'web of documents.' W3C standards such as XML were originally created, albeit rarely used, precisely in order to separate content and presentation (Connolly 1998).

Furthermore, the purpose of the Semantic Web is to expand the scope of the Web itself. Most of the world's digital information is not natively stored in hypertext. Instead, it is stored in databases and other non-hypertext documents and spreadsheets. While this information is slowly but surely migrating towards the Web, as more and more of this information is being exposed to the Web via scripts that automatically and dynamically convert data from databases into HTML, the Semantic Web imagines that by having a common knowledge representation language across the entire Web, all sorts of information that previously were not on the Web can become part of the Web. This makes the Semantic Web not a different and parallel Web to the hypertext Web, but an extension of the current Web, where hypertext serves as just one possible language.

3.1   A Brief History of Knowledge Representation

The creation of the Semantic Web then depends on the creation of at least one (if not multiple!) knowledge representation language for the Web, and so the Semantic Web inherits both the successes and failures of previous efforts to create knowledge representation languages in artificial intelligence. The earliest work in digital knowledge representations was spear-headed by John McCarthy's attempts to formalize elements of human knowledge in first-order predicate logic, where the primary vehicle of intelligence was to be considered some form of inference

(1959). These efforts reached their apex in Hayes's "Naive Physics Manifesto," which called for parts of human understanding to be formalized as first-order logic. Although actual physics was best understood using mathematical techniques such as differential equations, Hayes conjectured that most of the human knowledge of physics, such as "water must be in a container for it not to spill," could be conceptualized better in first-order logic (1979). Hayes took formalization as a grand long-term challenge for the entire AI community to pursue: "we are never going to get an adequate formalization of common sense by making short forays into small areas, no matter how many of them we make" (Hayes 1979). While many researchers took up the grand challenge of Hayes in various domains, soon a large number of insidious problems were encountered, primarily in terms of the expressivity of first-order logic and its undecidability of inference. In particular, first-order logic formalizations were viewed as not expressive enough, being unable to cope with temporal reasoning as shown by the Frame Problem, and so had to be extended with fluents and other techniques (McCarthy and Hayes 1969). Since the goal of artificial intelligence was to create an autonomous human-level intelligence, another central concern was that predicate calculus did not match very well with how humans actually reasoned. For example, humans often use default reasoning, and various amendments must be made for predicate calculus to support this (McCarthy 1980). Further efforts were made to improve first-order logic with temporal reasoning to overcome the Frame Problem, as well as the use of fuzzy and probabilistic logic to overcome issues brought up by default reasoning and the uncertain nature of some knowledge (Koller and Pfeffer 1998). Yet as predicted by Hubert Dreyfus, it seemed none of these formal solutions could solve the fundamental epistemological problem that all knowledge was in front of an immense background of a world that *itself* seemed to resist formalization (Dreyfus 1979).

Under increasing criticism from its own former champions like McDermott, first-order predicate calculus was increasingly abandoned by those in the field of knowledge representation (1987). McDermott pointed out that formalizing knowledge in logic requires that all knowledge be formalized as a set of axioms and that "it must be the case that a significant portion of the inferences we want... are deductions, or it will simply be irrelevant how many theorems follow deductively from a given axiom set" (1987). McDermott found that in practice neither can all knowledge be formalized and that even given some fragment of formalized knowledge, the inferences drawn are usually trivial or irrelevant (1987). Moving away from first-order logic, the debate focused on what was the most appropriate manner for AI to model human intelligence. Some researchers championed a *procedural* view of intelligence that regarded the representation as itself irrelevant if the program could successfully solve some task given some input and output. This contrasted heavily with earlier attempts to formalize human knowledge that it was called the *declarative versus procedural* debate. Champion of procedural semantics Terry Winograd stated that "the operations on symbol structures in a procedural semantics need not correspond to valid logical inferences about the entities they represent" since "the symbol manipulation processes themselves are primary, and the rules of logic and mathematics are seen as an abstraction from a limited set of them" (1976). While the procedural view of semantics first delivered impressive results through programs like SHRDLU (Winograd 1972), since the 'semantics' were ad-hoc and task-dependent, procedural semantics could not be used outside the limited domain in which they were created. Furthermore, there became a series of intense debates on whether these programs often purported to do what they wanted even within their domain, as Dreyfus critiqued that it was ridiculous that just because a program was labelled 'understand' that it did actually in any way understand (1979). Interestingly enough, the debate between declarative and procedural semantics is, under the right formal conditions, a red herring since the Curry-Howard Isomorphism states that given the right programming language, there is a tight coupling between logical proofs and programs so that the simplification of proofs can be equivalent to steps of computation (Wadler 2001).

Within AI, research began into other forms of declarative knowledge representation languages besides first-order logic that were supposed to be in greater concordance with human intelligence and that could serve as more stable substrates for procedural knowledge-based systems. Most prominent among these alternatives were *semantic networks*, "a graphic notation for representing knowledge in patterns of interconnected nodes and arcs"(Sowa 1987). Semantic networks are as old as classical logic, dating back to Porphyry's explanation of Aristotelian categories (Sowa 1987), although their first self-described usage was as a common knowledge-representation system for machine-translation systems by Masterman (1961). Motivated by a correspondence with natural language, semantic networks were used by many systems in natural language processing, such as the work of Wilks in resolving ambiguities using preference semantics and the work of Schank using conceptual dependency graphs to discover identical sentences regardless of their syntactic form (Schank 1972; Wilks 1975). Soon semantic networks were being used to represent everything from human memory to first-order logic itself (Quillian 1968; Sowa 1976). The approach of semantic networks was given some credence by the fact that often when attempting to make diagrams of 'knowledge,' humans often start by drawing circles connected by lines, with each component labelled with some human-readable description. A semantic network about 'The architect of the Eiffel Tower was Gustave Eiffel' is given in Fig. 3.1. Note that it refers declaratively to things in the world, but uses 'natural-language-like' labels on its nodes and edges.

When researchers attempted to communicate or combine their knowledge representation schemes, no-one really knew what the natural language description 'meant' except the author, even when semantic networks were used as a formal language. The 'link' in semantic networks was interpreted in at least three different ways (Woods 1975) and no widespread agreement existed on the most common sort-of link, the IS-A link, which could represent both subclassing, instantiation, close similarity, and more. This led to an assault on semantic networks by champions of first-order logic like Hayes, who believed that by providing a formal semantics that defined 'meaning', first-order logic at least allowed knowledge representations to be transportable across domains, and that many alternative knowledge representations could be re-expressed in first order-logic (Hayes 1977). In response, the field of knowledge representation bifurcated into separate disciplines. Many of the

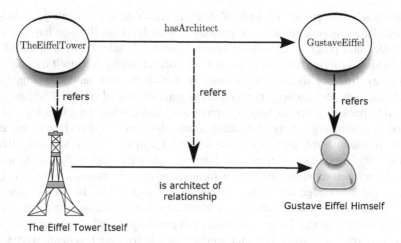

Fig. 3.1 An example semantic network

former champions of logic currently do not believe that human intelligence can be construed as logical inference, but researchers still actively pursue the field as it is of crucial importance to many systems, such as those used in mathematical proof-proving, and it is still used in many less ambitious knowledge-reasoning systems such as ISO Common Logic (Delugach 2007).

The classical artificial intelligence programme, while fixated on finding a formal language capable of expressing human knowledge, had ignored the problem of tractable inference. This problem came to attention abruptly when KRL, one of the most flexible knowledge representation languages pioneered by Winograd was found to have intractable inference even on simple problems of cryptarithmetic, despite its representational richness.[1] Furthermore, while highly optimized inference mechanisms existed for first-order logic, first-order predicate logic was proven to be undecidable. These disadvantages of alternative representational formats and first-order logic led many researchers, particularly those interested in *an alternative "slot and value" knowledge representation language* known as **frames** to begin researching the decidability of their inference mechanisms (Minsky 1975). This research into frames then evolved into research on **description logics**, where the trade-offs between the tractability and expressivity were carefully studied (Levensque and Brachman 1987). The goal of the field was to produce a logic with decidable inference while maintaining maximum expressivity. Although the first description-logic system, KL-ONE, was proven to have undecidable inference for even subsumption, later research produced a vast proliferation of description logics with carefully categorized decidability and features (Brachman and Schmolze 1985; Schmidt-Schauss 1989).

---

[1] Personal communication with Henry S. Thompson.

Ultimately, the project of artificial intelligence to design a single knowledge representation system suitable for creating human-level intelligence has not yet succeeded and progress, despite occassional bursts of enthusiasm, is doubtful at best. With no unifying framework, the field of artificial intelligence itself fragmented into many different diverse communities, each with its own family of languages and techniques. Researchers into natural language embraced statistical techniques and went back to practical language processing tasks, while logicians have produced an astounding variety of different knowledge representation languages, and cognitive scientists moved their interests towards dynamical systems and specialized biologically-inspired simulations. The lone hold-out seemed to be the Cyc project, which continued to pursue the task of formalizing all 'common-sense' knowledge in a single knowledge representation language (Lenat 1990). In one critique of Cyc, Smith instead asked what lessons knowledge representation languages could learn from hypertext, "Forget intelligence completely, in other words; take the project as one of constructing the world's largest hypertext system, with Cyc functioning as a radically improved (and active) counterpart for the Dewey decimal system. Such a system might facilitate what numerous projects are struggling to implement: reliable, content-based searching and indexing schemes for massive textual databases," a statement that strangely prefigures not only search engines, but the revitalization of knowledge representation languages due to the Semantic Web (1991).

3.2   The Resource Description Framework (RDF)

What makes knowledge representation language on the Web *different* from classical knowledge representation? Berners-Lee's early thoughts, as given in the first World Wide Web Conference in Geneva in 1994, were that "adding semantics to the Web involves two things: allowing documents which have information in machine-readable forms, and allowing links to be created with relationship values" (Berners-Lee 1994b). Having information in "machine-readable forms" requires a knowledge representation language that has some sort of relatively content-neutral language for encoding (Berners-Lee 1994b). The parallel to knowledge representation in artificial intelligence is striking, as it also sought to find one universal encoding, albeit encoding human-intelligence. The second point, of "allowing links," means that the basic model of the Semantic Web will be a reflection of the Web itself: the Semantic Web consists of connecting resources by links. The Semantic Web is then easily construed as a descendant of semantic networks from classical artificial intelligence, where nodes are resources and arcs are links. Under the aegis of the W3C, the first knowledge representation language for the Semantic Web, the **Resource Description Language** (RDF) was made a W3C Recommendation, and it is clearly inspired by work in AI on semantic networks. This should come as no surprise, for RDF was heavily inspired by the work of R.V. Guha on the Meta-Content Framework (MCF) (Guha 1996). Before working on MCF, Guha was chief lieutenant of the Cyc project, the last-ditch Manhattan project of classical artificial intelligence (Guha and Lenat 1993). There are nonetheless some key differences between semantic networks and RDF, as RDF was built in accordance with the Principles of Web Architecture that were explained in Chap. 2, as detailed in the next subsections.

3.2.1 RDF and the Principle of Universality

Semantic networks fell out of favor because of their use of ambiguous natural language terms to identify their nodes and arcs, which became a problem when semantic networks were transported between domains and different users, a problem that would be fatal in the decentralized and multi-lingual environment of the Web (Woods 1975). According to the Principle of Universality, since a resource can be *anything*, then a component of the knowledge representation language should be considered a resource, and thus can be given a URI. Instead of labelling the arcs and nodes with natural language terms, in RDF all the arcs and nodes can be labelled with URIs. Although few applications had ever taken advantage of the fact before RDF, URIs could be minted for things like the Eiffel Tower *qua* Eiffel-Tower, an absolute necessity for knowledge representation. Since the sense of statements in knowledge representation is usually about content in the world outside the Web, this means that the Semantic Web crucially depends on the rather strange fact that URIs can refer to things outside the Web.

This does not restrict the knowledge-representation language to merely referring to things that we would normally consider outside of the Web, since normal web-pages use URIs as well, and so the Semantic Web can easily be used to refer to normal web-pages. This has some advantages, as it allows RDF to be used to model the relationships between web-accessible resources and even mix certain kinds of relationships. This sort of "meta-data" is exemplified by the relationship between a web-page and its human author, in which both the author and the page would both be denoted by URIs using RDF. Lastly, this ability to describe everything with URIs leads to some unusual features, for RDF can then model its own language constructs using URIs, and make statements about its own core language constructs. However, just as all components of RDF may be considered resources, just as all resources may not have URIs, all components of RDF may not have URIs. For example, a string of text or a number may be a component of RDF, and these are called **literals** by RDF. In RDF specified anonymous resources are not given a URI, and these are called **blank nodes**. Yet it would be premature to declare that the deployment of URIs in RDF signals a major improvement over natural language labels, for URIs can be just as ambiguous as natural language labels by themselves. However, various theories of semantics as well as engineering like the 'follow-your-nose' principle were theorized to solve the problem of ambiguity.

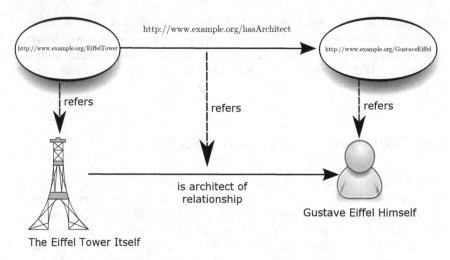

Fig. 3.2 An example RDF statement

3.2.2 RDF and the Principle of Linking

The second step in Berners-Lee's vision for the Semantic Web, "allowing links to be created with relationship values," follows straightforwardly from the application of the Principle of Universality to knowledge representation. Since RDF is composed of resources, and any resource may link to another resource, then any term in RDF may be linked to another term. This linking forms the heart of RDF, as it allows disparate URIs to be linked together in order for statements in RDF to be made. The precise form of a statement in RDF is a ***triple***, which consists of two resources connected by a link, as shown in Fig. 3.2. This use of RDF shows off the flexibility of using URIs and links for reference instead of access. Lastly, this use of URIs and links *outside* Web representations like those of hypertext web-pages shows the flexibility of the linking paradigm, as RDF is an example of the use of the idea of a *linkbase* that was developed in the hypertext community, in particular in the *Microcosm* hypertext system, a pre-Web forebear that failed due to not being based on open standards and also not being based on the Internet (Fountain et al. 1990).

Web representations *in some form of Semantic Web language* such as RDF are called **Semantic Web documents**. There are several options for encoding Semantic Web documents. The W3C standardized encoding of RDF is the verbose XML format 'RDF/XML' although a simpler encoding called *Turtle* exists. In Turtle, a triple is three space-delimited terms (the subject, predicate, and object) ended in a period:

http://www.example.org/EiffelTower
http://www.example.org/hasArchitect
http://www.example.org/Gustave_Eiffel

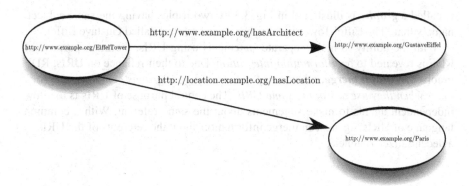

Fig. 3.3 Merging RDF triples

Using namespaces,[2] one abbreviates the example triple to ex:EiffelTower ex:hasArchitect ex:Gustave_Eiffel. As compared to Fig. 3.1, the *only* noticeable difference between RDF and a classical semantic network is the use of URIs.

There are some restrictions to linking on the Semantic Web. As opposed to the vast numbers and kinds of links possible in XLink, linking on the Semantic Web is directed, like hyperlinks (DeRose et al. 2001). *The starting resource in the triple* is called the ***subject***, while *the link itself* is called the ***predicate***, and *the ending resource in the triple* is the ***object***. The predicate is usually a role as opposed to an arc role. The major restriction on the Semantic Web is that the subject must be a URI or a blank node, and the predicate must also be a URI. The object, on the other hand, is given the most flexibility, as it may either be a URI, a blank node, or a literal. This predicate-argument structure is a well-known and familiar structure from logic, linguistics, and cognitive science. Triples resemble the binary predicates in propositional logic needed to express facts, relationships, and the properties of individuals. Furthermore, triples seem similar to simple natural language sentences, where the subject and objects are nouns and the predicate is a verb.

From the perspective of the traditional Web, the main feature of RDF is that links in RDF themselves have a required role URI. It is through this role that URIs are given to relationships outside the Web in RDF. For example, the relationship of 'is architect of' between Gustave Eiffel and the Eiffel Tower could be formalized as a link (as shown in Fig. 3.2), as could the relationship between Tim Berners-Lee and the creation of his web-page. In RDF, URIs can refer to these abstract relationships, even if these URIs may not be accessible in the same sense as web-pages. In that manner, RDF predicates are unlike links in traditional hypertext systems. Similarly, a triple by itself can only state a simple assertion, but webs of links may be made between triples to explain complex statements. A set of triples that share resources

---

[2]So that ex="http://www.example.org/".

is called a *graph*, as illustrated in Fig. 3.3 by two triples having the same subject, namely that 'The Eiffel Tower in Paris has as an architect called Gustave Eiffel.'

With the ability to make separate statements using URIs, the main purpose of RDF is revealed to be *information integration*. Due to their reliance on URIs, RDF graphs can **graph merge**, when *two formerly separate graphs combine with each other when they use any of the same URIs*. The central purpose of URIs is to allow independent agents to make statements about the same referent. With a common language of URIs, agents can merge information about the referents of the URIs in a decentralized manner.

3.2.3   RDF and the Principle of Self-description

Once the Principle of Universality and the Principle of Linking are obeyed, the Principle of Self-Description naturally follows, and RDF is no exception. Self-description is a crucial advantage of RDF in decentralized environments, since an agent by following links can discover the context of a triple needed for its interpretation. As witnessed by the Brachman and Smith survey of knowledge representation systems, a bugbear of semantic networks was their inability to be transferred outside of the closed domain and centralized research group that designed them (Brachman and Smith 1980). The crucial context for usage of a particular semantic network was always lost in transfer, so that what precisely "IS-A" means could vary immensely between contexts, such as the difference between a sub-class relationship or individual identity (Brachman 1983). By providing their own method of self-description, RDF triples can be transported from one context to another, at least in an ideal world where normal conditions, such as when the URIs in the triple can be used to access a web-page describing its content, and correct media types are used.

The hypertext Web, when every resource is linked together, provides a seamless space of linked documents. For example, the W3C tries to deploy its own internal infrastructure in a manner compatible with the principles of Web architecture. Its e-mail lists are archived to the Web, and each e-mail is given a URI, so an agent may follow links seamlessly from one e-mail message to another, and by following links can launch applications to send e-mail, discover more about the group, and in new e-mails reference previous topics. Likewise, an initiative called "Linked Data" attempts to deploy massive public data-sets as RDF, and its main tenet is to follow the Principle of Self Description (Bizer et al. 2008). The hope is that the Semantic Web can be thought of as a seamless web of linked data, so that an agent can discover the interpretation of Semantic Web data by just following links. These links will then go to more data which may host formal definitions or informal natural language descriptions and multimedia depictions. For example, if one finds an RDF triple such as `ex:EiffelTower ex:hasArchitect ex:Gustave_Eiffel`, one can discover more information about the Eiffel Tower, like a picture of it or the fact that construction was finished in 1889, by accessing http://www.example.org/EiffelTower.

Since RDF is supposed to be an all-purpose knowledge representation system for the Web, RDF statements themselves can also be described using RDF. RDF itself has a namespace document,[3] which provides a description of RDF in RDF itself. In other words, RDF can be meta-modeled using RDF itself, in a similar manner to the use of reflection in knowledge representation and programming languages (Smith 1984). For example, the notion of an RDF predicate has its own URI,[4] and is defined there as "the predicate of the subject RDF statement." The same holds for almost all RDF constructs, and a conformant RDF processor can derive from any RDF triple a set of axiomatic triples that define RDF itself, such as `rdf:predicate rdf:type rdf:Property` (all RDF predicates are of the type property). For a statement like `ex:EiffelTower ex:hasArchitect ex:Gustave_Eiffel`, an agent can infer `ex:hasArchitect rdf:type rdf:predicate`, which states in RDF that an architect relationship is a predicate in an RDF triple. However, usually RDF is not hosted according to the Principle of Self-Description. Use of the media type `application/rdf+xml` is not consistent usually, and the namespaces URI of specifications like the RDF Syntax namespace just allow access of to some RDF triples, which is useless to a machine incapable of understanding RDF in the first place, instead of a more useful RDDL document (Borden and Bray 2002). A version of RDDL in RDF (Walsh and Thompson 2007), with an associated GRDDL transform, makes it possible for Semantic Web agents to follow namespace documents to associated resources (Connolly 2007).

3.2.4 RDF and the Open World Principle

The Principle of the Open World is the fundamental principle of inference on the Semantic Web. A relatively simple language for declaring sub-classes and sub-properties, RDF Schema, abbreviated as RDF(S), was from the beginning part of the vision of the Semantic Web and developed simultaneously with RDF. Yet determining how to specify exactly what other triples may be inferred from a given RDF triple is a non-trivial design problem, since it requires adding an inference mechanism to a semantic network, which historically in AI featured little or no inference. Those that do not remember the history of artificial intelligence are bound to repeat it, and the process of specifying inference in RDF led to an almost complete repeat of the 'procedural versus declarative' semantics debate. The original RDF specification defined its inference procedure by natural language and examples. Yet differing interpretations of the original RDF specification led to decidedly different inference results, and so incompatible RDF processors. This being unacceptable for a Web standards organization, the original defender of formal semantics in artificial

---

[3] At http://www.w3.org/1999/02/22-rdf-syntax-ns#.

[4] At http://www.w3.org/1999/02/22-rdf-syntax-ns#predicate.

intelligence, Pat Hayes, oversaw the creation of a declarative, formal semantics for RDF and RDF(S) in order to give them a principled inference mechanism.

The Open World principle was considered to be a consequence of the lack of centralized knowledge implied by the decentralized creation of URIs and links as given by the Principles of Universality and Linking. The parallel to the removal of centralized link indexes is that on the Semantic Web, "we remove the centralized concepts of absolute truth, total knowledge, and total provability, and see what we can do with limited knowledge" (1998c). Hayes argued, in a similar fashion as he had argued in the original 'procedural versus declarative' semantics debate in AI, that the Semantic Web should just use standard first-order predicate logic. Yet while Berners-Lee accepted the need for a logic-based semantics, he argued against Hayes for the Principle of Open World and monotonicity, and the formal semantics of RDF was designed to obey the Open World Assumption (Hayes 2002). The reason for maintaining the Open World Assumption was that adding triples in a graph merge should never change the meaning of a graph so one could never retract information by simply adding more triples, or invalidate previously-made conclusions. This monotonicity is considered key, since otherwise every time an RDF triple was merged into a graph the interpretation of the graph could change and so the entire graph might have to be re-interpreted, a potentially computationally expensive operation. By having a design that allows only monotonic reasoning, RDF allows interpretations to be changed incrementally in order to scale well in the potentially unbounded partial information of the Web. Hayes himself eventually came to agree with Berners-Lee on the issue, noting that reasoning on the Semantic Web "needs to always take place in a potentially open-ended situation: there is always the possibility that new information might arise from some other source, so one is never justified in assuming that one has 'all' the facts about some topic" (2002).

RDF Schema is on the surface a very simple modeling and inference language (Brickley and Guha 2004). Due to the Open World assumption, unlike schemas in relational databases or XML Schemas, RDF Schemas are not prescriptive, but merely descriptive, and so an agent cannot validate RDF triples as being either consistent or inconsistent with an RDF Schema (Thompson et al. 2004). They cannot make the information given by a triple itself change, but only enrich the description of an existing triple. RDF Schema adds two main features to RDF. First, RDF(S) provides a notion of *class*, or a set of resources. Then RDF(S) allows any resource to be given membership in classes and declare sub-classes (or subsets) of a class that inherit all the triples created to describe the class. Second, RDF(S) also allows properties to have sub-properties and for properties to have types for domains and ranges, such that in a triple the subject is the domain and the object is the range of a property. Imagine that the property ex:hasArchitect has the range ex:Person and domain ex:Building. Note that RDF Schemas are not auto-matically applied to triples even if they are mentioned in a triple, such that for a state-ment like ex:Eiffel_Tower ex:hasArchitect ex:Gustave_Eiffel, the fact that the domain of ex:hasArchitect is buildings and the range is people, is not known unless the RDF Schema is automatically imported and so merged with the triple itself. An RDF(S)-aware agent that has retrieved the RDF Schema can deduce from the triple that `ex:Gustave_Eiffel rdf:type ex:Person`, namely that Gustave Eiffel is indeed a person. This sort of simple reasoning is again encoded as a set of axiomatic triples and rules for inference and semantic conditions for applying these axioms to infer more triples. See the RDF Formal Semantics for full details (Hayes 2004). From here on out, the acronym 'RDF' refers to both RDF and RDF(S), whose formal semantics are given together (Hayes 2004).

In practice, the Principle of the Open World has surprising results. One of the ramifications in RDF is that there is no proper notion of false, but only the notion that something is either inferred or not, and if it is not inferred, it may simply be undefined. Although it seems straightforward, in practice this leads to surprising results. Take the following example: 'Gustave is the father of Valentine,' which in RDF is `ex:Gustave ex:fatherOf ex:Valentine`. Is George also the father of Valentine (`ex:George ex:fatherOf ex:Valentine`)? Operating under the closed world assumption, the answer would be no. Yet operating under the Open World Principle, that statement would be possible, for there is no restriction that someone can only have a single father, and in RDF(S) stating such a restriction is impossible. This restriction is possible in the *Web Ontology Language* (abbreviated OWL, in an obscure reference to A.A. Milne), an open-world extension of RDF that allows restrictions, such as cardinality, to be placed on predicates. However, even if one sets the cardinality of the `ex:fatherOf` predicate to one (so that a person could have at most one father), the results would be surprising: the reasoner would conclude that `ex:George` and `ex:Gustave` refer to the same individual. In contrast to the expected behaviour of many other inference engines, including people, there is no *Unique Name Assumption, the assumption that each unique name refers to a unique individual*, due to the Open World Principle. The Unique Name Assumption, while very useful for counting, makes an implicit assumption about each name referring to only one individual, and if an individual cannot be found that satisfies the name then that individual must not exist. This further reinforces the tendency of URIs on the Semantic Web, despite their global scope, to be ambiguous, a point we shall return to.

3.2.5 RDF and the Principle of Least Power

Insofar as it is applied to the Semantic Web, the Principle of Least Power is strangely counter-intuitive: traditionally knowledge representation languages were always striving for greater power, yet the Semantic Web begins with RDF, a language purposefully designed to be the least powerful language. The true bet of the Semantic Web is then on triples as the most basic language upon which other languages can be based. The challenge for the Principle of Least Power is how to build the rest of the Semantic Web by expanding on the language of triples.

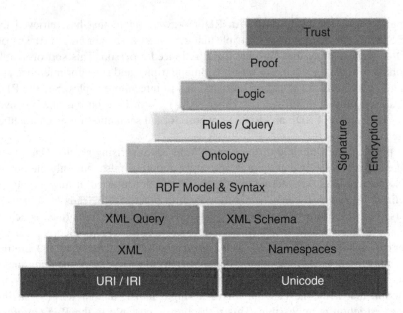

Fig. 3.4 The Semantic Web stack

Inspired by the Principle of Least Power, he envisaged that each language would extend and build upon lower-level languages. On top of RDF, Berners-Lee envisaged a whole stack of more expressive languages being constructed. Although the vagarities of the standardization process have caused various changes in the 'Semantic Web stack' and numerous conflicting versions exist, the original and most popular version of the Semantic Web stack is given in Fig. 3.4 (Gerber et al. 2008). The W3C has commenced standardization efforts in a number of these areas, and research in almost all levels of the stack has begun. The majority of the research has focused on extending the Semantic Web with "ontologies" based on description logic like OWL. As should be suspected given their heritage in artificial intelligence, most of the work in description logic applied to OWL has focused on determining the most expressive possible language that preserves decidable inference. OWL itself works well with the Open World Principle, since it only makes an inference by adding inferred statements and classifications, and so remains monotonic. While almost any possible triple is acceptable in RDF, OWL allows users to design ontologies that can even add constraints, such as cardinality and data-typing, that can make some RDF triples inconsistent with a given OWL ontology. Another part of the Semantic Web, originally unforeseen, is the query language *SPARQL*, a query language for RDF similar to the popular database query language SQL (Prud'hommeaux and Seaborne 2008). Current work is focused on *Rule Interchange Format*) (RIF), a rule-language similar to Prolog for both serializing normal rules and operating over RDF data (Boley and Kifer 2008). Other higher-levels on the Semantic Web stack such as 'Unifying Logic' remain mysterious, if poetic and evocative.

3.3 Information and Non-information Resources

One question is whether or not there should be some way to distinguish between URIs used to access web-pages and Semantic Web documents, and URIs used as names for things like physical entities and abstract concepts that are not 'on the Web.' This latter class of URIs, URIs that are used as names for entities and abstract concepts, are called *Semantic Web URIs*. Should a URI be able to both name a non-Web accessible thing in addition to accessing a representation of the thing? This is a difficult question, as it seems the class of web-pages and physical people should be disjointed (Connolly 2006). The W3C TAG took on this question, calling it the *httpRange-14* issue, which was phrased as the question: what is the range of the HTTP dereference function? (Connolly 2006).

The TAG defined a class of resources on the Web called an 'information resource,' which is a resource "whose essential characteristics can be conveyed in a message" (Jacobs and Walsh 2004). In particular, this means that an *information resource* is a *resource that can be realized as an information-bearing message, even with multiple encodings.* A resource is defined by its sense (content), not the encoding of its Web representations. So information resources would naturally include web-pages and so resources on the hypertext Web, as well as most digital things. However, there are *things that cannot be realized digitally by a message,* but only described or depicted by digital information. These things are *non-information resources.* Their only realization is themselves. Many analogue things therefore are non-information resources. It appears that this distinction between information resources and non-information resources is trying to get at the heart of the distinction between a resource being a web-page *about* the Eiffel Tower and a resource *for* the Eiffel Tower itself. A web-page is an information resource, but the Eiffel Tower itself is a non-information resource, as is the text of *Moby Dick* or the concept of red.

The distinction is more subtle than it first appears. The question is not whether something *is* accessible on the Web, but whether it *can be* accessible on the Web by being *in theory* transmitted as an encoding, and therefore Web representation, in a message. For example, imagine a possible world where the Eiffel Tower does not have a web-page. In this world, it would seem counter-intuitive to claim that the web-page of the Eiffel Tower is then not an information resource just because it happens not to *exist* at this moment. This is not as implausible as it sounds, for imagine if the Eiffel Tower's web server went down, so that http://www.tour-eiffel.fr returned a 404 status code. A more intuitive case is that of the text of *Moby Dick.* Is the text of *Moby Dick* an information resource? If the complete text of Moby Dick isn't on the Web, one day it might be. However, a particular collector's edition of *Moby Dick* could not be an information resource, since the part of that resource isn't the text, but the physical book itself. Are ordinary web developers expected to have remarkably scholastic discussions about whether or not something is *essentially* information before creating a Semantic Web URI?

Both a web-page about the Eiffel Tower and the text of *Moby Dick* are, on some level of abstraction, carrying information about some content in some encoding.

So, if any information resource is any resource which can have its content realized as a Web representation, then information resources *must* be on some level digital so that they can be encoded as Web representations. Then both the text of *Moby Dick* and a web-page about the Eiffel Tower are information resources, even if they are not currently Web-accessible. Digital information can be transmitted via digital encodings, and so *can* in theory be on the Web by being realized as Web representations, even if the resource does not allow access to Web representations at a given time. Lastly, a particular edition of Moby Dick, or Moby Dick in French, or even some RDF triples about *Moby Dick*, are all information resources, with various encodings specified at certain levels of abstraction. It appears that the best story we have to tell about the rather clumsy term 'non-information resource' is that a non-information resource is a thing that is *analogue* and so resists direct digital encoding, but can only be indirectly encoded via representations of the thing in a suitable language. This would then at least be the rather odd combination of physical entities and abstract concepts. So the Eiffel Tower itself, Tim Berners-Lee himself, the integers, and a particular book at a given point in space-time (i.e. on a particular shelf!) are all non-information resources.

Should there be a class to which a web-page about the Eiffel Tower belongs but the text of some as-of-yet unwritten novel does not? In other words, it seems that the class of **information resources** is too large, and we need a term for things that are actually accessible over the Web at a given time. We call this kind of thing a **Web resource**, *an information resource that has accessible Web representations that realize its information.* A Web resource can then be thought of as a mapping from time of request to a series of Web representation responses, where the information realized by those Web representations *are* the Web resource. This definition is close in spirit to the original pre-Semantic Web thinking behind resources in IETF 1630, as well as in IETF RFC 2616 where a 'resource' is defined as "a network data object or service " and coherent with Engelbart's original use of the term 'resource' (Engelbart and Ruilifson 1999; Fielding et al. 1999). A **Semantic Web resource** is *a resource that allows access to Semantic Web documents.*

The distinction between information resources and non-information resources has real effects. When the average hacker on the streets wants to add some information to the Semantic Web, the first task is to mint a new URI for the resource at hand, and the second task is to make some of this new information available as a Web representation. However, should a Web representation be accessible from a URI for a non-information resource? If so, would this confuse the non-information resource itself with a Web resource that merely represents that resource. Yet how else would fulfilling the Principle of Self-Description for Semantic Web resources be possible? To refuse to allow access to any Web representations would make the Semantic Web completely separate from the Web. Non-information resources need **associated descriptions**, *resources that have as their primary purpose the representation, however incomplete, of some non-information resource.* In other words, associated descriptions are classical examples of metadata. According to the TAG, since the associated description is a separate thing from the non-information resource it represents, the non-information should be given a separate URI. This would fulfill

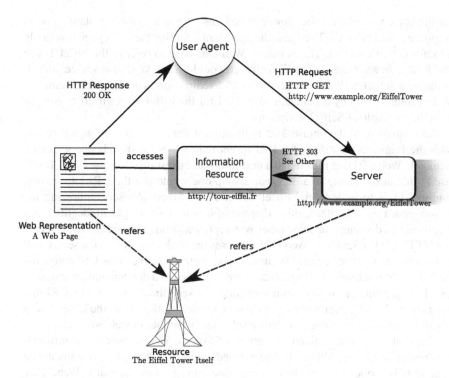

Fig. 3.5 The 303 redirection for URIs

the common-sense requirement that the URI for a thing itself on the Semantic Web should be *separate* from the URI for some information about the thing.

The TAG officially resolved *httpRange-14* by saying that disambiguation be-tween these two types of resource should be done through the 303 See Other HTTP header. The official resolution to Identity Crisis by the TAG is given below as:

- If an HTTP resource responds to a GET request with a 2xx response, then the resource identified by that URI is an information resource;
- If an HTTP resource responds to a GET request with a 303 (See Other) response, then the resource identified by that URI could be any resource;
- If an HTTP resource responds to a GET request with a 4xx (error) response, then the nature of the resource is unknown.

To give an example, let's say an agent is trying to access a Semantic Web URI that names a non-information resource, the Eiffel Tower itself, as illustrated in Fig. 3.5. Upon attempting to access that resource with an HTTP GET request using its Semantic Web URI, since the Eiffel Tower itself is not an information resource, no Web representations are directly available. Instead, the agent gets a 303 See Other that in turn redirects them to a documentation resource that hosts Web representations about the Eiffel Tower, such as the information resource for the homepage of the Eiffel Tower. When this URI returns the 200 status code in response to an HTTP GET request, the agent can infer that the homepage is actually an information resource. The Semantic Web URI used to refer to the Eiffel Tower itself, http://www.example.org/EiffelTower, could be any kind of resource, and so could be a Semantic Web resource. This 303 redirection then allows the Semantic Web resource given by a Semantic Web URI for the Eiffel Tower itself to comply with the Principle of Self-Description.

An alternative to the obtuse 303 redirection is the *hash convention*, where one uses the fragment identifier of a URI to get redirection for free. If one wanted a Semantic Web URI that referred to a non-information resource like the Eiffel Tower itself without the hassle of a 303 redirection, one would use the URI http://www.tour-eiffel.fr/# to refer to the Eiffel Tower itself. Since browsers, following the follow-your-nose algorithm, either dispose of it or treat the fragment identifier as a fragment of a document or some other Web representation, if an agent tries to access via HTTP GET a Semantic Web URI that uses the hash convention, the server will not return a 404 Not Found status code, but instead resolve to the URI before the hash, http://www.tour-eiffel, which can then be treated as a documentation resource. In this way, Semantic Web inference engines can keep the Semantic Web URI that refers to the Eiffel Tower itself and an associated description about the Eiffel Tower separate by taking advantage of some predefined behaviour in web browsers.

While at first these distinctions between Semantic Web resources and information resources seems ludicrously fine-grained, clarifying them and pronouncing an official W3C policy on them had an immense impact on the Semantic Web, since once there was definite guidelines on how to publish information on the Semantic Web, users could start creating Semantic Web URIs and connecting them to relevant documentation resources. The TAG's decision on redirection was made part of a tutorial for publishing Semantic Web information called *How to Publish Linked Data on the Web* (Bizer et al. 2007).

3.4   An Ontology of Web Architecture

The primary use of a formal ontology in the context of Web architecture is to allow us to formally model the various distinctions used in specifications and debates. Although some other formal logic that deals with actions and events may be more suitable for modelling the temporal transactions of client-server interactions on the Web, an ontology is necessary in order to capture the various distinctions given in specifications first. As even the primary architects of the Web find themselves confused about the distinctions between 'entities' in HTTP and 'representations' in Web architecture (Mogul 2002), this ontology could be of use as a reference to anyone interested in understanding or even extending existing Web specifications as well as those interested in correctly implementing best practices that are dependent on rather obscure corners of Web architecture, such as Linked Data's 303 redirects. A first attempt to formally model Web concepts was the *Identity, Resources, and*

Entity ontology (IRE) (Presutti and Gangemi 2008), which has evolved in the
The Identity of Resources on the Web (IRW) ontology presented here via several
iterations (Halpin and Presutti 2009).

IRW is a small ontology at the core of an ontology network. More specifically,
IRW defines the core concepts of the Web architecture and can be extended by
specialized ontology modules in order to address more specific Web domains such
as HTTP transactions and Linked Data. IRW reuses existing ontologies, some of
which are ontology design patterns (Gangemi and Presutti 2009). The following list
summarizes the prefixes that are used in the ontology and associates them with their
respective ontologies. Terms in IRW ontology will be given in `teletype` font, and
if no namespace is given, we will assume the `irw:` namespace.

Prefix	URI
`irw:`	`purl.org/NET/irw/#`
`ir:`	`ontologydesignpatterns.org/cp/owl/ir.owl#`
`comp:`	`ontologydesignpatterns.org/cp/owl/componency.owl#`
`http:`	`ontologydesignpatterns.org/ont/web/http2irw.owl#`
`ldow:`	`ontologydesignpatterns.org/ont/web/ldow2irw.owl#`
`tag:`	`ontologydesignpatterns.org/ont/web/tag2irw.owl#`
`ont:`	`w3.org/2006/gen/ont#`
`rdfs:`	`w3.org/2000/01/rdf-schema#`
`rdf:`	`w3.org/1999/02/22-rdf-syntax-ns#`
`owl:`	`w3.org/2002/07/owl#`

Notice that the stable version of the ontology can also be accessed via its PURL.
The latest version of the IRW ontology is available online.[5] While the IRW
ontology in full cannot be graphically explicated due to lack of space on a printed
page, the primary classes and properties are given in Fig. 3.6. The IRW-related
elements needed for the example of 303 redirection are given in Fig. 3.5. The IRW
ontology defines the class `Resource` to be equivalent to `rdfs:Resource`[6] as
it expresses the same intuition.

3.4.1 Resources and URIs

The notion of a URI is modeled as a class, `URI`. As XML Schema data-types for
URIs are not extensible, modeling URIs as a class allows us to talk about different
kinds of URIs, such as IRIs (Internationalized Resource Identifiers) and Semantic
Web URIs. A property `identifies` can then connect a URI to a resource. Since

---

[5]At http://ontologydesignpatterns.org/ont/web/irw.owl#.
[6]Notice that the ontology is encoded in OWL2.

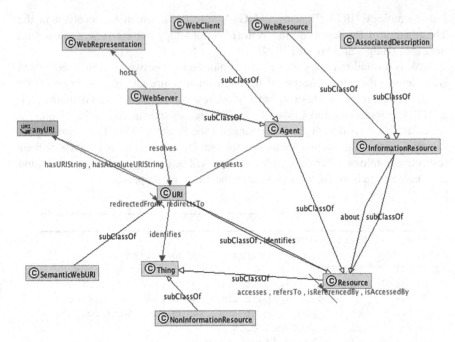

Fig. 3.6 The main elements of the IRW network of ontologies is illustrated as a graph. Boxes with the symbol "C" are classes, while those with a *small arrow* inside are datatypes. Arcs labelled as "subClassOf" represent `rdfs:subClassOf` relations between classes. The other arcs are either object properties or datatype properties, depending on the range node. The direction of an *arc* indicates the domain and range of the property. Two *arrows* that meet on their edges indicate a relation whose domain and range is the given by the same class

we want to associate a URI with character strings (possibly with the XML Schema data-type for URIs) such as 'http://www.example.org,' we also have a property called `hasURIString`. This property has various (functional) sibling children such as one relating IRIs to URIs, so that an IRI given in the Japanese character can be a URI. The core properties we include are `hasRelativeURIString` and `hasAbsoluteURIString` for the conversion of relative URIs to absolute URIs.

- **Resource**: An OWL Class. "Anything that might be identified by a URI" (Jacobs and Walsh 2004). This class is meant to express the same intuition of `rdfs:Resource` hence it is defined as equivalent to `rdfs:Resource`.

  - `owl:equivalentTo rdfs:Resource`

- **URI**: An OWL Class. An abbreviation for Uniform Resource Identifier. "A global identifier in the context of the World Wide Web" (Jacobs and Walsh 2004). Any identifier that follows the role given in IETF RFC 3986 can be an instance of this class, even if it is an IRI that has a conversion to a URI or uses a scheme such as

URN (Moats 1997) or URL (Berners-Lee et al. 1994) that has been subsumed by the concept of URIs.[7]

- rdfs:subClassOf Resource
- identifies exactly 1 Resource

- **identifies**: An OWL Object Property. The relationship between a URI and a resource. It can be functional as one should "assign distinct URIs to distinct resources" although some users of this ontology may wish to not use this constraint and so use the refersTo property (Jacobs and Walsh 2004).

  - owl:inverseOf isIdentifiedBy
  - rdfs:domain URI
  - rdfs:range Resource
  - rdfs:subPropertyOf refersTo
  - owl:FunctionalProperty

- **accesses**: An OWL Object Property. The relationship between a resource and another resource where the former provides a causal pathway to the latter.

  - owl:inverseOf isAccessedBy
  - rdfs:domain Resource
  - rdfs:range Resource
  - owl:TransitiveProperty

- **refersTo**: An OWL Object Property. The relationship between a resource and another resource where the former may be immediately causally disconnected from the latter but still 'stand in' for it in a syntactic expression. Note that reference in the logicist position is an aspect of an interpretation of the syntax of an ontology, not a property of the use of an ontology itself. So this is actually a meta-property that attempts to make explicit the *intended* interpretation of an agent.

  - owl:inverseOf isReferencedBy
  - rdfs:domain Resource
  - rdfs:range Resource

3.4.2 Information Resources

There is a controversial sub-class of Resource outlined in AWWW known as 'information resources.' The AWWW defines the notion of **information resource** as "a resource which has the property that all of its essential characteristics can be

---

[7]Note that this class has itself a URI that is the irw class name for URI in the IRW namespace, but concrete individual URIs are instances of this class and could be any URI.

conveyed in a message" (2004), modelled in IRW as `InformationResource`. This definition has widely been thought of as unclear, and defining what set of individuals belong in this class and what do not has been a source of perpetual debate on various list-servs. In order to clarify this notion we decided to reuse a known ontology pattern i.e. the *Information Realization* content ontology pattern, referred to with prefix `ir:`. Remarkably, this content ontology pattern is extracted from the DOLCE Ultra Light ontology[8] and is implemented also in the Core Ontology for Multimedia (COMM)[9] for addressing a similar modeling issue. The reuse of such a content pattern also supports interoperability with other ontologies that reuse it. This pattern-based approach to ontology design is a strength of IRW.

Notice that the `ir:` is very small, two classes and two object properties, hence it is convenient to simply directly import all of the *Information Realization* pattern. An `InformationResource` is viewed to be equivalent to the notion of *information object* from `ir:`, such as a musical composition, a text, a word, or a picture. An information object is an object defined at a level of abstraction, independently from how it is concretely realized. This means an information resource has, via the `ir:realizes` property (with inverse `ir:isRealizedBy`), at least one `ir:InformationRealization`, a concrete *realization*. The fact that any information resource's "essential characteristics can be conveyed in a single message" implies that everything from a bound book to the electric voltages that encode an HTTP message can be a realization of an information resource (Jacobs and Walsh 2004). Furthermore, the property `about` (and inverse property, `isTopicOf`) expresses the relationship between an information resource and other resource (or resources) that an information resource is 'about.'

Examples of realizations are descriptions of a resource using natural language or depictions of a resource using images. Information resources can be, but not necessarily, identified (accessed or referred to) by a URI. In this manner, the text of Moby Dick can be an information resource since it could be conveyed as a single message in English, and can be realized by both a particular book or a web-page containing that text. Thus, the definition of information object and information realization can be thought of as similar to the classic 'type-token' division in philosophy of mind between an object given on a level of abstraction and some concrete thing which realizes that abstraction, where that single abstraction may have multiple realizations. This is similar, but broader than the class-individual distinction as one may want to model the 'token' or 'realization' itself as a class. As such, it's also broader than the *TBox* and *ABox* distinction from description logic.

- **InformationResource**: An OWL Class. "A resource which has the property that all of its essential characteristics can be conveyed in a message" (Jacobs and Walsh 2004).

---

[8]http://www.ontologydesignpatterns.org/ont/dul/DUL.owl
[9]http://comm.semanticweb.org/

- `rdfs:subClassOf Resource`
- `ir:isRealizedBy min 1 ir:InformationRealization`
- `owl:equivalentTo ont:InformationResource`
- `owl:equivalentTo ir:InformationObject`, which is defined by `ir:` as "A piece of information, such as a musical composition, a text, a word, a picture, independently from how it is concretely realized" (Gangemi 2008).

- **`ir:InformationRealization`**: An OWL Class. Imported from `ir:`. "A concrete realization of an expression, e.g. the written document containing the text of a law" (Gangemi 2008). This is equivalent to the broader notion of **representation** as defined in AWWW, "data that encodes information about resource state" (Jacobs and Walsh 2004).
- **`ir:realizes`**: An OWL Object Property. Imported from `ir:`. "A relation between an information realization and an information object, e.g. the paper copy of the Italian Constitution realizes the text of the Constitution" (Gangemi 2008).

- `owl:inverseOf ir:isRealizedBy`
- `rdfs:domain ir:InformationRealization`
- `rdfs:range ir:InformationObject`

- **about**: An OWL Object Property. An intentional relationship between an information resource and another resource. Note that this property is wider than the inverse functional `foaf:primaryTopic` and `foaf:isPrimaryTopicOf` properties of the `Friend of a Friend (FOAF)` vocabulary,[10] which could be considered sub-properties of this property, as the about property makes no claims about whether a topic is primary or not.

- `owl:inverseOf: isTopicOf`
- `rdfs:domain InformationResource`
- `rdfs:range Resource`

3.4.3 Web Resources and Web Representations

Up until this section, the work done by IRW has, outside of mentioning URIs, not been specific to the Web per se, but explicating the more general ideas of information and resources that apply equally as well to books as to web-pages. In this section, we further specialize IRW to the Web domain by considering the notion of 'representations' that can be transferred over a protocol such as HTTP. To avoid confusion with the broader philosophical notion of representation, we call this term from Web architecture **web representations** instead. Also, it is possible our use of the term 'representation' is narrower than the AWWW's use, which could be

---

[10]The `foaf:` prefix stands for http://xmlns.com/foaf/0.1/.

equivalent to the notion of any information realization in the large, while our use of the term is instead for representations sent over the Web using HTTP. Furthermore, one can distinguish **web resources** (WebResource) as a subset of information resources that are *under normal conditions* usually web-accessible, i.e. the server is not down, the browser works normally, etc.

In terms of HTTP, a WebRepresentation is an entity (associated with various entity headers and an entity body) that is also subject to content negotiation and so may be transferred as multiple entities. This is because, as given in IETF RFC 2616, a Web representation may be defined as "an entity included with a response that is subject to content negotiation" such that "there may exist multiple representations associated with a particular response status" (Fielding et al. 1999). Therefore, we define WebRepresentation as a sub-class of a more general Entity class as defined by HTTP RFC 2616 (Fielding et al. 1999). The term 'entity' could be confusing as it is often used in many other philosophical and technical contexts. However, in HTTP an **entity** may be the information given by either an HTTP request or response, but a Web representation, by virtue of being a 'representation' of a resource, is only for an HTTP response. A web representation is thus a kind of entity that is about the state of a resource as defined in AWWW (Jacobs and Walsh 2004), but there are entities that only request the state of resources or indicate that requests can or cannot be fulfilled. For example, an HTTP POST request or even a 404 response are entities but they do not necessarily represent the state of a particular web resource. An entity may be transferred as the request or response of many particular actions by a client. For example, different URIs may return the same entity, such as when one URI hosts a copy of a resource given by another URI. In order to model the complexity of headers and bodies in HTTP entities, we use another popular content ontology pattern, the *Composition* pattern, referred to as comp:. This pattern, extracted from the DOLCE Ultra Lite ontology,[11] allows us to model a non-transitive component-whole relationship, which however implies (by subsumption) a transitive part-of relation.

- **http:Entity**: An OWL Class. "The information transferred as the payload of a request or response" (Fielding et al. 1999). "An entity consists of metainformation in the form of entity-header fields and content in the form of an entity-body" (Fielding et al. 1999).

  - rdfs:subClassOf ir:InformationRealization
  - comp:hasComponent exactly 1 http:EntityHeader
  - comp:hasComponent max 1 http:EntityBody

- **http:EntityBody**: An OWL Class. Whatever information is sent in the request or response is in "a format and encoding defined by the entity-header fields" (Fielding et al. 1999). Also called in HTTP the 'content' of a message (Fielding et al. 1999).

  - http:hasMediaType o http:MediaType

---

[11]http://www.ontologydesignpatterns.org/ont/dul/DUL.owl.

- **http:EntityHeader**: An OWL Class. "Entity-header fields define meta-information about the entity-body or, if no body is present, about the resource identified by the request" (Fielding et al. 1999). Sometimes called in HTTP "meta-information" (Fielding et al. 1999). Various fields of the entity header can define status codes (`http:StatusCode`), encoding (`http:MediaType`), language (`http:ContentLanguage`), creation (`http:CreationDate`), date of modification (`http:ModificationDate`), and so on.

  - `rdfs:subClassOf ir:InformationRealization`
  - `http:hasComponent min 1 http:EntityHeaderField`

- **http:hasHeaderFieldValue**: An OWL Object Property. A relation between an entity header field and its field values. It is specialized by several properties, each representing an entity header field such as `http:hasStatusCode` and `http:hasContentType`.

  - `rdfs:domain http:HeaderField`

- **WebRepresentation**: An OWL Class. A sequence of octets, along with representation metadata describing those octets, that constitutes a record of the state of the resource at the time when the representation is generated (Berners-Lee et al. 2005). Note that the term 'representation' is used for this class in IETF RFC 3968, but has been changed to 'web representation' to separate it from the more general notion of 'representation' in philosophy (Jacobs and Walsh 2004)

  - `rdfs:subClassOf http:Entity`
  - `locatedOn min 1 WebServer`

- **WebResource**: An OWL Class. "A network data object or service" (Fielding et al. 1999). As such, this is a resource that is accessible via the Web (Hayes and Halpin 2008). Therefore, a web resource must have at least one URI and be realized by at least one web representation.

  - `rdfs:subClassOf InformationResource`
  - `isIdentifiedBy min 1 URI`
  - `ir:isRealizedBy min 1 WebRepresentation`

3.4.4 Media Types

One intriguing problem, central to the notion of Web representations and resources, is the connection between media types and resources. Very little work has been done in this area, likely due to the lack of use of content negotiation in general on the hypertext Web. For example, instead of using content negotiation to return versions of the same resource in multiple languages, many sites use explicit links. The only substantial work so far on this issue has been Berners-Lee's note *Generic*

Resources where he outlines an ontology of types of resources conditioned by how the resource varies over HTTP requests (Berners-Lee 1996a). Berners-Lee has informally said that a **generic resource** is equivalent to information resources, since the important part of a generic resource is the information itself, not any particular realization of the information. For example, a resource like 'the weather report for Los Angeles' is a generic resource, as is the text of Moby Dick in any language. However, the 'weather report for Los Angeles today' is not a generic resource as it is indexed to a particular temporal junction, nor is Moby Dick in a particular language like English. Resources may also vary over time. For example, the text of Moby Dick will be the same over time and so be **time-invariant**, but the resource for the 'weather report for Los Angeles' will change over time and so be **time-specific** (Berners-Lee 1996a). Furthermore, resources may vary over media-types. For example, the same information may be given in some custom XML dialect or RDF or the same depiction may be given in different formats like JPG and SVG. These resources are all imported from Berners-Lee's *ont* ontology.[12] There are also **fixed resources** that regardless of aspects like time and natural language always return the same representation. For example, a resource for Moby Dick that always provided the same edition in the same language as plain text would be a fixed resource. The idea of a fixed resource is surprisingly common, as it equates a single web-page with a resource and so matches the folk psychology of most users of the Web.

- `ont:TimeSpecificResource`: An OWL Class. A resource of which all representations are in the same version. Representations of the resource will not change as a result of the resource being updated to a version with time. The dates of creation and of last modification of such a resource would be expected to be the same.

  - `rdfs:subClassOf InformationResource`
  - `owl:disjointWith ont:TimeGenericResource`
  - `ir:realizedBy only (WebRepresentation ∧`
    `(comp:hasComponent exactly 1 CreationDate) ∧`
    `(comp:hasComponent exactly 1 LastModificationDate))`

- `ont:LanguageSpecificResource`: An OWL Class. A resource of which all representations are in the same natural language.

  - `rdfs:subClassOf InformationResource`
  - `owl:disjointWith ont:LanguageGenericResource`
  - `ir:realizedBy only (WebRepresentation ∧`
    `(comp:hasComponent exactly 1 ContentLanguage))`

---

[12]http://www.w3.org/2006/gen/ont

- **ont:ContentTypeSpecificResource**: An OWL Class. A resource of which all representations are encoded in the same Internet media-type, also called 'content-type.'

    - rdfs:subClassOf InformationResource
    - owl:disjointWith ont:ContentGenericResource
    - realizedBy only (WebRepresentation ∧ (comp:hasComponent only (EntityBody encodedIn exactly 1 MediaType)))

- **ont:FixedResource**: An OWL Class. A resource whose representation type and content will not change under any circumstances.

    - owl:equivalentTo (ont:ContentTypeSpecificResource ∧ ont:LanguageSpecificResource ∧ ont:TimeSpecificResource)

3.4.5 Hypertext Web Transactions

The typical Web transaction is started by an agent, given in IRW by a class Agent, which is some client like a browser in the context of the Web (Jacobs and Walsh 2004). This agent can issue a **request** (requests) through an entity (http:sendsEntity) containing a header field with, as value, the URI that the request is acting upon (hasRequestedURI). This path is modeled in IRW by means of a property chain axiom, asserted in the module devoted to HTTP, i.e. http:. Note that requests serves as a hook to the alignment of IRW with *HTTP in RDF*[13] as a URI corresponds to a response executed by a server which returns an entity which includes a status code (http:StatusCode). Hence, we also introduce the class WebServer for the generic notion of a **web server**, which has a resolves property. The property represents the resolution of a URI to a concrete web server, which currently is done by mapping a URI to an IP address or addresses via the Domain Name System (DNS).[14]

Each WebServer resolves at least one URI, and for the resolution to be successful, the web server has also to be the **location of** i.e. it hosts, at least one WebRepresentation. This indicates that a web server concretely can respond to an HTTP request with a particular web representation. Since requests and resolves are all sub-properties of the transitive property accesses, this part of the ontology models the physical and causal pathway between a given request for a URI and a response with a web representation.

---

[13]http://www.w3.org/TR/HTTP-in-RDF10/.
[14]Although caching complicates this in actual deployments.

The entity given in the request may have a preferred media-type, and the response should have a media-type as well. The media-type, such as 'application/xml' or 'application/rdf+xml,' tells the agent how to interpret the entity body of the response. Media-types are modeled in IRW through the class MediaType. The relationship between an http:MediaType and an http:Entity is given by the encodes relationship. Note that each web representation has a single media-type.

A URI may also have a redirectsTo property, a sub-property of accesses, that we can use to model HTTP redirection. This can be done via a number of different techniques, ranging from a 'Content-Location' HTTP entity header to a 300-level HTTP status code, and to model these we rely on the *HTTP-in-RDF* ontology.[15] Note that, even in the light of the W3C TAG's *httpRange-14* decision, redirection can also be used between information resources that have nothing to do with the Semantic Web. So, the domain and range say nothing about the type of resource.

- **Agent**: An OWL Class. A human or a program that establishes connections for the purpose of sending requests (Fielding et al. 1999). In the W3C AWWW, an agent is "a person or a piece of software acting on the information space on behalf of a person, entity, or process" (Jacobs and Walsh 2004).

  – rdfs:subClassOf Resource

- **requests**: An OWL Object Property. "The act of issuing a request message from a client to a server that includes, within the first line of that message, the method to be applied to the resource, the identifier of the resource, and the protocol version in use" (Fielding et al. 1999). A request action is a flow itself characterized by an agent that sends an entity that includes a URI; this is expressed in IRW by a property chain axiom.

  – rdfs:subPropertyOf accesses
  – rdfs:domain Agent
  – rdfs:range URI
  – http:sendsEntity o comp:hasComponent o
    http:hasRequestedURI

- **WebServer**: An OWL Class. "An application program that accepts connections in order to service requests by sending back responses" (Fielding et al. 1999). Note that "any server may act as an origin server, proxy, gateway, or tunnel, switching behavior based on the nature of each request" (Fielding et al. 1999). A web server hosts at least one web representation and resolves at least one URI.

  – rdfs:subClassOf Agent
  – hosts min 1 WebRepresentation
  – resolves min URI

---

[15]http://www.w3.org/TR/HTTP-in-RDF10/.

- **resolves**: An OWL Object Property. The relationship between a web server that hosts a web representation, and the URI of the resource realized by that web representation.

  - owl:inverseOf resolvesTo
  - rdfs:subPropertyOf accesses
  - rdfs:domain WebServer
  - rdfs:range URI
  - hosts o ir:realizes o isIdentifiedBy

- **locatedOn**: An OWL Object Property. A relation between a web representation and a web server, indicating that the entity can be obtained by an HTTP request to the web server.

  - owl:inverseOf hosts
  - rdfs:domain WebRepresentation
  - rdfs:range WebServer

- **encodedIn**: An OWL Object Property. The relationship between an information realization and its encoding. In the case of entities its range is the entity's media type. So given an entity that has a component with a content type header field set to a certain media type, that entity is encodedIn that media type.

  - owl:inverseOf encodes
  - rdfs:domain ir:InformationRealization
  - comp:hasComponent o irw:hasValueMediaType

- **redirectsTo**: An OWL Object Property. The relationship between two URIs wherein any requested entity is forwarded to the URI given as the object of this property.

  - owl:inverseOf redirectedFrom
  - rdfs:subPropertyOf accesses
  - rdfs:domain URI
  - rdfs:range URI

3.4.6 Modeling the Semantic Web and Linked Data

The Semantic Web is supposed to use URIs not only for hypertext documents but also for abstract concepts and things. In order to model explicitly the redirection solution to the 'Identity Crisis' by the W3C TAG, two distinct sub-properties of redirectsTo have been added in a specific module of IRW[16] associated with prefix tag:. This module contains the tag:redirects303To property and the

---

[16]http://www.ontologydesignpatterns.org/ont/web/tag2irw.owl.

tag:redirectsHashTo property. The former models the TAG's 'solution' to *httpRange-14* while the latter represents the hash convention. With these kinds of re-directions in hand, we can now model the typical Semantic Web transaction. A new sub-class of URI, SemanticWebURI is given. A **Semantic Web URI** refers to a resource that is not accessible on the Web such as the Eiffel Tower, and so the URI must redirect to another URI that can access an information resource containing data encoded in some Semantic Web language like RDF. Therefore, this kind of URI also has a constraint that it must have at least one redirectsTo property.

As mentioned earlier, in the 'Linked Data Tutorial' note, the kinds of resources referred to by a Semantic Web URI are called **non-information resources** (Bizer et al. 2007). Although this term is controversial (and explicitly not endorsed by Berners-Lee) and hard to define abstractly, operationally it simply means a resource that is not web-accessible that therefore should, to comply with the Linked Data initiative, use redirection to resolve to an information resource describing the non-information resource. Although the space of non-information resources is relatively large and hard to draw precise boundaries around, we list a few exemplars in order to serve as what Dennett would call "intuition-pumps" in order to help us understand this concept (Dennett 1981). In particular a new class called ldow:NonInformationResource is introduced, which represents things that cannot themselves – for whatever reason – be realized as a single digitally encoded message. Naturally, this class is disjoint with InformationResource. A number of different kinds of things may be NonInformationResources. Since this concept is the cause of much confusion and debate, it can obviously range over physical people, artifacts, places, bodies, chemical substances, biological entities, and the like – or to resources that are created in a social process and cannot be completely realized digitally such as legal entities, political entities, social relations, as well as the concept of a horse, and imaginary objects like unicorns or even functions over the integers.

An **associated description** (ldow:AssociatedDescription) is an information resource that can be accessed via redirection from a Semantic Web URI (Bizer et al. 2007). In DBpedia[17] dbpedia:/resource/Eiffel_Tower redirects to dbpedia:/data/Eiffel_Tower in RDF/XML, and to an HTML page at dbpedia:/page/Eiffel_Tower depending on the requested media type (Auer et al. 2007). This Linked Data typical scenario can be generalized as follows: a WebClient requests a SemanticWebURI x and the request is redirected (via hash or 303 redirection) to another URI that identifies a ldow:AssociatedDescription, which has one about property to a non-information resource. The typical Linked Data terminology is represented in a specific module of IRW referred to here by the prefix ldow:.[18] The associated description is typically created in order to describe its associated non-information resource. For an illustrated example of these classes in action, refer to Fig. 3.5.

---

[17] Prefix dbpedia: is used for the namespace http://dpedia.org.

[18] http://ontologydesignpatterns.org/ont/web/ldow2irw.owl

- **SemanticWebURI**: An OWL Class. A URI used to identify any resource that is not accessible on the Web.

  - rdfs:subClassOf URI
  - identifies only NonInformationResource
  - redirectsTo min 1 (URI and identifies only ldow:AssociatedDescription)

- **NonInformationResource**: An OWL Class. All resources that are not information resources.

  - rdfs:subClassOf Resource
  - owl:disjointWith InformationResource

- **ldow:AssociatedDescription**: An OWL Class. A resource that exists primarily to describe a non-web accessible resource.

  - rdfs:subClassOf WebResource
  - redirectedFrom some SemanticWebURI
  - isAbout exactly 1 ldow:NonInformationResource

- **tag:redirects303To**: An OWL Object Property. A redirection that uses the HTTP 303 status code.

  - owl:inverseOf redirected303From
  - rdfs:domain URI
  - rdfs:range URI
  - rdf:type owl:FunctionalProperty

- **tag:redirectsHashTo**: An OWL Object Property. A redirection that works via the fragment identifier being removed from the URI.

  - owl:inverseOf redirectedHashFrom
  - rdfs:domain URI
  - rdfs:range URI

3.5   The Semantic Web: Good Old Fashioned AI Redux?

Despite its apparent utility in crafting formal ontologies, at the present moment the Semantic Web has not taken off as part of the wider Web. To many, it has seemed that the Semantic Web was nothing but a second coming of classical artificial intelligence. As put by Yorick Wilks, "Some have taken the initial presentation of the Semantic Web by Berners-Lee, Hendler and Lassila to be a restatement of the Good Old Fashioned AI agenda in new and fashionable World Wide Web terms" (2008a). So why would the Semantic Web succeed where classical knowledge representations failed? The first reason would be a difference in the underlying intellectual project. A second reason would be a difference in technology.

The difference of the project is one both of scope and goal. The Semantic Web is, at first glance at least, a more modest project than artificial intelligence. To review the claims of artificial intelligence in order to clarify their relation to the Semantic Web, we are best served by remembering the goal of AI as stated by John McCarthy at the 1956 Dartmouth Conference, "the study is to proceed on the basis of the conjecture that every aspect of learning or any other feature of intelligence can in principle be so precisely described that a machine can be made to simulate it" (McCarthy et al. 1955). However, 'intelligence' itself is not even vaguely defined. The proposal put forward by McCarthy gave a central role to "common-sense," so that "a program has common sense if it automatically deduces for itself a sufficient wide class of immediate consequences of anything it is told and what it already knows" (1959).

In contrast, the Semantic Web does not seek to replicate human intelligence and encode all common-sense knowledge in some universal representational scheme. The Semantic Web instead leaves "aside the artificial intelligence problem of training machines to behave like people" but instead tries to develop a representation language that can *complement* human intelligence, for "the Web was designed as an information space, with the goal that it should be useful not only for human-human communication, but also that machines would be able to participate and help" (Berners-Lee 1998c). Despite appearances, the Semantic Web is in the spirit of Licklider and Engelbart rather than McCarthy, Minsky, and even latter-day proponents of AI like Brooks. Berners-Lee is explicit that the project of encoding human intelligence is not part of the problem, as the Semantic Web "does not imply some magical artificial intelligence which allows machines to comprehend human mumblings. It only indicates a machine's ability to solve a well-defined problem by performing well-defined operations on existing well-defined data" (Berners-Lee 1998c). Instead, the Semantic Web is an intellectual project whose goal is philosophically the opposite of artificial intelligence, the creation of new forms of collective intelligence. As phrased by Licklider, this would be a "man-machine symbiosis," in which in "the anticipated symbiotic partnership, men will set the goals, formulate the hypotheses, determine the criteria, and perform the evaluations. Computing machines will do the routinizable work that must be done to prepare the way for insights and decisions" (1960).

While the goals of the Semantic Web are different, it does still employ the same fundamental technology as classical artificial intelligence: knowledge representation languages. As put by Berners-Lee, "The Semantic Web is what we will get if we perform the same globalization process to knowledge representation that the Web initially did to hypertext" (Berners-Lee 1998c). Yet there is a question about whether or not knowledge representation *itself* might be the problem, not just scale. As put by Karen Spärck Jones, one of the founders of information retrieval, "there are serious problems about the core [Semantic Web] idea of combining substantive formal description with world-wide reach, i.e. having your cake and eating it, even if the cake is only envisaged as more like a modest sponge cake than the rich fruit cake that AI would like to have" (2004). So the problem may lie in the very use of *knowledge representation language* itself. So far we have shown that the properties of at least RDF as a knowledge representation language puts the emphasis on 'Web' as opposed to 'Semantic' in the Semantic Web, as it has a number of properties – a graph structure, the ability to make unconstrained statements, and the like – that have their basis in the tradition of the Web, rather than knowledge representation in AI. As the Web has proved to be extraordinarily successful, the hope of the Semantic Web is that any knowledge representation language which is based on the same principles as the Web may fare better than its ancestors in artificial intelligence. However, these changes in the formalism of RDF due to the influence of the Web are all relatively minor, and while counter-intuitive to traditional knowledge representation, they have yet to be vindicated as the Semantic Web has not yet reached widespread use.

Overlooked by Spärck Jones in her critique of the Semantic Web, the only substantive difference between traditional knowledge representation and the Semantic Web is the central role of URIs. Just as the later principles of Web architecture build upon the Principle of Universality, so the Semantic Web builds on top of the use of URIs as well. The true bet of the Semantic Web is *not* a bet on the return of knowledge representation languages, but a bet on the universality of URIs, namely that agents in a decentralized and global manner can use URIs to share meaning even about non-Web accessible things. As this use of URIs as the basic element of meaning is central to the Semantic Web, and as it is a genuinely *new* technical claim, it is precisely in the understanding of the status of meaning and reference of URIs that any new *theoretical* claim must be made. Furthermore, it is precisely within the realm of URIs that any *technical* claim to advance must be made.

Chapter 4
Theories of Semantics on the Web

> *Meaning is what essence becomes when it is divorced from the object of reference and wedded to the word.*
>
> W.V.O. Quine *(1951)*

4.1 The Identity Crisis

How can agents determine what a URI identifies? To use a word more familiar to philosophers, how can anyone determine what a URI refers to or means? On the pre-Semantic Web, a URI trivially identifies the hypertext web-pages that the URI accesses. On the Semantic Web, a whole new cluster of questions, dubbed the *Identity Crisis*, emerges. Can a URI for the Eiffel Tower be used to refer to the Eiffel Tower in Paris itself? If one just re-uses a URI for a web-page of the Eiffel Tower, then one risks the URI being ambiguous between the Eiffel Tower itself and a particular representation of the Eiffel Tower. If one gives the Eiffel Tower *qua* Eiffel Tower its own URI, should that URI allow access to any information, such as a hypertext web-page? In the realm of official Web standards, the jury is still out. In the specification of RDF, Hayes notes that "exactly what is considered to be the 'meaning' of an assertion in RDF or RDF(S) in some broad sense may depend on many factors, including social conventions, comments in natural language" so unfortunately "much of this meaning will be inaccessible to machine processing" such that "a full analysis of meaning" is "a large research topic" (Hayes 2004).

The comment in the RDF Semantics specification glosses over a huge argument. Unsurprisingly, the reason there is no standardized way to determine the meaning of a URI is because, instead of a single clear answer, there is a conceptual quagmire dominated by two positions in the development of RDF. The first position, the *direct reference position*, is that the meaning of a URI is whatever was intended by the owner. The owner of the URI should be able to unambiguously declare and communicate the meaning of any URI, including a Semantic Web URI. In this position, the referent is generally considered to be some individual unambiguous

H. Halpin, *Social Semantics: The Search for Meaning on the Web*,
Semantic Web and Beyond 13, DOI 10.1007/978-1-4614-1885-6_4,
© Springer Science+Business Media New York 2013

single thing, like the Eiffel Tower or the concept of a unicorn. This viewpoint is the one generally held by many Web architects, like Berners-Lee, who imagine it holds not just for the Semantic Web, but the entire Web. The second position, which we call the *logicist position* due to its more clear roots in non-modal logic, is that for the Semantic Web, the meaning of a URI is given by whatever things satisfy the model(s) given by the formal semantics of the Semantic Web. Adherents of this position hold that the referent of a URI is ambiguous, as many different things can satisfy whatever model is given by the interpretation of some sets of sentences using the URI. This position is generally held by logicians, who claim that the Semantic Web is entirely distinct from the hypertext Web, with URIs serving as nothing more than particularly funny symbols.

These two antagonistic positions were subterranean in the development of the Semantic Web, until a critical point was reached in an argument between Pat Hayes, the AI researcher primarily responsible for the formal semantics of the Semantic Web, and Berners-Lee. This argument was provoked by an issue called 'Social Meaning and RDF' and was brought about by the following draft statement in the *RDF Concepts and Abstract Syntax Recommendation*, "the meaning of an RDF document includes the social meaning, the formal meaning, and the social meaning of the formal entailments" so that "when an RDF graph is asserted in the Web, its publisher is saying something about their view of the world" and "such an assertion should be understood to carry the same social import and responsibilities as an assertion in any other format" (2004). During the period of comments for the RDF Working Drafts, Bijan Parsia commented that the above-mentioned sentences do not "really specify anything and thus can be ignored" or are "dangerously underthought and underspecified" and so should be removed (Parsia 2003). While at first these sentences about the meaning of RDF seemed to be rather harmless and in concordance with commonsense, the repercussions on the actual implementation of the Semantic Web are surprisingly large, since "an RDF graph may contain 'defining information' that is opaque to logical reasoners. This information may be used by human interpreters of RDF information, or programmers writing software to perform specialized forms of deduction in the Semantic Web" (Klyne and Carroll 2004). In other words, a special type of *non-logical* reasoning can therefore be used by the Semantic Web.

An example of this extra-logical reasoning engendered by the fact that URIs identify 'one thing' is as follows. Assume that a human agent has found a URI for the Eiffel Tower from DBpedia, and so by accessing the URI a Semantic Web agent can discover a number of facts about the Eiffel Tower, such as that it is in Paris and that its architect is Gustave Eiffel, and these statements are accessed as an RDF graph (Auer et al. 2007). However, a human can have considerable background knowledge about the Eiffel Tower, such as a vague belief that at some point in time it was the tallest building in the world. This information is confirmed by the human agent employing the follow-your-nose algorithm, where by following the subject of any triple, the human would be redirected to the hypertext Wikipedia article about the Eiffel Tower, where the agent discovers via a human-readable description that the Eiffel Tower was in fact the tallest building until 1930, when it was superseded in height by New York City's Chrysler building. This information is *not* explicitly in the RDF graphs provided. It is furthermore difficult to even phrase this sort of temporal information in RDF. Furthermore, the human agent discovers another URI for the Eiffel Tower, an RDF version of Wordnet in the file `synset-Eiffel_Tower-noun-1.rdf` (van Assem et al. 2006). When the human agent accesses this URI, there is little information in the RDF graph except that this URI is used for a noun. However, the human-readable `gloss` property explains that the referent of this URI is 'a wrought iron tower 300 m high that was constructed in Paris in 1889; for many years it was the tallest man-made structure.' Therefore, the human agent believes that there is indeed a singular entity called the 'Eiffel Tower' in Paris, and that this entity was in fact at some point the tallest building in the world, and so the two URIs are equivalent in some sense, although the URIs do not formally match. What the 'Social Meaning' clause was trying to state is that the human should be able to *non-logically* infer that both URIs refer to the Eiffel Tower in Paris, and they use this information to merge the RDF graphs, resulting in perhaps some improved inferences in the future.

This use-case was put forward primarily by Berners-Lee, and the W3C RDF Working Group decided that deciding on the relationship between the social and formal meaning of RDF was beyond the scope of the RDF Working Group to decide, so the RDF Working Group appealed to the W3C TAG for a decision. As TAG member Connolly noticed, they "didn't see a way to specify how this works for RDF without specifying how it works for the rest of the Web at the same time" (Berners-Lee 2003b). In particular, Berners-Lee then put forward his own viewpoint that "a single meaning is given to each URI," which is summarized by the slogan that a URI "identifies one thing" (2003c). In response, Hayes said that "it is simply untenable to claim that all names identify one thing" (2003a). Furthermore, he goes on to state that this is one of the basic results of the knowledge representation community and twentieth century linguistic semantics, and so that the W3C cannot by fiat render the judgment that a URI identifies one thing. Berners-Lee rejects Hayes's claim that the Semantic Web must somehow build upon the results of logic and natural language, instead claiming that "this system is different from natural language: we designed it such that each URI identifies one and only one concrete thing in the real world or one and only one globally shared concept" (2003a). At this point, in exasperation, Hayes retorted that "I'm not saying that the 'unique identification' condition is an unattainable ideal: I'm saying that it doesn't make sense, that it isn't true, and that it could not possibly be true. I'm saying that it is *crazy*" (2003b). While Hayes did not explain his own position fully, as he was the editor of the formal semantics of RDF and had the support of other logicians in the RDF Working Group, the issue deadlocked and the RDF Working Group was unable to come to a consensus. In order to move RDF from a Working Draft to a Recommendation, the W3C RDF Working Group removed all references to social meaning from the RDF documents.

One should be worried when two prominent researchers such as Berners-Lee and Hayes have such a titanic disagreement, where no sort of consensus agreement seems forthcoming. Yet who is right? Berners-Lee's viewpoint seems intuitive and easy to understand. However, from the standpoint of the formal semantics of logic, the argument would seem to have been won by Hayes. Still, there is reason to pause to consider the possibility that Berners-Lee is correct. First, while his notion may seem counter to 'common-sense' within formal logic, it should be remembered that as far as practical results are concerned, the project of logic-based modelling of common-sense knowledge in classical artificial intelligence inaugurated by Hayes earlier is commonly viewed to be a failure by current researchers in AI and cognitive science (Wheeler 2005). In contrast, despite the earlier and eerily similar argument that Berners-Lee had with original hypertext academic researchers about broken links and with the IETF about the impossibility of a single naming scheme for the entire Internet, the Web is without a doubt an unparalleled success. While in general the intuitions of Berners-Lee may seem to be wrong according to academia, history has proven him right in the past. Therefore, one should take his pronouncements seriously.

The Identity Crisis is not just a conflict between merely two differing individual opinions, but a conflict between two entire disciplines: the nascent discipline of 'Web Science' as given by the principles of Web architecture, and that of knowledge representation in AI and logic (Berners-Lee et al. 2006). Berners-Lee's background is in the Internet standardization bodies like the IETF, and it is primarily his intuitions behind Web architecture. Hayes, whose background in logic jumpstarted the field of knowledge representation in artificial intelligence, should be taken equally seriously. If two entire fields, who have joined common-cause in the Semantic Web, are at odds, then trouble at the level of *theory* is afoot.

Troubles at levels of theory invariably cause trouble in practice. So this disagreement would not be nearly as worrisome were not the Semantic Web itself in such a state of perpetual disrepair, making it practically unusable. In a manner disturbingly similar to classical artificial intelligence, the Semantic Web is always thought of as soon-to-be arriving, the 'next' big thing, but its actual uses are few and far between. The reason given by Semantic Web advocates is that the Semantic Web is suffering from simple engineering problems, such as a lack of some new standard, some easily-accessible list of vocabularies, or a dearth of Semantic Web-enabled programs. That the Semantic Web has not yet experienced the dizzying growth of the original hypertext Web, even after an even longer period of gestation, points to the fact that something is fundamentally awry. The root of the problem is the dependence of the Semantic Web on using URIs as names for things non-accessible from the Web.

Far from being a mandarin metaphysical pursuit, this problem is the very first practical issue one encounters as soon as one wants to actually use the Semantic Web. If an agent receives a graph in RDF, then the agent should be able to determine an interpretation. The inference procedure itself may help this problem, but it may instead make it worse, simply producing more uninterpretable RDF statements. The agent could employ the follow-your-nose algorithm, but what information, if any, should be accessible at these Semantic Web-enabled URIs? If a user wants to add some information to the Semantic Web, how many URIs should they create? One for the representation, and another for the referent the representation is *about*? Should the same URI for the Eiffel Tower itself be the one that is used to access a web-page about the Eiffel Tower?

URIs on the Semantic Web can be thought of as analogous to natural language *names*, as names in natural language can be used to refer as well. Therefore, what needs to be done is to distinguish within analytic philosophy the various theories on naming and reference in general, and then see how these various theories either do or do not apply to the Semantic Web. What is remarkable is that the position of Hayes, the logicist position, corresponds to a well-known theory of meaning and reference, the 'descriptivist theory of reference' attributed to early Wittgenstein, Carnap, Russell, and turned into its pure logical form by Tarski (Luntley 1999). However, it is common currency in philosophical circles that the descriptivist theory of reference was overthrown by the 'causal theory of reference' championed by Kripke and extended by Putnam (Luntley 1999). It is precisely this causal theory of reference that Berners-Lee justifies in his direct reference position. Thus, the curious coincidence is that both opposing positions on the Semantic Web correspond to *equally* opposing positions in philosophy. Understanding these positions belongs primarily to the domain of philosophy, even if Hayes and especially Berners-Lee do not articulate their positions with the relevant academic citations. In this manner, the precise domain of philosophy that the Identity Crisis falls under is the philosophy of language. The purpose of the rest of this chapter is then the full explication of these two theories of reference in philosophy of language, and then to inspect their practical success (or lack thereof) in the context of the Semantic Web, while at the end offering a critique of both, paving the way for a third theory of meaning.

4.2   Sense and Reference

The original theory of meaning we shall return to is Frege's original controversial theory of sense and reference as given in *Sinn und Bedeutung* (Frege 1892).[1] This theory is no longer particularly popular, although it has had some revival with an odd dualist variation under the 'two-dimensionalism' of Chalmers (2006),[2] and this is likely because Frege himself was quite cryptic with regards to any definition of 'sense.' The key idea lies in Frege's contention that the meaning of any representational term in a language is determined by what Frege calls the "sense" of the sentences that use the term, rather than any direct reference of the term (1892). According to Frege, two sentences could be the same only if they shared the same

---

[1] The ambiguous translation of this work from original German has been a source of great philosophical confusion. While the word 'Sinn' has almost always been translated into 'sense,' the word 'Bedeutung' has been translated into *either* 'reference' or 'meaning,' depending on the translator. While 'Bedeutung' is most usually translated into the fuzzy English word 'meaning' by most German speakers, the *use* to which Frege puts it is much more in line with how the word 'reference' is used in philosophy. So in the tradition of Michael Dummett, we will translate Frege's 'Bedeutung' into 'reference' rather than 'meaning' (Dummett 1973).

[2] Likely Frege himself would not be considered a dualist, but a monist with objective meaning given in the world.

sense. Take for example the two sentences "Hesperus is the Evening Star" and "Phosphorus is the Morning Star" (Frege 1892). Since the ancient Greeks did not know that 'The Morning Star is the same as the Evening Star,' they did not know that the names 'Hesperus' and 'Phosphorus' share the same referent when they baptized the same star, the planet Venus, with two different names (Frege 1892). Therefore, Frege says that these two sentences have distinct 'senses' even if they share the same referent. Frege pointed out that, far from being meaningless, statements of identity that would be mere tautologies from the point of view of a theory of reference are actually meaningful if one realizes different terms can have distinct senses. One can understand a statement like 'The Morning Star is the Evening Star' without knowing that both refer to Venus, and one may only know that the 'Morning Star' refers to Venus and by learning the 'Morning Star' and the 'Evening Star' are not distinct senses but a single sense, one can do actual *meaningful cognitive work* by putting these two senses together. While the idea of a notion of 'sense' seems intuitive from the example, it is famously hard to define, even informally. Frege defines 'sense' in terms of the mysterious *mode of presentation*, for "to think of then being connected with a sign (name, combination of words, letters), besides that to which the sign refers, which may be called the reference of the sign, also what I should like to call the sense of the sign, wherein the mode of presentation is contained" (1892). This statement has caused multiple decades of debate by philosophers of language like Russell and Kripke who have attempted to banish the notion of sense and simply build a theory of meaning from the concept of reference. One thing is clear, that the sense is *not* an **idea**, *an inner and subjective mental representation of a referent*.

Regardless of what precisely 'sense' is, Frege believed that the notion of sense is what allows an agent to understand sentences that may not have a referent, for "the words 'the celestial body most distant from Earth' has a sense, but it is very doubtful there is also a thing they refer to... in grasping a sense, one certainly is not assured of referring to anything" (Frege 1892). So it is the concept of sense that should be given priority over reference. This is not to deny the role of reference whatsoever, since "to say that reference is not an ingredient in meaning is not to deny that reference is a consequence of meaning... it is only to say that the understanding which a speaker of a language has of a word in that language... can never consist merely in his associating a certain thing with it as its referent; there must be some particular *means* by which this association is effected, the knowledge of which constitutes his grasp of its sense" (Dummett 1973).

Sense is in no way an 'encoded' referent, since the referent is distal from the sense. Instead, the sense of a sentence should naturally lead an agent to correctly guess the referents of the representational sentence. Yet how could this be detected? Again, sense is sense strictly 'in the head' with no effect on behavior. As put by Wittgenstein, "When I think in language, there aren't 'meanings' going through my mind in addition to the verbal expressions: the language is itself the vehicle of thought" (Wittgenstein 1953). Sense is the bedrock upon which meaning is constructed, and must be encoded in a language. In fact, according to Frege, sense can only be determined from a sentence in a language, and the sense of a sentence almost always requires an understanding of a whole network of other sentences in a given discourse.

So, how can sense be determined, or at least detected? After all, almost *anything* counts as meaningful behavior. While sense determination is a difficult and context-ridden question that seems to require some full or at least 'molecular' language understanding, one account of sense detection so far is given by the earlier notion of assertoric content of Dummett, which is simply that an agent can be thought of as interpreting to a sense if they can answer a number of "yes-no" binary questions about the sense in a way that makes 'sense' to other agents speaking the language (Dummett 1973). There is a tantalizing connection of Dummett's assertoric content as answers to binary questions to the information-theoretic reduction of uncertainty through binary choices (bits), as the content of information cannot be derived without enough bits in the encoding. Overall, Dummett's notion of sense as grounded in actual language use naturally leads to another question: Is sense objective?

The reason the notion of sense was thought of as so objectionable by many philosophers like Russell and Kripke was that sense was viewed as a private, individual notion, much like the Lockean notion of an *idea*. Frege himself clearly rejects this, strictly separating the notion of a sense from an individual subjective idea of a referent, which he refers to as an 'idea.' Far from a mere subjective idea or impression of a referent, Frege believed that sense was inherently *objective*, "the reference of a proper name is the object itself which we designate by using it; the idea which we have in that case is wholly subjective, in between lies the sense, which is indeed no longer subjective like the idea, but is yet not the object itself" (1892). A sense is objective insofar as it is a shared part of an inherently public language, since a sense is the "common property of many people, and so is not a part of a mode of the individual mind. For one can hardly deny that mankind has a common store of thoughts which is transmitted from one generation to another" (1892). While the exact nature of a sense is still unclear, its main characteristic is that it should be whatever is *objectively shared* between those competent in the use of names in a language.

Ever since Frege's attempted to define it, this notion of meaning as an objective sense has been considered counter-intuitive and controversial, and so with a few exceptions most philosophers of language would rather throw the notion of sense out the window and instead ground theories of meaning in subjective impressions of 'sense-data.' Furthermore, unlike Fregean sense, these theories of semantics have actually been debated in the context of the Web. So before buying into a Fregean notion of sense on the Web, let's see how these alternatives to sense fare in their encounter with the Web.

4.3 The Logicist Position and the Descriptivist Theory of Reference

The origin of logicist semantics is in what is popularly known as the descriptivist theory of reference. In this theory of reference, the referent of a name is given by whatever satisfies the descriptions associated with the name. Usually, the descriptions are thought to be logical statements, so a name is actually a disguised logical description. The referent of the name is then equivalent to the set of possible things, given normally by a mathematical model, such that all statements containing the name are satisfied. To explain a bit further, *formal languages* are languages with an explicitly defined syntax at least, and also possibly (although not always) a model-theoretic semantics. The purpose of these formal languages can be interpretation by computers. Many computer languages not considered to be programming languages are languages insofar as they have some normative or even informal interpretation, such as HTML. Furthermore, due to some biases against computer languages being put on the same footing as natural language, sometimes the term *format* is used as a synonym for computer-based language.

As mentioned earlier, an act of interpretation is usually thought of as a mapping from some sentences in a language to the content of some state-of-affairs in a world. This world is often thought to be the everyday world of concrete trees, houses, and landscapes that humans inhabit. Informally an interpretation can be considered to be a mapping from sentences to the physical world itself, a mapping rather ironically and appropriately labelled 'God Forthcoming' (Halpin 2004). However, often we do not have access to the world itself and it is unclear if a simplistic definition such as "the truth of a sentence consists in its agreement with (or correspondence to) reality" makes any sense, for "all these formulations can lead to various misunderstandings, for none of them is sufficiently precise and clear" (Tarski 1944). In an attempt to define a formal notion of truth, Tarksi defined the interpretation of a language, which he terms the "object" language, in terms of a "meta-language" (1944). If both the language and the meta-language are suitably formalized, the interpretation of the language can then be expressed in terms of the satisfaction of a mathematical model, where *satisfaction* can be defined as *an interpretation from sentences to a mathematical model that defines whether or not every sentence in the language can be interpreted to content*, which in the tradition of Frege is usually thought of as a 'truth' value (i.e. the content is simply the value 'true.'). In this way, formal semantics is distinguished from the jungle of informal semantics by having a precisely defined mathematical model 'stand-in' for the vague and fuzzy world or some portion thereof. While Tarksi originally applied this only to suitably formal languages, others such as Montague have tried to apply this approach, with varying degrees of success and failure, to natural language. To summarize, *model-theoretic semantics* is a semantics where *an interpretation of a language's sentences is to a mathematical model*. The *model* is *a mathematical structure, possibly a representation of the world or the language itself*. The relationship is summarized below in Fig. 4.1, where the relationship between the model and the world is thought to be distal (such that the model *represents* the world). This is not always the case, as in the model can be thought of as ranging over the world itself.

The adequacy of models is usually judged by whether or not they fulfill the purposes to which the language is designed, or whether or not their behaviour adequately serves as a model of some portion of the world. Given a model-theoretic semantics, an interpretation can be given as "a minimal formal description of those aspects of a world which is just sufficient to establish the truth or falsity of any

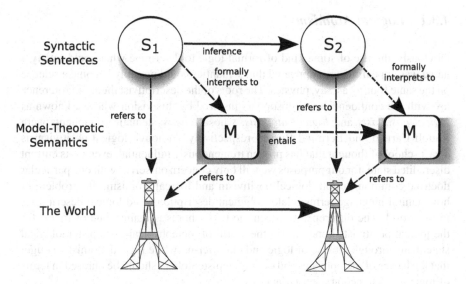

Fig. 4.1 Models, entailment, and inference

expression" in the language (Hayes 2004). While again the history and debate over these terms is outside the scope of this thesis, in general the original notion, as pioneered by Carnap (1947), is that a certain *kind of thing may only be described*, and so given an **intension**, while the *things that satisfy this description* (which may be more than one thing) are **extensions**. Sentences are **consistent** *if they can be satisfied*, they are **inconsistent** if otherwise. Lastly, note that an **entailment** is *where an interpretation of one sentence to some content always satisfies the interpretation of another sentence to some content*, i.e. the first statement entails the second. In contrast, an **inference** is a *syntactic relationship where one sentence can be used to construct another sentence in a language*. In detail, as shown in Fig. 4.1, the syntactic inference mechanisms over time produce more valid inferences, and because these inferences 'line up' with entailments, they also may accurately describe the world outside the formal system. Ideally, this model also 'lines-up' with the world, so the inferences give one more correct statements about the world. Models can be captured in various ways. We have primarily described a denotational semantics, but often axiomatic and operational semantics are equally powerful formalisms. Inference can usually be accomplished by some local inference procedure, like a computer program. The inference procedure of a language is **sound** *if every inferred sentence can be satisfied* (i.e. the inference mechanism preserves 'truth'), and it is **complete** *if every satisfied sentence can be shown to be entailed* (i.e. all 'true' statements can be proven). This is necessarily a quick overview of the large field of formal semantics, but the general notions are illustrated in Fig. 4.1 as the parallel between the causal relationships of the syntactic sentences and their interpretations to a model that *semantically* refers to the world.

4.3.1 Logical Atomism

Obviously, the use of some kind of formal logic to determine what could satisfy a name was appealing, as it appeared that semantics could possibly become a science on the same footing as, say, physics. The roots of the descriptivist theory of reference lay with the confluence of philosophers inspired by this vision who are known as *logical positivists* and *logical atomists*, whose most systematic proponents were Rudolf Carnap and Bertrand Russell respectively. Although logical positivism is a vast school of thought that has proven tremendously influential, even in its current discredited state, for our purposes we will only concern ourselves with one particular doctrine common to both logical positivism and logical atomism, the problem of how natural language terms relate to logical descriptions, and logical descriptions to the world. The difference between the two schools is mainly one of focus, for the logical positivists hoped to rid the world of metaphysical and epistemological statements through the use of logic and empiricism, while logical atomists thought that the basics of metaphysics and even our epistemology should be phrased in terms of logic over elementary sense-data.

The logical positivists and Bertrand Russell were inspired by Wittgenstein's early philosophical work in the *Tractatus Logico-Philosophicus*. In it, Wittgenstein strongly argues for *logical atomism*, that *logic* is the true language of the world; "logic is not a body of doctrine, but a mirror image of the world" for "the facts in logical space" are the world (1921). So logical statements are "laid against reality like a measure" (1921). This is possible because the world is metaphysically determinate at its base, being composed of "simple" and "unalterable" objects that "make up the substance of the world" so that "the configuration of objects produces states of affairs" where "the totality of existing states of affairs is the world" (Wittgenstein 1921). In other words, there is no – as Brian Cantwell Smith would put it – "flex" or "slop" in this picture, no underlying "metaphysical flux" that somehow resists easily being constrained into these fully determinate "objects" (1996). Although the nature of the world consists of *true* logical facts, humans, since they "picture facts" to themselves, can nonetheless make *false* logical statements, since these pictures merely "model reality" (Wittgenstein 1921). Contrary to his own logical atomist teacher Russell, Wittgenstein thought that the primary job of the logician is then to state true facts, and "what we cannot speak about" in the form of true logical statements "we must pass over in silence," a phrase he believed was consistently misinterpreted by logical positivism (Wittgenstein 1921). Note that unlike the more mature standpoint of Hayes, the early logical atomism of Wittgenstein allowed *logical statements* to directly refer to single things in the world, i.e. young Wittgenstein and the logical positivists reified *the formal model* to *be the world* itself.

Carnap's ultimate goal was to use this logical empiricism to render any scientific hypothesis either verifiable by sense experience or not. According to Carnap, in his *The Logical Structure of the World*, all statements (at least, "scientific" statements with "cognitive content") can be reduced to logical statements, where the content of this logical language is given by sensory experiences (1928). These "elementary experiences" (called *eigenpsychische* by Carnap) cannot be directly described, as they are irreducible, but only described by a network of logical predicates that treat these experiences as logical constants (Carnap 1928). For examples of these kinds of sentences, one would not say "The Eiffel Tower is made of reddish iron." One would say something more elementary like 'hard thing here now' or 'redness here now' when bumping one's toe against the brute fact of the Eiffel Tower. Then these sense-data – which were considered a priori true due to their verification by sense experience – could be built up into larger complex sentences and names via logic. Since natural language is part of the world, the structure of language too must be logical, and range over these elementary sense experiences. In this regard, names are given to their referents by concordance with a logical structure ranging over these elementary sensory experiences. Carnap's project was similar in spirit to Chomsky's syntactic theory of language, but focused on semantics rather than syntax: Carnap hoped to develop a semantic and logical definition of meaning that would validate only sentences with 'meaning' and dispose of all metaphysical notions, which would naturally include likely most of Hegel and perhaps even Fregean sense.

Bertrand Russell begins the logical atomist investigation of the connection between logic and names in language is his landmark investigation *On Denoting* with a deceptively simple question: "is the King of France bald?" (Russell 1905). To what referent does the description "the King of France" refer to? (Russell 1905) Since in Russell's time there was no King of France, it could not refer to anything like what Carnap later called "elementary sense data" (Carnap 1928). In this regard, Russell makes a crucial distinction. According to Russell, elementary sensory experiences are known through *acquaintance*, in which we have some sort of direct 'presentation of' the thing (Russell 1905). According to Russell, these statements of acquaintance with directly present sensory data employ what are known as Russellian demonstratives (such as 'this' or 'that') as exemplified by the statement "That is the Eiffel Tower." Yet knowledge of a thing can be based on *descriptions*, which are those "things we only reach by means of denoting phrases" (Russell 1905). Russell believed that "all thinking has to start from acquaintance, but it succeeds in thinking *about* many things with which we have no acquaintance" via the use of description (Russell 1905). Russell was most interested in whether those things with which we have direct acquaintance can be considered true or false, or whether a more mysterious third category such as 'nonsense' is needed. Russell opts to reject creating imaginary but true 'things' as well as any third category, but instead holds that statements such as "the King of France is bald" are false, since "it is false that there is an entity which is now the King of France and is bald" (Russell 1905). This solution then raises the alarming possibility that "the King of France is not bald" may also come out false, which would seem to violate the Law of the Excluded Middle. So, Russell counters this move by introducing the fact that "the King of France is bald" is actually a complex logical statement involving scope and quantification, namely $(\exists x.F(x) \wedge G(x)) \wedge (\forall y.F(y) \rightarrow x = y)$, where F is "being the King of France" and G is "being bald" (Russell 1905). According to the analysis, 'The King of France' is merely a *disguised* complex logical statement. Furthermore, this treatment can be extended to proper names such as 'Sir Walter

Scott,' who can be identified with 'the author of Waverly,' so that instead of being a tautology, even a proper name of a person, even if known through acquaintance, is sort of short-hand for a large cluster of logical statements. To use our previous example, the 'Eiffel Tower' can be thought of as a short-hand for not only that 'there exists an entity known as the Eiffel Tower' but also the logical statement that 'the aforementioned entity had Gustave Eiffel as its architect.' If someone did not know that 'the aforementioned entity was also the tallest building in the world up until 1930,' one could then make a statement such as 'The Eiffel Tower is identical to the tallest building in the world up until 1930' without merely stating a tautology, and such a statement would add true and consistent knowledge to a hearer who was not previously aware of the fact.

As sensible as Russell's programme appeared, there are difficulties in building any theory of reference on, as Quine put it, such a "slender basis" as elementary sense-data and logic (1951). One obvious problem for any descriptive theory of names comes for the use of names of any "kind of abstract entities like properties, classes, relations, numbers, propositions," for such entities could not have an interpretation for any content using such a simple sensory epistemology (Carnap 1950). Carnap's *Empiricism, Semantics, and Ontology* made an argument for basing such entities purely on linguistic form itself. Carnap believed that, despite the difficulty of determining the interpretation of names for abstract entities, "such a language does not imply embracing a Platonic ontology but is perfectly compatible with empiricism" (1950). His position was that while "if someone wishes to speak in his language about a new kind of entity, he has to introduce a system of new ways of speaking, subject to new rules," which Carnap calls the "construction of a linguistic framework for the new entities in question." From *within* a linguistic framework, Carnap claimed that to commit to any statement about the "existence or reality of the total system of the new entities" was to make a "pseudo-statement without cognitive content" (1950). This particular position of Carnap's was eventually devastated, as Quine showed that even the most unremarkable of sensory expressions such as 'redness here now' were undermined by multiple problems. For example, there is the issue of indeterminacy of translation, in which even the verbal expression of sense experiences assumes a common background, but one can imagine many cases where two creatures would utter "redness here now" in reaction to actually different sensory stimuli (imagine a human with color-blindness). Also, there is the problem where even our sense experiences are not 'raw' but influenced by a complex holistic network of propositions – one does not experience 'hard iron here now' but the Eiffel Tower itself (Quine 1951).

4.3.2 Tarski's Formal Semantics

Tarski abandoned the quaint epistemology of logical atomism in terms of direct acquaintance with sensory data and defined reference purely in terms of mathematical logic in his *The Concept of Truth in Formal Languages* (Tarski 1935). Reference was just defined as a consequence of the truth *only* in terms of satisfaction of a formal language (Tarski 1935). To set up his exposition, Tarski defines two languages, the first being the syntactic *object language L* and the second being the meta-language *M*. The *meta-language* should be more expressive such that it can describe every sentence in the object language, and furthermore, that it contain axioms that allow the truth of every sentence in the object language to be defined. In his first move, Tarski defines the formal conception of truth as 'Convention T,' namely that for a given sentence s in L, there is a statement p in M that is a theorem defining the truth of s, that is, the truth of s is determined via a translation of s into M (Tarski 1935). Tarski then later shows that truth can be formally defined as "s is true if and only if p" (Tarski 1944). For example, if the object language is exemplified by a sentence uttered by some speaker of English and the meta-language was an English description of the real world; 'The Eiffel Tower is in Paris' is true if and only if the Eiffel Tower is in Paris. The sentence 'The Eiffel Tower is in Paris' must be satisfied by the Eiffel Tower *actually being* in Paris. While this would at first seem circular, its non-circularity is better seen through when the object language is not English, but another language such as German. In this case, "'Der Eiffelturm ist in Paris' is true if and only if the Eiffel Tower is in Paris." However, Tarski was not interested in informal languages such as English, but in determining the meaning of a new formal language via translations to mathematical models or other formal languages with well-known models. If one was defining a formal semantics for some fragment of a knowledge representation language like RDF, a statement such as http://www.eiffeltower.example.orgex:locationex:Paris is true if and only if $\exists ab.R(a,b)$ where R, a, and b are given in first-order predicate logic.

If one is defining a formal Tarski-style semantics for a language, what should one do when one encounters complex statements, such as 'the Eiffel Tower is in Paris and had as an architect Gustave Eiffel'? The answer is at the heart of Tarski's project, the second component of Tarski's formal semantics is to use the principle of compositionality so that any complex sentence can have its truth conditions derived from the truth conditions of its constituents. To do this, the meta-language has to have finitely many axioms, and each of the truth-defining theorems produced by the meta-language have to be generated from the axioms (Tarski 1935). So, the aforementioned complex sentence is true if and only if $\exists ab.R(a,b) \wedge Q(a,c)$, where Q can be the *architect of* relationship, c can be Gustave Eiffel and a the Eiffel Tower. Tarski's theory as explained so far only deals with 'closed' sentences, i.e. sentences containing no variables or quantification. The third and final component of Tarski's formal semantics is to use the notion of satisfaction via extension to define truth (Tarski 1935). For a sentence such as 'all monuments have a location,' we can translate the sentence to $\forall a \exists l.monument(a) \rightarrow hasLocation(a,l)$ which is true if and only if there is an extension x from the world that satisfies the logical statements made about a. In particular, Tarski has as his preferred extensions infinite ordered pairs, where the ordered set could be anything (Tarski 1935). For formal languages, a model-theoretic semantics with a model composed by set theory was standard. For example, the ordered pairs in some model of $\langle Eiffel\ Tower, Paris \rangle$

would satisfy, as would (*ScottMonument, Edinburgh*) but not (*Paris, Eiffel Tower*). However, there is no reason why these models could not be "God Forthcoming," things in the real world itself, albeit given in set-theoretic terms (Smith 1996). To summarize Tarksi's remarkably successful programme, model-theoretic semantics can produce a theory of truth that defines the semantics of a sentence in terms of the use of a translation of the sentence into some formal language with a finite number of axioms, then using compositionality to define the truth of complex sentences in terms of basic sentences, and finally determining the truth of those basic sentences in terms of what things in a model satisfy the extensions of the basic sentences as given by the axioms. This work marks the high-point of the logical programme, as all questions of meaning are reduced to questions about giving the interpretation of a sentence in terms of a formal notion of truth. This notion of truth is not restricted by the logical atomist's epistemology of elementary sense data, but instead can range over any possible formal language and any possible world. This victory is not without its costs, since while Tarski provides the best account of the relationship between logical descriptions and the world by simply removing all questions that cannot be phrased formally, formal semantics by itself leaves unsolved the fundamental question about how natural language relates to our experience of the world. Ignoring a problem does not make it go away. So when confronted with this vexing problem, champions of formal semantics often revert to the Russellian doctrine of direct acquaintance, thereby returning to the original problems that caused Tarski to abandon epistemology.

4.3.3   Logical Descriptions Unbound on the Web

While the descriptivist theory of reference seems distant from the Identity Crisis of the Web, it is in fact central to the position of Hayes and the Semantic Web as a whole. This is primarily because Hayes's background was in formal logic, with his particular specialty being the creation of Tarski-style semantics for knowledge representation languages. What Hayes calls the "basic results in twentieth century linguistic semantics" that Berners-Lee's dictum that "URIs identify one thing" violates is the interpretation of URIs in a Tarski-style formal semantics (Hayes 2003a). For the logicist position, the *semantics* in the Semantic Web derive from the Tarski-style formal semantics Hayes created for the Semantic Web (Hayes 2004).

Before delving into the formal semantics of RDF, it should be noticed that these semantics are done by extension, like most other formal languages (Hayes 2004). However, the semantics of RDF are purposefully quite weak (they do not allow arithmetic or constructs like the negation of a class), and so RDF avoids logical paradoxes like the encoding of Gödel sentences. Yet in order to make RDF triples as flexible as possible, RDF includes features normally associated with higher-order logic such as "a property may be applied to itself" and classes "may contain themselves" (Hayes 2004). This is handled semantically by having first an interpretation map the URI to an individual. Then unlike standard first-order logic, this individual then maps to different extensions depending on the role the URI is playing as a property or class in the triple. A simple example should suffice to give a flavour of the formal semantics, where a relation is just another kind of individual. What is the formal semantics of ex:EiffelTower ex:architect ex:Gustave_Eiffel? To simplify slightly, Hayes defines the formal semantics in terms of set theory, where there is a set of resources that compose the model of the language, a set of properties, and a set of URIs that can refer to resources. The interpretation of any RDF statement is then given as an extensional mapping from the set of properties to the powerset of resources, to the set of pairs of resources. So, given a set-theoretic model consisting of elements (given by italics) *Gustave Eiffel* and *the Eiffel Tower* and *being the architect of*, then ex:EiffelTower $\models$ *the Eiffel Tower*, ex:Gustave_Eiffel $\models$ *Gustave Eiffel* and ex:architect $\models$ *being the architect of*, so that the entire triple maps to a set of pairs: ex:EiffelTower ex:architect ex:Gustave_Eiffel $\models$ *(..., (the Eiffel Tower, Gustave Eiffel), ...)*. Common-sense human intuitions will likely have this interpretation map to ex:EiffelTower ex:architect ex:Gustave_EiffelTower, and using the axioms defined in the RDF formal semantics a few new triples can be inferred, such as ex:architect rdf:type rdf:Property, i.e. *being an architect of* is a property of something.

However, the inherent pluralism of the Tarski approach to models also means that another equally valid interpretation would be the inverse, i.e. the mapping of ex:EiffelTower to *Gustave Eiffel* and ex:Gustave_Eiffel to *the Eiffel Tower*. In other words, ex:architect $\models$ *being the architect of*, so that the entire triple maps to a set of pairs ex:EiffelTower ex:architect ex:Gustave_Eiffel $\models$ *(..., (Gustave Eiffel, Eiffel Tower), ...)*. Due to the unconstrained nature of RDF, ex:architect has no 'natural' relationship to anything in particular, but could easily be assigned either *the Eiffel Tower* or *Gustave Eiffel* just as easily as *being the architect of*. Furthermore, the model could just as easily be given by something as abstract as the integers *1* and *2*, and an equally valid mapping would be for ex:EiffelTower $\models$ *1* and ex:Gustave_Eiffel $\models$ *2*, so that ex:architect $\models$ *being the architect of*, so that the entire triple maps to a set of pairs ex:EiffelTower ex:architect ex:Gustave_Eiffel $\models$ *(..., (1,2), ...)*. Indeed, the extreme pluralism of a Tarski-style semantics shows that, at least if all one has is a single lone triple statement, that triple can be satisfied by any model. This is no mere oddity of formal languages, this would also hold for any lone sentence in a language like English – such as "Gustave Eiffel is the architect of the Eiffel Tower" – as long as one subscribed to a Tarski-style semantics for natural language. As the number of triples increased, the amount of possible things that satisfy the model is thought to decrease, but in such a loose language as RDF, Hayes notes that it is "usually impossible to assert enough in any language to completely constrain the interpretations to a single possible world, so there is no such thing as 'the' unique interpretation" (Hayes 2004). This descriptivist theory of reference, where descriptions are logical statements in RDF, is illustrated in Fig. 4.2.

Fig. 4.2 The descriptivist theory of reference for URIs

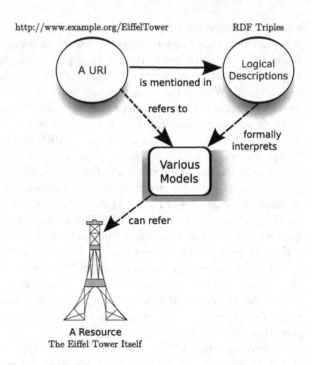

A Resource
The Eiffel Tower Itself

While Hayes makes no claim that access to some web-pages via URIs is not possible, he claims that such access to Web representations is orthogonal to the question of what a URI could refer to, since "the architecture of the Web determines access, but has no direct influence on reference" (Hayes and Halpin 2008). Furthermore, Hayes's logical understanding of ambiguity parts path with natural language understandings of ambiguity: Hayes claims that reference to resources is completely *independent* of whatever Web representations can be accessed, even if those contain logical expressions. While much credit should be given to Hayes for creating a logical semantics for RDF, the problem of connecting these descriptions to the world outside of the Web falls outside formal semantics and so opens up a seemingly uncrossable abyss between the logical descriptions and sensory data. One seemingly easy way out of this abyss is to revert to the doctrine of Russellian direct acquaintance, also known as ostentation. In moments, Hayes himself seems to subscribe to the logical atomist epistemology of Russell, as he says that "reference can either be established by description or ostention" with ostention being defined as the use of a Russellian demonstrative (like 'that' or 'this') identifying a particular "patch of sense data" via a statement such as 'that is the Eiffel Tower' (Hayes 2006). Since most of the things referred to by names are not accessible, reference can only be determined by description, and these descriptions are inherently ambiguous as regards any sense-data (Hayes and Halpin 2008).

As our example showed, RDF in general says so little inferentially that many different models can satisfy almost any given RDF statement. Therefore, Hayes considers it essential to ditch the vague word 'identify' as used in URIs, and distinguish between the ability of URIs to access and refer. While access is constrained by Web architecture, according to Hayes, reference is absolutely unconstrained except by formal semantics, and so "the relationship between access and reference is essentially arbitrary" (Hayes and Halpin 2008). From this philosophical position, the Identity Crisis dissolves into a pseudo-problem, for the same URI can indeed access a web-page and refer to a person unproblematically, as they no longer have to obey the dictum to identify one thing. Hayes compares this situation to that of *overloading*, using a single name to refer to multiple referents, and instead of being a problem, "it is a way of using names efficiently" and not a problem for communication, as "natural language is rife with lexical ambiguity which does not hinder normal communication," as these ambiguities can almost always be resolved by sufficient context (Hayes and Halpin 2008). Overall, the argument of Hayes against Berners-Lee in the Identity Crisis is the position of keeping the formal semantics of reference separate from the engineering of the Web.

4.4 The Direct Reference Position and the Causal Theory of Reference

The alternative slogan of Berners-Lee, that "URIs identify one thing," may not be completely untenable after all (Berners-Lee 2003c). It appears to even be intuitive, for when one says 'I went to visit the Eiffel Tower,' one believes one is talking about a very *particular* thing in the *real* world called the 'Eiffel Tower,' not a cluster of descriptions or model of the world. The direct theory of reference of Berners-Lee has a parallel in philosophy, namely Saul Kripke's 'causal theory of reference,' the widely-known argument against the descriptivist theory of reference, and so the reliance upon the purely formal semantics of Hayes (Kripke 1972). In contrast to the descriptivist theory of reference, where the content of any name is determined by ambiguous interpretation of logical descriptions, in the *causal theory of reference* any name refers via some causal chain directly to a referent (Kripke 1972).

4.4.1 Kripke's Causal Theory of Proper Names

The causal theory of reference was meant to be an attack on the descriptivist theory of reference attributed to Russell, and its effect in philosophy has been to discredit any neo-Russellian descriptivist semantics for proper names. Unsurprisingly, the causal theory of reference also has its origin in logic, since Kripke as a modal logician felt a theory of reference was needed that could make logical statements about things in different logically possible worlds (Kripke 1972). However, while Kripke did not directly confront the related position of Tarski, his argument does nonetheless attempt to undermine the ambiguity inherent in Tarski's model-theoretic semantics, although a Tarski-style semantics can merely 'flatten' models of possible worlds into a singular model. Still, as a response in philosophy of language, it is accepted as a classical refutation of the descriptivist theory of reference.

In Kripke's *Naming and Necessity*, an agent fixes a name to a referent by a process called *baptism* in which the referent, known through direct acquaintance, is associated with a name via some local and causally effective action by the agent (Kripke 1972). Afterwards, a historical and causal chain between a current user of the name and past users allows the referent of a name to be transmitted unambiguously through time, even in *other possible worlds*. For example, a certain historical personage was given the name 'Gustave Eiffel' via a rather literal baptism, and the name 'Gustave Eiffel' would still refer to that baptized person, even if he had not been the architect of the Eiffel Tower, and so failed to satisfy that definite description. Later, the causal chain of people talking about 'Gustave Eiffel' would identify that very person, even after Gustave Eiffel was dead and gone. Descriptions aren't entirely out of the picture on Kripke's account; they are necessary for disambiguation when the context of use allows more than one interpretation of a name, and they figure in the process by which things actually get their names, if the thing cannot be directly identified. However, this use of descriptions is a mere afterthought with no causal bearing on determining the referent of the name itself, for as Kripke puts it, "let us suppose that we do fix the reference of a name by a description. Even if we do so, we do not then make the name synonymous with the description, but instead we use the name rigidly to refer to the object so named, even in talking about counterfactual situations where the thing named would not satisfy the description in question" (Kripke 1972). So what is crucial is not satisfying any description, but the act of baptism and the causal transmission of the name.

4.4.2 Putnam's Theory of Natural Kinds

Kripke's examples of the causal theory of reference used proper names, such as 'Cicero' or 'Aristotle,' and he did not extend his analysis to the whole of language in a principled manner. However, Hilary Putnam, in his *The Meaning of 'Meaning,'* extends Kripke's analysis to all sorts of names outside traditional proper names, and in particular Putnam uses for his examples the names of natural kinds (Putnam 1975). Putnam was motivated by an attempt to defeat what he believes is the false distinction between intension and extension. The set of logical descriptions, which Putnam identifies with a "psychological state," that something must satisfy to be given a name is the *intension*, while those things in a given interpretation that actually satisfy these descriptions, are the *extension* (Putnam 1975). Putnam notices that while a single extension can have multiple intensions it satisfies, such as the Eiffel Tower both being "in Paris" and "a monument," a single intension is supposed to have the same extension in a given interpretation. If two people are looking for a "monument in Paris," the Eiffel Tower should satisfy them both, even though the Eiffel Tower can also have many other possible descriptions.

Putnam's analysis can be summarized as follows: Imagine that there is a world "very much like Earth" called 'Twin Earth.' On Twin Earth "the liquid called 'water' is not H_2O but a different liquid" whose chemical formula is abbreviated as XYZ, and that this XYZ is "indistinguishable from water at normal temperatures and pressures" since it "tastes like water and quenches thirst like water" (Putnam 1975). A person from Earth would *incorrectly* identify XYZ for their normal referent of water, as it would satisfy all their descriptions. In this regard, this shows that meanings "ain't in the head" but are in fact determined, not by individual language use or descriptions, but by some indexical relationship to "stuff that is like water around here" normally. That "stuff" *should* get its name and meaning from *experts*, since "probably every adult speaker even knows the necessary and sufficient condition 'water is H_2O,' but only a few adult speakers could distinguish water from liquids which superficially resembled water... in case of doubt, other speakers would rely on the judgment of these 'expert' speakers" who would ideally test XYZ and determine that it was indeed, not water" (Putnam 1975). Indeed, less outlandish examples, such as the difference between "beech trees" and "elm trees" are trotted out by Putnam to show that a large amount of our names for things, perhaps even extending beyond natural kinds, are actually determined by expert knowledge (Putnam 1975). In this way, Kripke's baptism can extend to almost all languages, and scientists can be considered a special sort of naming authority capable of baptizing all sorts of things with a greater authority than everyone else. As even Putnam explicitly acknowledges "Kripke's doctrine that natural-kind words are rigid designators and our doctrine that they are indexical are but two ways of making the same point" (Putnam 1975).

4.4.3 Direct Reference on the Web

This causal theory of reference is naturally close to the direct reference position of Berners-Lee, whose background is in expert-created databases. He naturally assumes the causal theory of reference is uncontroversial, for in database schemas, what a term *refers to* is a matter best left to the expert designer of the database. So Kripke and Putnam's account of unambiguous names can then be transposed to the Web with a few minor variations in order to obey Berners-Lee's "crazy" dictum that "URIs identify one thing" regardless of interpretation or even accessible web-page (Berners-Lee 2003c). While it may be a surprise to find Berners-Lee to be a closet Kripkean, Berners-Lee says as much, "that the Web is not the final arbiter of meaning, because URI ownership is primary, and the look-up system of HTTP is... secondary" (Berners-Lee 2003c). There is also an element of Grice in the direct theory of reference, for the *intended* interpretation and perhaps even purpose of the owner is the one that really matters to Berners-Lee, not any publicly accessible particular Web representation (Grice 1957). However, ultimately Berners-Lee has far more in common with the causal theory of reference, since although the URI

Fig. 4.3 The causal theory   http://www.example.org/EiffelTower
of reference for URIs

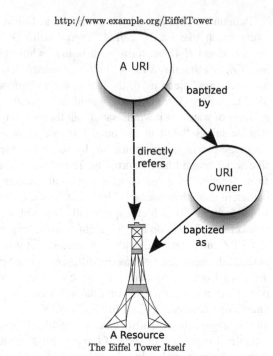

A Resource
The Eiffel Tower Itself

owner's intention determines the referent, after the minting of the new URI for the
resource, the intended interpretation is somehow never supposed to vary (Berners-
Lee 1998a).

To apply the causal theory of reference as to URIs, baptism is given by the
registration of the domain names, which gives a domain name and legally binding
set of IP addresses, such as example.org, a legally binding owner. Of course, the
natural question then would be if this Kripkean practice can then be extended
to entire URIs such as http://www.example.org/Eiffel? For most domain names a
specific policy given by the owner could set the allowed referents for the creation
of URIs that involve the domain name in question, perhaps as embodied in some
software system. One could imagine several variations on this theme, from the
URIs being controlled indirectly by systems-programmers to URIs outsourced to
the general public in the form of a user-generated URI registry with a single top-
level domain. Regardless of the details, the referent of a URI is established by fiat
by the owner(s), and then optionally can be communicated to others in a causal
chain in the form of publishing a web-page accessible from the URI or by creating
Semantic Web statements about the URI. This causal theory of reference for URIs
is illustrated in Fig. 4.3.

In this manner, the owner of the URI can thereby determine the referent of the
URI and communicate it to others, but ultimately the act of baptism, and so the
determination of the referent, are in the hands of the owner of the URI, the self-
professed 'expert' in the new vocabulary term introduced to the Semantic Web by

his URI, and the owner has no real responsibility to host any Web representations at the URI. Since the owner can causally establish a name for a non-Web accessible thing via simply minting a new URI without hosting *any* web-page, under the causal theory of reference the Semantic Web can be treated as having a giant translation manual mapping URIs directly to referents, where the URIs refer directly to objects in the world outside of the Web. Realistically, if an agent got a URI like http://www.example.org/Gustave_Eiffel and one wanted to know what the URI referred to, one could use a service such as whois to look up the owner of the URI, and then contact the owner of the URI if there was any doubt in the matter. Yet since obviously such URIs cannot access things outside the Web and contacting the owner every time a URI is to be used is absurd, what kinds of web-pages, if any, should this giant Semantic Web dictionary return? If it returns no web-page, how can a user-agent distinguish a URI for a referent outside the Web from that of a URI for a web-page? This question is partially answered by Berners-Lee in a solution called '303 redirection,' where a distinct URI is given to the thing-in-of-itself, and then when this URI is accessed by an agent such as a web-browser, a particular Web mechanism called the 303 Header redirects to the agent to another URI for a web-page describing the resource, either in RDF or in HTML, or both. However, this mechanism has been considered difficult to use and understand, "analogous to requiring the postman dance a jig when delivering an official letter" (Hayes 1977).

4.5 Sense and Reference on the Web

The Semantic Web has still not experienced the tremendous growth of the hypertext Web, and the primary reason appears to be this impasse at the Identity Crisis. For the first few years of its existence (2001–2006), in general the arguments of Hayes prevailed, and the URIs used in RDF graphs did not access any web-pages. However, in this phase of its existence, the Semantic Web did not progress beyond yet another little-used knowledge representation language. In the last few years (2006–2012), the Semantic Web has experienced phenomenal growth under the term 'Linked Data,' as Berners-Lee's position has had more acceptance and users have started deploying RDF using actual URIs. This growth is estimated as billions of RDF triples, including large-scale projects by the biomedical community and in government data in using the Semantic Web, seems to have implicitly validated Berners-Lee's direct reference position. Yet that is far from true; what is apparent from any analysis of the Semantic Web is that there appear to be *too many* URIs for some things, while *no* URIs for other things (Halpin and Lavrenko 2011b). As differing users export their data to the Web in a decentralized manner, new URIs are always minted, so running the risk of fracturing the Semantic Web into isolated 'semantic' islands instead of becoming a unified web, as the same URIs are not re-used. The critical missing element of the Semantic Web is some mechanism that allows users to come to agreement on URIs and then share and re-use them, a problem ignored both by the logical and direct reference positions on semantics. Given the practical failure of both approaches, one should be suspicious that something is *theoretically* wrong as well.

The philosophical root of the problem may be that both Russell and Kripke – and so both Berners-Lee and Hayes – reject the notion of 'sense.' The Fregean distinction between 'sense' and 'reference' that provoked both Russell and Kripke's intellectual projects to build an entire theory of meaning on top of only reference, where Frege held that the meaning of any term in a language is determined by the sense of the sentences that use the term, rather than any direct reference of the term (Frege 1892). It is precisely this notion that sense is 'objective' that allows us to begin to construct a new position in the next chapter. Yet how does this notion of sense play out? Dummett provides an insightful hint: "Frege's thesis that sense is objective is thus implicitly an anticipation of Wittgenstein's doctrine that meaning is use" (Dummett 1993a). So we must outline a third position, the position of social semantics that takes the objective notion of 'sense' and Wittgenstein's analysis of "meaning as use" as its foundation (Wittgenstein 1953). Determining how sense can be objective – and *computational* – is the task at hand.

Chapter 5
The Semantics of Tagging

You philosophers ask questions without answers, questions that have to remain unanswered to deserve being called philosophical. According to you, answered questions are only technical matters. That's what they were to begin with.

Jean Lyotard *(1988)*

5.1 Making Sense of Tagging

During the last decade the Web has become a space where increasing numbers of users create, share and store content, leading it to be viewed not only as an "information space" (Berners-Lee 1996b) but also a "social space" (Hendler and Golbeck 2008). This new step in the evolution of the Web, often referred to as the 'Web 2.0,' was shaped by the arrival of the different services that came into existence to support users to easily publish content on the Web, such as photos (Flickr), bookmarks (del.icio.us), movies (YouTube), blogging (Wordpress), and others allow users to *tag* URIs with keywords to facilitate retrieval both for the acting user and for other users. Almost simultaneously with the growth of user-generated content on the Web came a need to create order in this fast-growing unstructured data. Tagging refers to the labeling of resources by means of free-form descriptive natural language keywords, and tagging has become the predominant method for organizing, searching and browsing online web-pages, as well as any other resource. Sets of categories derived based on the tags used to characterize some resource are commonly referred to as folksonomies. This approach to organizing online information is usually contrasted with the formal ontologies used by the Semantic Web, as in collaborative tagging systems where users themselves annotate resources by tags they freely choose and thus form a 'flat space of names' without the predefined and hierarchical structure characteristic of the Semantic Web ontologies.

H. Halpin, *Social Semantics: The Search for Meaning on the Web*,
Semantic Web and Beyond 13, DOI 10.1007/978-1-4614-1885-6_5,
© Springer Science+Business Media New York 2013

As shown earlier, the Semantic Web has so far been attached to classical theories of semantics that are based on a rejection of the idea of an objective Fregean 'sense' in favor of an approach based purely on reference. The usual critique of Fregean sense has been that the notion of some objective yet common notion of sense is at least cryptic and even anti-scientific. Yet with the development of collaborative tagging systems, it seems we at long last have an organic notion of a Fregean sense developing that is both objective and common in the form of tagging. In tagging, for each URI a number of users attach tags to particular URIs, and this common set of tags can be considered the Fregean sense of the URI. This technique has already been applied to problems such as ontology mapping (Togia et al. 2010). While there are some difficulties with this viewpoint, namely that collaborative tagging systems usually conflate a URI with whatever web representations are accessible by that URI (and thus violate the Semantic Web dictum to separate representations from resources and their URIs), such conflation does not at all disqualify tagging as a candidate for a computational theory of sense. First, one can imagine that tagging could be applied to the associated descriptions of Semantic Web URIs, and that these tags would then directly apply to the non-information resource of that URI. To strike deeper, one could also hold that the entire division between Semantic Web URIs and URIs for ordinary hypertext web-pages is fundamentally misbegotten, with 303 redirection being a completely unnecessary HTTP roundtrip. However, it should be also noted that while the Semantic Web has yet to reach widespread usage, collaborative tagging systems are now part and parcel of most major web-sites, and their use seems to be increasing rather than decreasing.

There are concrete benefits to the tagging approach compared to the Semantic Web's traditional focus on formal ontologies. The flexibility of tagging systems is thought to be an asset; tagging is a post-hoc categorization process, in contrast to a pre-optimized classification process such as expert-generated taxonomies. In defining this distinction, Jacob (2004) believes that "categorization divides the world of experience into groups or categories whose members share some perceptible similarity within a given context. That this context may vary and with it the composition of the category is the very basis for both the flexibility and the power of cognitive categorization." Philosophically, tagging is akin to late Wittgenstein's notion of 'family-resemblance' (Wittgenstein 1953). Classification, on the other hand "involves the orderly and systematic assignment of each entity to one and only one class within a system of mutually exclusive and non-overlapping classes; it mandates consistent application of these principles within the framework of a prescribed ordering of reality" (Jacob 2004), a tradition going back to Aristotle (Sowa 1987). Other authors argue that tagging enables users to order and share data more efficiently than using classification schemes; the free-association process involved in tagging is cognitively much more simple than decisions about finding and matching existing categories (Butterfield 2004). Additionally, proponents of tagging systems show that users of tagging systems only need to agree on the general meaning of a tag in order to provide shared value instead of the more difficult task of agreeing on a specific, detailed taxonomy (Mathes 2004).

Yet, what are the *semantics* of a tagging system? A number of problems stem from organizing information through tagging systems, including ambiguity in the meaning of tags and the use of synonyms which creates informational redundancy. Interestingly, Semantic Web ontologies like *NiceTag* have been developed to address the issues of ambiguity in tagging systems by formalizing the tagging process itself, often by linking a particular tag to a Semantic Web URI (Monnin et al. 2010). While this may clarify the intended meaning of the tag, this approach does not thereby in some semi-magical manner give semantics to the tag. Also, it seems the most interesting question for our approach is not what the referent of a particular tag act, but whether or not the *collective* sum of individual tagging acts can serve as an objective notion of sense. Since each tag for a given web resource (such as a web-page) is repeated a number of times by different users, for any given tagged resource there is a distribution of tags and their associated frequencies. The collection of all tags and their frequencies ordered by rank frequency for a given resource is the *tag distribution* of that resource, which is our candidate for a Fregean sense.

So then, the important open question concerning the use of collaborative tagging to organize metadata is whether the system becomes *stable* over time. By *stable*, we mean that users have collectively developed some implicit consensus about which tags best describe a site, and these tags do not vary much over time. Only this will allow tags to be used as an adequate computational theory of neo-Fregean sense, since otherwise tagging would be subjective rather than objective. We will assume that these tags that best describe a resource will be those that are used most often, and new users mostly reinforce already-present tags with similar frequencies. Since users of a tagging system are not acting under a centralized controlling vocabulary, one might imagine that no coherent categorization schemes would emerge at all from collaborative tagging. In this case, tagging systems, especially those with an open-ended number of non-expert users like del.icio.us,[1] would be inherently unstable such that the tags used and their frequency of use would be in a constant state of flux. If this were the case, identifying coherent, stable structures of collective sense produced by users with respect to a site would be difficult or impossible.

The hope amongst proponents of collaborative tagging systems is that stable tag distributions, and thus, possibly, stable categorization schemes, might arise from these systems. Again, by *stable* we do not mean that users stop tagging the resource, but instead that users collectively settle on a group of tags that describe the resource well and new users mostly reinforce already-present tags with the same frequency as they are represented in the existing distribution. Online tagging systems have a variety of features that are often associated with complex systems such as a large number of users and a lack of central coordination. These types of systems are known to produce a distribution known as a power-law over time. A crucial feature of some power laws – and one that we also exploit in this work – is that they can be produced by scale-free networks. So regardless of how large the system

---

[1] http://del.icio.us, which as of 2011 redirects to http://delicious.com/

grows, the shape of the distribution remains the same and thus *stable*. Researchers have observed, some casually and some more rigorously, that the distribution of tags applied to particular resources in tagging systems follows a power-law distribution where there are a relatively small number of tags that are used with great frequency and a great number of tags that are used infrequently (Mathes 2004). If this is the case, tag distributions may provide the stability necessary to draw out useful information structures.

This chapter is organized as follows. In the first part, we examine how to detect the emergence of stable 'consensus' distributions of tags assigned to individual resources. In Sect. 5.2 we demonstrate a method for empirically examining whether tagging distributions follow a power-law distribution. In Sect. 5.2.4 we show how this convergence to a power-law distribution can be detected over time by using the Kullback-Leibler divergence. We further empirically analyze the trajectory of tagging distributions before they have stabilized, as well as the dynamics of the long tail of tag distributions. In the second part, we examine the applications of these stable power-law distributions. In Sect. 5.3, we examine if this power-law is the result of tag suggestions. In Sect. 5.4 we demonstrate how the most frequent tags in a distribution can be used in inter-tag correlation graphs (or folksonomy graphs) to chart their relation to one another. Section 5.5 shows how these folksonomy graphs can be (automatically) partitioned, using community-based methods, in order to extract shared tag vocabularies. Finally, Sect. 5.6 provides an independent benchmark to compare our empirical results from collaborative tagging, by solving the same problems using a completely different data set: search engine query logs.

5.1.1 Related Work

Existing research on tagging has explored a wide variety of problems, ranging from fundamental to more practical concerns – and much of this research is not relevant to our task at hand, such as discovering the best interfaces for presenting tags to users (Halvey and Keane 2007) or using tags to extract data such as event and place locations from tagged photos (Rattenbury et al. 2007). In a direction of work that bears directly on the larger question of the semantics of collective tagging systems, Mika (2005) addresses the problem of extracting taxonomic information from tagging systems in the form of Semantic Web ontologies, but fails to address the stability of collective tagging. More of interest is the study of Shen and Wu on the structure of a tagging network for del.icio.us data which examines network characteristics of the tagging system such as the degree distribution (the distribution of the number of other nodes each node is connected to) and the clustering coefficient (based on a ratio of the total number of edges in a subgraph to the number of all possible edges) (Shen and Wu 2005). Shen and Wu do indeed find that the a snapshot of an entire tagging network is indeed scale-free and has the features Watts and Strogatz (1998) found to be characteristic of small world networks: small average path length and relatively high clustering coefficient.

Fig. 5.1 Tripartite graph structure of a tagging system. An edge linking a user, a tag and a resource (website) represents one tagging instance

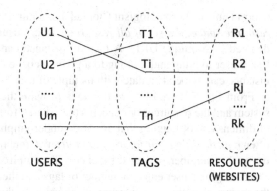

USERS   TAGS   RESOURCES
                   (WEBSITES)

However, we are more interested in the tags applied to individual URIs. An early line of research that has attempted to formalize and quantify the underlying dynamics of collaborative tagging systems is Golder and Huberman (2006), which also make use of del.ici.ous data. They show the majority of sites reach their peak popularity, the highest frequency of tagging in a given time period, within 10 days of being saved on del.icio.us (67% in their data set), though some sites are rediscovered by users (about 17% in their data set), suggesting stability in most sites but some degree of 'burstiness' in the dynamics that could lead to cyclical patterns of stability characteristic of chaotic systems. Importantly, Golder and Huberman find that the distribution of tags within a given site stabilizes over time, usually around 100 tagging events. They do not, however, examine what type of distribution arises from a stabilized tagging process, nor do they present a method for determining the stability of the distribution which we see as central to understanding the possible utility of tagging systems. Thus, the first task should be to determine the stability of tagging systems.

5.1.2 The Tripartite Structure of Tagging

To begin, we review the conceptual model of generic collaborative tagging systems theorized in order to make predictions about collaborative tagging systems based on empirical data and based on generative features of the model (Mika 2005).

There are three main types of entities that compose any tagging system:

- The users of the system (people who actually do the tagging)
- The tags themselves
- The resources being tagged (in this case, the websites)

Each of these can be seen as forming separate spaces consisting of sets of nodes, which are linked together by edges (see Fig. 5.1). The first space, the **user space**, *consists of the set of all users of the tagging system*, where each node is a user. The second space is the **tag space**, *the set of all tags*, where a tag corresponds to a term ('music') or neologism ('toread') in natural language. The third space is the *resource space*, *the set of all resources*, where usually each resource is a website denoted by a unique URI.[2] A tagging instance can be seen as the two edges that link a user to a tag and that tag to a given website or resource. Note that a tagging instance can associate a date with its tuple of user, tag(s), and resource.

From Fig. 5.1, we observe that tags provide the link between the users of the system and the resources or concepts they search for. This analysis reveals a number of dimensions of tagging that are often under-emphasized. In particular, tagging is often *a methodology for information retrieval*, much like traditional search engines, but with a number of key differences. To simplify drastically, with a traditional search engine a user enters a number of tags and then an automatic algorithm labels the resources with some measure of relevance to the tags *pre-discovery*, displaying relevant resources to the user. In contrast, with collaborative tagging a user finds a resource and then adds one or more tags to the resource manually, with the system storing the resource and the tags *post-discovery*. When faced with a case of retrieval, an automatic algorithm does not have to assign tags to the resource automatically, but can follow the tags used by the user. The difference between this and traditional searching algorithms is twofold: collaborative tagging relies on human knowledge, as opposed to an algorithm, to directly connect terms to documents before a search begins, and thus relies on the collective intelligence of its human users to *pre-filter* the search results for relevance. When a search is complete and a resource of interest is found, collaborative tagging often requires the user to tag the resource in order to store the result in his or her personal collection. This causes a *feedback cycle*. These characteristics motivate many systems like del.icio.us and it is well-known that feedback cycles are one ingredient of complex systems (Bar-Yam 2003), giving further indication that a power-law in the tagging distribution might emerge.

5.2 Detecting Power Laws in Tags

This section uses data from del.icio.us to empirically examine whether intuitions regarding tagging systems as complex systems exhibiting power law distributions hold.

5.2.1 Power Law Distributions: Definition

A *power-law* is a relationship between two scalar quantities x and y of the form:

$$y = cx^{\alpha} + b \tag{5.1}$$

---

[2]Most systems such as del.icio.us store only the URI. The resource space, in this definition, represents whatever is being tagged, which may or may not be websites per se but resources themselves.

in which c and α are the constants that characterize the power-law and b being some constant or variable dependent on x that becomes constant asymptotically. The α exponent is the scaling exponent that determines the slope of the distribution before the long tail behavior begins. A power-law function can be transformed to a log–log scale. So (5.1) can also be written as:

$$\log y = \alpha \log x + \log c \qquad (5.2)$$

When written in this form, a fundamental property of power-laws becomes apparent; when plotted in log–log space, power-laws are straight lines. Therefore, the most simple and widely used method to check whether a distribution follows a power-law and to deduce its parameters is to apply a logarithmic transformation, and then perform linear regression in the resulting log–log space. The most widely used method to check whether a distribution follows a power-law is to apply a logarithmic transformation, and then perform linear regression, estimating the slope of the function in logarithmic space to be α. The least-square regression method, as done previously, has been shown to produce systematic bias due to fluctuations of the long tail (Clauset et al. 2007). To determine a power-law accurately requires minimizing the bias in the value of the scaling exponent and the beginning of the long tail via maximum likelihood estimation. See Newman (2005) for the technical details. To determine the α of the observed distributions, we fitted the data using the maximum likelihood method recommended by Newman (2005).

The intuitive explanation of power-law parameters in the domain of tagging is as follows: c represents the number of times the most common tag for that website is used, while α gives the power-law decay parameter for the frequency of tags at subsequent positions. Thus, the number of times the tag in position p is used (where $p = 1.25$, since we considered the tags in the top 25 positions) can be approximated by a function of the form:

$$Frequency(p) = \frac{c}{p^{-\alpha}} \qquad (5.3)$$

where $-\alpha > 0$ and $c = Frequency(p = 1)$ is the frequency of the tag in the first position in the tag distribution (thus, it is a constant that is specific for each site/resource).

5.2.2   Empirical Results for Power Law Regression for Individual Sites

For this analysis, we used two different data sets. The first data set contained a subset of 500 "Popular" sites from del.icio.us that were tagged at least 2,000 times (i.e. where we would expect a "converged" power law distribution to appear). The second data set considers a subset of another 500 sites selected randomly from the "Recent" section of del.icio.us. Both sections are prominently displayed on

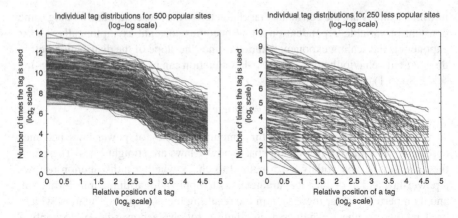

Fig. 5.2 Frequency of tag usage relative to tag position. For each site, the 25 most frequently used tags were considered. The plot uses a double logarithmic (log–log) scale. The data is shown for a set of 500 randomly-selected, heavily tagged sites (*left*) and for a set of 500 randomly-selected, less-heavily tagged sites (*right*)

the del.icio.us site, though "Recent" sites are those tagged within the short time period immediately prior to viewing by the user and "Popular" sites are those which are heavily tagged in general.[3] While the exact algorithms used by del.icio.us to determine these categories are unknown, they are currently the best available approximations for random sampling of del.icio.us, both of heavily tagged sites and of a wider set of sites that may not be heavily tagged.

The mean number of users who tagged resources in the "Popular" data set was 2074.8 with a standard deviation of 92.9, while the mean number of users of the "Recent" data set was 286.1 with a standard deviation of 18.2. In all cases, the tags in the top 25 positions in the distributions have been considered and thus all of our claims refer to these tags. Since the tags are rank-ordered by frequency and the top 25 is the subset of tags that are actually available to del.icio.us users to examine for each site, we argue that using the top 25 tags is adequate for this examination.

Results are presented in Fig. 5.2. In all cases, logarithm of base 2 was used in the log–log transformation.[4]

As shown by Newman and Girvan (2004) and others, the main characteristic of a power law is its slope parameter α. On a log–log scale, the constant parameter c only gives the "vertical shift" of the distribution with respect to the y-axis. For each of the sites in the data set, the corresponding power law function was derived and the

---

[3] All data used in the convergence analysis was collected in the week immediately prior to 19 Nov 2006.

[4] Note that the base of the logarithm does not actually appear in the power law equation (c.f. (5.1)), but because we use empirical and thus possibly noisy data, this choice might introduce errors in the fitting of the regression phase. However, we did not find significant differences from changing the base of the logarithm to e or 10.

slopes of each (α parameters) were compared. The slopes indicate the fundamental characteristic of the power laws, as vertical shifts can and do vary significantly between different sites.

Our analysis shows that for the subset of heavily tagged sites, the slope parameters are very similar to one another, with an average of $\alpha = -1.22$ and a standard deviation ± 0.03. Thus, it appears that the power law decay slope is relatively consistent across all sites. This is quite remarkable, given that these sites were chosen randomly with the only criteria being that they were heavily tagged. This pattern where the top tags are considerably more popular than the rest of the tags seems to indicate a fundamental effect of the way tags are distributed in individual websites which is independent of the content of individual websites. The specific content of the tags themselves can be very different from one website to another and this obviously depends on the content of the tagged site.

For the set of less-heavily tagged sites, we found the slopes differed from each other to a much greater extent than with the heavily tagged data, with an average $\alpha = -5.06$ and standard deviation ± 6.10. Clearly, the power law effect is much less pronounced for the less-heavily tagged sites as opposed to the heavily tagged sites, as the standard deviation reveals a much poorer fit of the regression line to the log–log plotted aggregate data. For sites with relatively few instances of tagging, the results reveal mostly noise.

5.2.3 Empirical Results for Power-Law Regression Using Relative Frequencies

In the previous section, we applied power law regression techniques to individual sites, using the number of hits for a tag in a given position in the distribution. In this section, we examine the aggregate case where we no longer use the raw number of tags (because these are not directly comparable across sites), and instead use the relative frequencies of tags. The relative frequency is defined as the ratio between the number of times a tag in a particular position is used for a resource and the total number of times that resource is tagged.[5] Thus, relative frequencies for a given site always sum to one. These relative frequencies based on data from all 500 sites of the "Popular" data set were then averaged. Results are presented in Fig. 5.3.

As before, a power-law was derived in the log–log space using least-means squares (LMS) regression. This power law was found to have the slope $\alpha = -1.25$. The regression error, computed through the LMS method in the normal, not logarithmic space, was found to be 0.038. Note that the LMS regression error computation only makes sense when converted back in the normal space, since in the log–log space exponents are negative and, furthermore, deviations on the y-axis denote actual error only after the exp_2 function is applied. This corresponds to an

---

[5] To be more precise, the denominator is taken as the total number of times the resource is tagged with a tag from the top 25 positions, given available data.

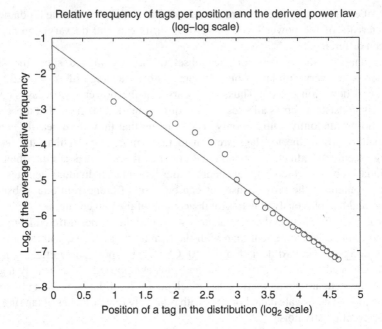

Fig. 5.3 Average relative frequency of tag usage, for the set of 500 "Popular" sites from above. On the y-axis, the logarithm of the relative frequency (probability) is given (The plot uses a double logarithmic (log–log) scale, thus on the y-axis values are negative since relative frequencies are less than one)

LMS error rate in the power law regression of 3.8% over the total number of tags in the distribution, which is low enough to allow us to conclude that tag distributions do follow power laws.

We note, however, that there is a deviation from a perfect power law in the del.icio.us data in the sense that there is a change of slope after the top seven or eight positions in the distribution. This effect is also relatively consistent across the sites in the data set. This may be due to the cognitive constraints of the users themselves or an artifact of the way the del.icio.us interface is constructed, since that number of tags are offered to the users as a suggestion to guide their search process. Nevertheless, given that the LMS regression error is rather low, we argue the effect is not strong enough to change the overall conclusion that tag distributions follow power laws.

5.2.4 The Dynamics of Tag Distributions

While earlier we provided a method for detecting a power-law distribution in the tags of a site or collection of sites, now we move to another aspect of the problem, namely how the shape of these distributions develops in time from the tagging actions of the individual users. First, we examine the how power-law distributions form at the top (the first 25 positions) of tag distributions for each site. For this, we employ a method from information theory, namely the Kullback-Leibler divergence. Second, we study the dynamics of the entire tag distributions, including all tags used for a site, and we show that the relative weights of the top and tail of tag distributions converge to stable ratios in the data sets.

5.2.4.1 Kullback-Leibler Divergence: Definition

In probability and information theory, the Kullback-Leibler divergence (also known as "relative entropy" or "information divergence") represents a natural distance measure between two probability distributions P and Q (in our case, P and Q are two vectors representing discrete probability distributions). Formally, the Kullback-Leibler divergence between P and Q is defined as:

$$D_{KL}(P||Q) = \sum_x P(x) log \left(\frac{P(x)}{Q(x)} \right) \tag{5.4}$$

The Kullback-Leibler distance is a non-negative, convex function, i.e. $D_{KL}(P,Q) \geq 0, \forall P, Q$ (note that $D_{KL}(P,Q) = 0$ iff. P and Q coincide). Also, unlike other distance measures it is not symmetric, i.e. in general $D_{KL}(P,Q) \neq D_{KL}(Q,P)$.

5.2.4.2 Application to Tag Dynamics

We use two complementary ways to detect whether a distribution has converged to a steady state using the Kullback-Leibler divergence:

- The first is to take the relative entropy between every two consecutive points in time of the distribution, where each point in time represents some change in the distribution. Again, in our data, tag distributions are based on the rank-ordered tag frequencies for the top 25 highest-ranked unique tags for any one website. Each point in time was a given month where the tag distribution had changed; months where there was no tagging change were not counted as time points. Using this methodology, a tag distribution that was 'stable' would show the relative entropy converging to and remaining at zero over time. If the Kullback-Leibler divergence between two consecutive time points becomes zero (or close to zero), it suggests that the shape of the distribution has stopped evolving. This technique may be most useful when it is completely unknown whether or not the tagging of a particular site has stabilized at all.
- The second method involves taking the relative entropy of the tag distribution for each time step with respect to the final tag distribution, the distribution at the time the measurement was taken or the last observation in the data, for that site. This method is most useful for heavily tagged sites where it is already known or suspected that the final distribution has already converged to a power-law.

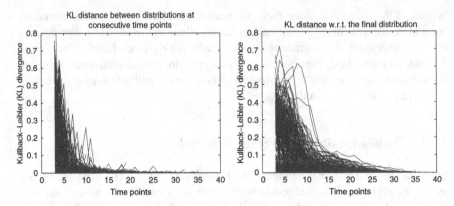

Fig. 5.4 (*left*). Kullback-Leibler divergence between tag frequency distributions at consecutive time steps for 500 "Popular" sites. (*right*). Kullback-Leibler divergence of tag frequency distribution at each time step with respect to the final distribution

The two methods are complementary; the first methodology would converge to zero if the two consecutive distributions are the same, and thus one could detect whether distributions converged if even temporarily. Cyclical patterns of stabilization and destabilization may be detected using this first method. The second method assumes that the final time point is the stable distribution so this method detects convergence only towards the final distribution. If both of these methods produce relative entropies that approach zero, then one can claim that the distributions have converged over time to a single distribution, the distribution at the final time point. Given our interest in distributions that have converged to power-laws, we are actually examining the dynamics of convergence to a power-law.

5.2.4.3   Empirical Results for Tag Dynamics

The analysis of the intermediate dynamics of tagging is considerably more involved than the analysis of final tag distributions. Because the length of the histories varies widely, there is no meaningful way to compute a cumulative measure across all sites as in Sect. 5.2, so our analysis has to consider each resource individually. In Fig. 5.4a, b, we plot the results for the convergence of the 500 "Popular" sites, on the basis that their final distribution must have converged to a power law, that their complete tagging history was available from the first tagging instances, and that this history was of substantial length. In the data set considered, up to 35 time points are available for some sites (which roughly corresponds to 3 years of data, since one time point represents 1 month).

There is a clear effect in the dynamics of the above distributions.[6] At the beginning of the process when the distributions contain only a few tags, there is a high degree of randomness, indicated by early data points. However, in most cases this converges relatively quickly to a very small value, and then in the final ten steps, to a Kullback-Leibler distance which is graphically indistinguishable from zero (with only a few outliers). If the Kullback-Leibler divergence between two consecutive time points (in Fig. 5.4a) or between each step and the final one (Fig. 5.4b) becomes zero or close to zero, it indicates that the shape of the distribution has stopped changing. The results here suggest that the power law may form relatively early on in the process for most sites and persist throughout. Even if the number of tags added by the users increases many-fold, the new tags reinforce the already-formed power law. Interestingly, there is a substantial amount of variation in the initial values of the Kullback-Leibler distance prior to the convergence. Future work might explore the factors underlying this variation and whether it is a function of the content of the sites or of the mechanism behind the tagging of the site. Additionally, convergence to zero occurs at approximately the same time period (often within a few months) for these sites.

The results of the Kullback-Leibler analysis provide a powerful tool for analyzing the dynamics of tagging distributions. This very well might be the result of the scale-free property of tagging networks, so that once the tagging of users has reached a certain threshold, regardless of how many tags are added, the distribution remains stable (Shen and Wu 2005). This method can be immensely useful in analyzing real-world tagging systems where the stability of the categorization scheme produced by the tagging needs to be confirmed.

5.2.4.4 Examining the Dynamics of the Entire Tag Distribution

In the previous sections, we focused on the distributions of the tags in the top 25 positions. However, heavily tagged or popular resources, such as those considered in our analysis, can be tagged several tens of thousands of times each, producing hundreds or even thousands of distinct tags. It is true that many of these distinct tags are simply personal bookmarks which have no meaning for the other users in the system. However, it is still crucial to understand their dynamics and the role they play in tagging, especially with respect to the top of the tag distribution. Some sources (e.g. Anderson 2006), have argued that the dynamics of long tails are a fundamental feature of Internet-scale systems. Here we were particularly interested in two questions. First, how does the number of times a site is tagged (including the long tail) evolve in time? Second, how does the relative importance of the head (top 25 tags) to the long tail change as tags are added to a resource?

---

[6]Note that in Fig. 5.4, the first two time points were omitted because their distribution involved few tags and were thus very highly random.

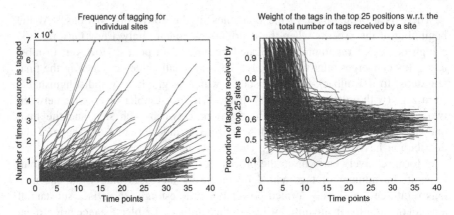

Fig. 5.5 (*left*). Cumulative number of times a resource is tagged for each time point. (*right*). Proportion of times a tag in the top 25 spots of the distribution has been used to tag a resource to the total number of times the resource has been tagged with any tag

Results for the same set of 500 "Popular" sites described above are shown in Fig. 5.5. Note that the tag distributions were reconstructed through viewing the tagging history of the individual site as available through del.icio.us and collecting the growth of this tagging distribution over time, thus allowing us to record the growth of tags outside the 25 most popular.

As seen in Fig. 5.5, the total number of times a site is tagged grows continuously at a rate that is specific to each site and this probably depends on its domain and particular context. Though the results are not shown here due to space constraints, a similar conclusion can be formulated for the number of distinct tags, given that the number of distinct tags varies considerably per site and does not seem to stabilize in time. However for virtually all of the sites in the data set considered, the proportion of times a tag from the top 25 positions is used relative to the total number of times that a resource is tagged did stabilize over time. So, while the total number of tags per resource grows continuously, the relative weight of the tags in the head of the tag distribution compared to the those in the long tail does stabilize to a constant ratio. This is an important effect and it represents a significant addition to our analysis of the stability of the top 25 positions, since it shows the relative importance of the long tail with respect to the head of the distribution does eventually stabilize regardless of the growth of tags in the long tail.

5.3 The Effect of Suggestions on Tagging

So far, we have explored the important question of whether a coherent, stable way of characterizing sense can emerge from collaborative tagging systems, and have presented several novel methods for analyzing data from such systems. We have shown that tagging distributions of heavily tagged resources tend to stabilize into power law distributions and present a method for detecting power law distributions in tagging data, and seen the emergence of stable power law distributions as an aspect of what may be seen as collective consensus around the categorization of information driven by tagging behavior. Thus groups of tags are indeed an adequate candidate for a notion of Fregean sense.

However, one could argue that the stabilization is just a mere artifact of tag suggestions. Tag suggestions are when a tagging system, instead of letting the user tag the resource, automatically (as the product of some algorithm) presents a list of 'suggested' tags for the user. The user can then easily accept these tags or choose through them, rather than choose their own. This could lead to the stabilization of the tagging system not as a product of the actual collaborative sense-making of users, but as an artificial and predictable result of the tag suggestion algorithm. However, the reasons behind the emergence of a power-law distribution in tagging systems are yet unknown, although explanations fall into two general categories. The first of these explanations is relatively simple: the tags stabilize into a power-law because users are imitating each other via tag suggestions put forward by the tagging system (Golder and Huberman 2006). The second and more recent explanation is that in addition to imitation, users share through a similar tag generation procedure based on the information on the webpage, most likely because the users have the same background knowledge (Dellschaft and Staab 2008). However, drawing these two influences apart has not yet been tested scientifically, which we will do. First let's inspect the existing explanations for tagging stabilization more deeply.

5.3.1 Models of Collaborative Tag Behavior

5.3.1.1 A Simple Model: The Polya Urn

The most elementary model of how a user selects tags when annotating a resource is simple imitation of other users. Note that 'imitation' in tagging systems means that the tags are being reinforced via a 'tag suggestion' mechanism, and so the terms imitation, reinforcement, feedback, and tag suggestion can be considered to be synonymous in the context of tagging systems. The user can imitate other users precisely because the tagging system tries to support the user in the tag selection process by providing tag suggestions based on tags other people used when tagging the same resource. There are minor variants of this theme, such as the possibility of using a combination of tags of other users in combination with a user's own previously used tags. In most tagging systems like del.icio.us these tag suggestions are presented as a list of tags that the user can select in order to add them to their tagging instance. The selections of tags from the tag recommendation forms a positive feedback loop in which more frequent tags are being reinforced, thus causing an increase in their popularity, which in turn causes them to be reinforced further and exposed to ever greater numbers of users. This simple type of explanation is easily amendable to preferential attachment models, also known as 'rich get richer' explanations, which are well-known to produce power-law distributions. Intuitively, the earliest studies of tagging observed that users imitate other pre-existing tags (Golder and Huberman 2006). Golder and Huberman proposed that the simplest model that results in a "power-law" would be the classical Polya urn model (2006). Imagine that there is an urn containing balls, each being one of some finite number of colors. At every time-step, a ball is chosen at random. Once a ball is chosen, it is put back in the urn along with another ball of the same color, which formalizes the process of feedback given by tag suggestions. As put by Golder and Huberman, "replacement of a ball with another ball of the same color can be seen as a kind of imitation" where each color of a ball is made equal to a natural language tag and since "the interface through which users add bookmarks shows users the tags most commonly used by others who bookmarked that URL already; users can easily select those tags for use in their own bookmarks, thus imitating the choices of previous users" (2006). Yet, this model is too limited to describe tagging, as it features only reinforcement of existing tags, not the addition of *new* tags.

5.3.1.2   Imitation and the Yule-Simon Model

The first model that formalized the notion of new tags was proposed by Cattuto (2006). In order for new tags to be added, a single parameter p must be added to the model, which represents the probability of a new tag being added, with the probability $\bar{p} = (1 - p)$ that an already-existing tag is reinforced by random uniform choice over all already-existing tags. This results in a Yule-Simon model, a model first employed by Yule (1925) to model biological genera and later Simon to model the construction of a text as a stream of words (Simon 1955). This model has been shown to be equivalent to the famous Barabasi and Albert algorithm for growing networks (Bornholdt and Ebel 2001). Yet the standard Yule-Simon process does not model vocabulary growth in tagging systems very well, as noticed by Cattuto as it produces exponents "lower than the exponents we observe in actual data" (Cattuto 2006).

Cattuto hypothesize that this is because the Yule-Simon model assumes users are choosing to reinforce ($\bar{p}$) tags uniformly from a distribution of *all* tags that have been used previously, so Cattuto concludes that "it seems more realistic to assume that users tend to apply recently added tags more frequently than old ones" (Cattuto 2006). This behavior could be caused by the exposure of a user to a feedback mechanism, such as the del.icio.us tag suggestion system. This suggestions exposes the user only to a subset of previously existing tags, such as those most recently added. Since the tag suggestion mechanism only encourages more recently-added tags to be re-enforced with a higher probability, Cattuto added a memory kernel with a power-law exponent to standard Yule-Simon model. This means that the weight of a previously existing tag being reinforced is weighted according to a power-law itself, so that a tag that has been applied x steps in the past is chosen with a probability $\bar{p}(x) = a(t)/(x + \tau)$, where $a(t)$ is a normalization factor and τ "is a characteristic time scale over which recently added words have comparable probabilities" (Cattuto 2006). While the parameter p controls the probability of reinforcing an existing tag, this second parameter τ, controls how fast the memory kernel decays and so over what time-scale a tag may likely count as 'new' and so be more likely to be reinforced. As Cattuto notes, "the average user is exposed to a few roughly equivalent top-ranked tags and this is translated mathematically into a low-rank cutoff of the power-law" (Cattuto 2006). This model produces an "excellent agreement" with the results of tag-correlation graphs (Cattuto 2006). It should be clear that the original Yule-Simon model simply parametrizes the probability of the imitation of existing tags. The modified Yule-Simon model with a power-law memory kernel also depends on the imitation of existing tags, where the probability of a previously-used tag is decaying according to a power-law function.

5.3.1.3 Adding Parameters and Background Knowledge

Although Cattuto's model is without a doubt an elegant minimal model that captures tag-correlation distributions well, it was not tested against tag-resource distributions (Cattuto 2006). Furthermore, as noticed by Dellschaft and Staab, Cattuto's model also does not explain the sub-linear tag vocabulary growth of a tagging system (2008). Dellschaft and Staab propose an alternative model, which adds a number of new parameters that fit the data produced by tag-growth distributions and tag-resource distributions better than Cattuto's model (2008). The main point of interest in their model is that instead of a new tag being chosen uniformly, the new tag is chosen from a power-law distribution that is meant to approximate "background knowledge." So besides "background knowledge" ($\bar{p}$), their model also features the inverse of "background knowledge," i.e. the "probability that a user imitates a previous tag assignment" (p) (Dellschaft and Staab 2008). In essence, Dellschaft and Staab have added (at least) two new parameters to a Yule-Simon process, and these additional parameters allow the reinforcement of existing tags to be more finely tuned. Instead of a single power-law memory kernel with a single parameter τ, these additional parameters allow the modeling of "an effect that is comparable to the fat-tailed access of the Yule-Simon model with memory" while keeping tag-growth sub-linear (Dellschaft and Staab 2008). The model proposed by Cattuto keeps the tag-growth parameter equal to 1 and so makes tag growth linear to p (Cattuto 2006). Yet for us, the most important advantage of Dellschaft and Staab over Cattuto's model is that their added parameters let their model match the previously unmatched observation by Halpin et al. of the frequency rank distribution made in Chap. 4. The match is not as close as the match with vocabulary growth and tag correlations, as resource-tag frequency distributions vary highly per resource, with the exception of the drop in slope around rank 7–10.

5.3.2   Experimental Design

What unifies all of these models is that they assume that imitation, usually assumed to be tag suggestions from the tagging system, has a major impact on the emergence of a power-law distribution. With concern to the modified Yule-Simon model and the more highly parametrized model that takes into account 'background knowledge,' different claims are made of where the imitated tags come from. Cattuto (2006) propose that they come from a random uniform distribution of tags while Dellschaft and Staab propose a more topic-related distribution that itself has a power-law distribution (Dellschaft and Staab 2008). However, just because a simple model based on imitation of tag suggestions can lead to a power-law distribution does not necessarily mean that tag suggestions are actually the mechanism that causes the power-law distribution to arise in tagging systems. The research question posed then is whether or not the tag suggestion mechanism is the main force behind the observed power-law distributions in tagging systems.

In order to measure the effects of tag suggestions on the tag behavior of users we developed a Web-based experiment in which users were asked to tag 11 websites, with two varying conditions: the 'tag suggestion' condition (Condition A) in which 7 tag suggestions were presented to the user, and a 'no tag suggestion' condition (Condition B) in which no tag suggestions were presented to the user. In this experiment we focus on del.icio.us again, as del.icio.us was the first to introduce a tag based collaborative bookmark system. The user interface used in our experiment presented the tag suggestions in a similar way to del.icio.us to avoid confusion. The 11 websites used in the experiment were selected according to two criteria. First, the topics of the web-pages needed to appeal to the general public. Second, the website needed to have over 200 tagging instances. The appeal to the general public was operationalized by randomly choosing sites that were tagged with the tag 'lifestyle' on del.icio.us. The tag "lifestyle" is a popular tag with 72,889 tagged web-pages as of October 2008. This was chosen in order to not bias our study to one particular specialized subject matter, and so exclude web-pages on del.icio.us that have a highly technical content. Specialized content may not lead to normal tagging behavior from users in the experiment who might not be familiar with the specialist subject matter. The second criteria, of using only web-pages with over 200 tagging instances, was chosen since it has been shown that stable power-law tag distributions emerge around the 100–150th tagging (Golder and Huberman 2006). We did not want the tag suggestions to be from non-stable tag distributions, as it has been shown that the variance between the top popular tags could vary widely before 100–150th tag. 11 web-pages were selected for this experiment, with the popular tags provided from del.icio.us and the number tags. Note that while the number of URIs in the experiment (11) may appear to be small, it is larger than previous experiments over tag suggestions (Suchanek et al. 2008) and will be shown to be sufficient to provide statistically significant results. It was far more critical for this experiment to get enough subjects in order for power-law distributions to be given the chance to arise without tag suggestions, and this would require at least 100 experimental subjects tagging each URI.

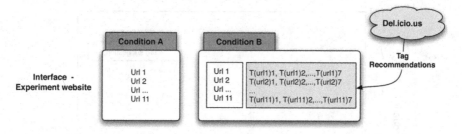

Fig. 5.6 Experimental design

Figure 5.6 shows the experimental design. In the 'no tag suggestion' condition (Condition A), as shown in Fig. 5.6, a user is presented the 11 websites he needs to tag without any form of tag suggestions. In the 'tag suggestion' condition (Condition B), also shown in Fig. 5.6, a user is presented the 11 websites with seven suggested tags. While the details of the tag suggestion algorithm applied by del.icio.us is unknown, for our experiment the suggested tags in Condition B were aggregated from del.icio.us and the seven suggested tags given by del.icio.us for each of the 11 websites. For the experiment the seven popular tags were aggregated and presented to the participants in a manner similar to how tags are suggested to users of del.icio.us, being shown to the user before they commence their tagging. Each of the 300 participants was randomly assigned to either the 'tag suggestion' or 'no tag suggestion' condition. Of these 300 users, 78 did not tag any website (37 in the 'tag suggestion' condition, 41 in the 'no tag suggestion' condition) and are therefore excluded from further analysis. The users were randomized over age, gender, computer, experience with the Web, and their past tagging usage.

5.3.3   Results

In total the 222 participants applied 7,250 tags over all websites in both conditions, with 3,694 tags applied in the 'tag suggestion' condition and 3,556 in the 'no tag suggestion' condition. On average every user in the 'tag suggestion' condition applied 32.69 ($S.D. = 9.77$) tags over all 11 URIs and for the no tag suggestion conditions 32.61 ($S.D. = 6.80$) tags over 11 URIs. Following the same methodology as done in Sect. 5.2, we averaged the tag-resource distributions for all 11 web-pages. This distribution in log–log space is given in Fig. 5.7. In a log–log scale, *both* conditions appear visually to exhibit power-law behavior.

5.3.3.1   Parameter Estimation via Maximum-Likelihood

Figure 5.8 shows the different α parameters for the 'tag suggestion' and 'no tag suggestion' conditions, as well as the α determined via aggregation of tagging data from del.icio.us for the 11 URIs, using the same maximum likelihood method

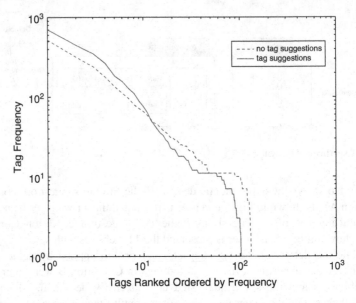

Fig. 5.7 Averaged tag-resource distributions for both experimental conditions on a log–log scale. The *solid line* depicts the 'tag suggestion' condition, the *dotted line* the 'no tag suggestion' condition

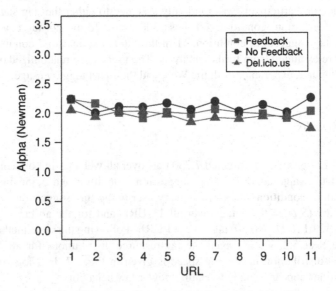

Fig. 5.8 *X axis* depicts the URI used in the experiment, *Y axis* depicts the different α values

employed in Sect. 5.2.1. Overall, for the 'no tag suggestion' condition, the average α was 2.1827 (S.D. 0.0799) while for the 'tag suggestion' condition the average α was 2.0682 (S.D. 0.0941). The α values for both conditions and the aggregated data from del.icio.us are situated in the interval $[1.732391 < \alpha < 2.249359]$. Figure 5.8 shows that both experimental conditions and the aggregated data from del.icio.us have similar exponents. Our results show that a similar α holds for both the 'tag suggestion' and 'no tag suggestion' condition.

5.3.3.2 Kolmogorov-Smirnov Complexity

Determining whether a particular distribution is a 'good fit' for a power-law is difficult, as most goodness-of-fit tests employ some sort of normal Gaussian assumption that is inappropriate for non-normal power-law distributions. However, the Kolmogorov-Smirnov Test (abbreviated as the 'KS Test') can be employed as a 'goodness-of-fit' test for any distribution without implicit parametric assumptions and is thus ideal for use measuring goodness-of-fit of a given finite distribution to a power-law function. Intuitively, given a reference distribution P (perhaps produced by some well-known function like a power-law) and a sample distribution Q of size n, where one is testing the null hypothesis that Q is drawn from P, then one simply compares the cumulative frequency of both P and Q and then the greatest discrepancy (the D-statistic) between the two distributions is tested against the critical value for n, which varies per function.

For a power-law distribution generating function, we can get a critical p-value by generating artificial data using the scaling exponent α and lower-bound equal to those found in the supposed fitted power-law distribution. A power-law is fit to this artificial data, and then the KS test is then done for each distribution that was artificially generated comparing it to its *own* fitted power-law. The p-value is then just the fraction of the amount of times the D-statistic is larger for the artificially-generated distribution than the D-statistic of the empirically-found distribution. Therefore, the larger the p-value, the more likely a genuine power-law has been found in the empirical data. According to Clauset, "once we have calculated our p-value, we need to make a decision about whether it is *small enough to rule out* the power-law hypothesis" (emphasis added) (2007). The power-law hypothesis is simply that the distribution was generated by a power-law generating function. The null hypothesis is that by chance a function would generate the power-law distribution observed in the empirical data. We shall also use $p \leq 0.1$.

The KS test for all 11 tagged web-pages, testing both the 'tag suggestion' and 'no tag suggestion' conditions, is given in Fig. 5.9. The average D statistic for the 'no tag suggestion' condition is 0.0313 (S.D. 0.0118) with $p = 0.48$ ($p > 0.1$, power-law found). For the 'tag suggestion' condition the average D-statistic is 0.0724 (S.D. 0.0256) with $p = 0.08$ ($p \leq 0.1$, no power-law found). These results show that the power-law function exhibited *only* in the 'no tag suggestion' condition is significant, the fit is closer for the 'no tag suggestion' condition than the 'tag suggestion' condition. The D-statistic showed a range from 0.0170 to 0.0552 for 'no tag suggestion' condition yet a range of 0.0428–0.1318 for 'tag suggestion.' Thus, the power-law only significantly appears without tag suggestions, and with tag suggestions a power-law cannot be reliably found. This is surprising, as tag

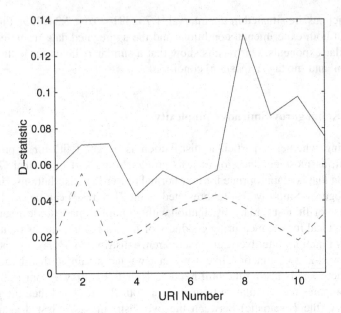

Fig. 5.9 *X axis* depicts the URI used in the experiment, *Y axis* depicts the different D Statistics from the KS Test. The *dotted line* is the 'no tag suggestion' condition, while the *solid line* is the 'tag suggestion' condition

suggestions do not only *not* cause the power-law to form, but it seems that they somehow prevent it from being formed. On the other hand, the 'no tag suggestion' condition results in a significantly good fit to a power-law. Therefore, the result is somewhat counter-intuitive, as according to our experimental data a simple tag-based suggestion mechanism is unlikely the main cause of the power-law formation.

5.3.4 Influence of Tag Suggestions on the Tag Distribution

Given that the KS test shows that there is a significant and perhaps counter-intuitive difference in the emergence of the power-law distributions between the conditions, we need a more fine-grained way to tell what the differences are in the distributions for the two conditions.

5.3.4.1 Ranked frequency distribution

In order to observe the micro-behavior of the 'tag suggestion' and 'no tag suggestion' distributions, we investigate whether or not the tag suggestion tags are 'forced' higher in the distribution, so leading to a more sparse long tail and an

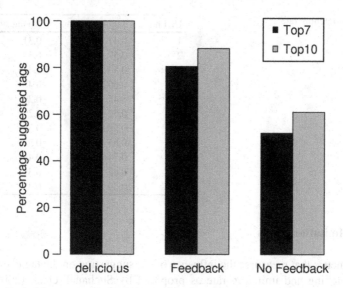

Fig. 5.10 Ranked frequency distribution repeating suggested tags

exaggerated top of the distribution in the 'tag suggestion' condition. In order to provide a measurement of the number of suggested tags in the top of the distribution, the percentage of suggested tags that were found in the top 7 and top 10 tags were calculated. We compared the percentage of suggested tags in the top 7 and top 10 ranks for both conditions with del.icio.us. For this we assume that the seven suggested tags provided by del.icio.us represent the top 7 tags in the ranked frequency distribution so that the percentage of suggested tags in the top 7 and top 10 ranks for del.icio.us is equal to 100%. We averaged the percentages for all URIs per experimental condition.

Figure 5.10 shows that for the percentage of suggested tags available in the top 7 rank for the 'tag suggestion' condition is 80.51% and for the 'no tag' suggestion condition 51.93%. This means that only half of the suggested tags can be found in the top 7 of the ranked frequency distribution in the 'no tag suggestion' condition. So unsurprisingly, in the 'tag suggestion' condition, we observed more of the suggested tags than in the 'no tag suggestion' condition. There is an influence of tag suggestions on the ranked position and the frequency of the suggested tags. Tag suggestions do influence the tag-resource distribution, as tag suggestion causes a net gain of nearly one in three tags being imitated that would otherwise not be. However, when users are not guided by tag suggestions and tag freely they still choose for themselves half of the tags that would have been otherwise suggested had they had a 'tag suggestion' mechanism available. Further we look at the availability of suggested tags in the top 10 as an indication of how dispersed the suggested tags are in the ranked frequency distribution for both conditions. For the top 10 rank Fig. 5.10 shows that the percentage of suggested tags in the 'tag suggestion' condition is 88.30% and for the "no tag suggestion" condition is 61.03%.

Table 5.1 Matching rate

URI no.	Tag suggestion	No tag suggestion
1	0.47	0.31
2	0.57	0.34
3	0.53	0.32
4	0.65	0.48
5	0.45	0.29
6	0.52	0.29
7	0.58	0.38
8	0.65	0.38
9	0.74	0.46
10	0.63	0.30
11	0.59	0.31

5.3.4.2   Imitation Rates

Another metric that measures the influence of tag suggestion on the tag distribution is the matching and imitation rate as proposed by Suchanek et al. (2008). The matching rate measures the proportion of applied tags that are available in the suggested tags. This metric provides insight into how the user is influenced by the tag suggestions provided by the tagging system. For our experiment the *matching rate (mr)* is being defined as:

$$mr(X) = \frac{\sum_{i=1}^{n} | T(X,i) \cap S(X) |}{\sum_{i=1}^{n} | T(X,i) |} \tag{5.5}$$

X denotes the tag suggestion method that is being used in both our conditions. The 'tag suggestion' condition provides 7 suggested tags while the 'no tag suggestion' condition provided no suggested tags. For a given URI, $T(X,i)$ denotes the set of tags at the ith tag entry and $S(X)$ denotes the suggested tags for that URI. For a tagging instance in which all tags are given by the suggested tags the matching rate will be 1.

The matching rate for the 11 URIs in the experiment and over the both conditions was calculated. The resulting matching rates can be found in Table 5.1. The 'no tag suggestion' condition serves as a reference point. The results in Table 5.1 show that users in the 'tag suggestion' condition are being influenced by the appearance of tag suggestions. The average matching rate for the 'tag suggestion' condition is 0.57 (S.D. 0.086) and for the 'no tag suggestion' condition 0.35 (S.D. 0.068). The main drawback of the matching rate is that it can't account for the application of suggested tags when tag suggestion is absent.

This ability to account for tag repetition even when the tag is missing is given by the *imitation rate (ir)*, defined by Suchanek et al. (2008):

$$\alpha_n(S) = \frac{prec_n(X,S) - prec_n(NONE,S)}{1 - prec_n(NONE,S)} \tag{5.6}$$

Table 5.2 Imitation rate

URI No.	Imitation rate
1	0.22
2	0.35
3	0.29
4	0.35
5	0.20
6	0.34
7	0.31
8	0.42
9	0.50
10	0.48
11	0.43

With $prec_n(X,S)$ defined as:

$$prec_n(X,S) = \frac{\sum_{i=1}^{n} |T(X,i) \cap S| \, [S(X,i) = S]}{\sum_{i=1}^{n} |T(X,i)| \, [S(X,i) = S]} \tag{5.7}$$

The term $prec_n(X,S)$ defines the proportion of applied tags that are available in the single tag suggestion set S. Since the tags S in our experiment are always static, $prec_n(X,S)$ is equal to the calculation of the matching rate for the tag suggestion condition in (5.5). $prec_n(NONE,S)$ defines the proportion of suggested tags that are available in the tags applied by the user when no tag suggestion is given. This is similar to the calculation of the matching rate for the 'no tag suggestion' condition. Therefore we can rewrite the imitation rate as:

$$ir = \frac{mr(ConditionA) - mr(ConditionB)}{1 - mr(ConditionB)} \tag{5.8}$$

Table 5.2 shows the imitation rates for the different experimental URIs. An imitation rate of 1 will denote full imitation. The results show that users tend to select suggested tags when they are available with a chance of 1 out of 3 with a mean imitation rate of 0.36 (S.D. 0.097).

Combining this insight with our previous work in KL divergence and looking at Fig. 5.7, it appears that the 'tag suggestion' condition 'compresses' the distribution that naturally arises without tag suggestions. This 'compression' of the distribution that the 'no tag suggestion' generates can be defined as highly frequent tags being reinforced more and less frequent tags reinforced less or not used at all, leading to more imitation in the top of the distribution and a 'shorter' long tail. It is because of this 'compression' caused by tag suggestions that the averaged 'no tag suggestion' distributions do not significantly fit power-law distributions while the averaged 'tag suggestion' distribution does fit a power-law distribution. Taking a 'scale-free' power-law as an ideal stable tag distribution, rather counter-intuitively a simple tag suggestion scheme based on frequency may actually hurt rather than help the stabilization of tagging as a power-law distribution.

5.3.4.3   Tag Suggestions Do Not Cause Tag Stabilization

This experiment provides a first step that leads to a new interpretation of the accepted theories and models that explain the emergence of power-laws in tagging systems. Common wisdom in tagging suggested that the power-law was unlikely to form without tag suggestions. As put by Marlow, Boyd, and others, "a convergent folksonomy is likely to be generated when tagging is not blind," blind tagging being tagging without tag suggestions (2006). The results show that the tags of users *without* tag suggestions converge into a power-law distribution. Moreover, a power-law function fits *more closely* the behavior of users when the users are *not* given tag suggestions than when the users are given tag suggestions. This means that tag suggestions distort the power-law function that would already naturally occur when users tag blindly without tag suggestions. These results are not unexpected. After all, *words in natural language naturally follow a power-law*, and there exist purely information-theoretic arguments why this is the case (Mandelbrot 1953).

This helps clarify a number of experimental results from previous experiments in tagging. First, this result clarifies how the power-law distribution was observed by Cattuto even before del.icio.us began using tag suggestions via the tag interface (Cattuto 2006). Second, it also helps explain how the majority of users in Suchanek et al.'s experiment had a high matching rate, even when in their report-back most of them said they didn't use or even notice tag suggestions (Suchanek et al. 2008). Our experiment does have a number of limitations, in particular our experiment should be extended to deal with more web-pages as well as expert and non-expert users dealing with different kinds of expert subject matters. In this situation, tag suggestions may have more of an influence on tagging behavior. Although the presented results indicate that some of the previous assumptions underlying the emergence of power-laws do not hold, a power-law distribution alone does not provide the necessary information needed to determine the role of tag suggestion on tag behavior. One line of research that seems promising is to understand how humans categorize in general, which could easily influence how they decide which tags to use to annotate web-pages. While the large amount of tagging data on the web made it easy to develop simple mathematical models of human behavior, it seems that a more detailed understanding of what users are *actually* doing is needed, the role of language in the use of the Web by human agents. Therefore, we need to inspect the collective use of language in tags more thoroughly to get a grasp of what is occuring with tagging systems as a kind of sense.

5.4   Constructing Tag Correlation Graphs

While earlier we have discovered the kinds of tag frequency distributions that emerge from the collective tagging actions of individual users, as well as the dynamics of this process of sense-making, we have come into a key problem. If the tag stabilization simply reflects the large-scale dynamics of English language usage, then the result is not very surprising. However, tags are often domain specific terms, and thus may not actually reflect English language use. Therefore, it would be useful to see if any latent sense could be extracted from the stabilized tag distributions, and if those latent structures reflected the domain-specific organization of information. We look at one of the most simple latent structures that can be derived through collaborative tagging: inter-tag correlation graphs (or, perhaps more simply, 'folksonomy graphs'). We discuss the methodology used for obtaining such graphs and then illustrate our approach through an example domain study.

5.4.1 Methodology

The act of tagging resources by different users induces, at the tag level, a simple distance measure between any pair of tags. This distance measure captures a degree of co-occurrence which we interpret as a similarity metric, between the content represented by the two tags. The collaborative filtering (Sarwar et al. 2001; Robu and Poutré 2006) and natural language processing (Manning and Schutze 2002) literature proposes several distance or similarity measures that can be employed for such problems. The metric we found most useful for this problem is *cosine distance*. Note that this should not be interpreted as a conclusion on our part that cosine distance is always an optimal choice for this problem. This issue probably requires further research on larger data sets.

Formally, let T_i, T_j represent two random tags. We denote by $N(T_i)$ and $N(T_j)$ respectively the number of times each of the tags was used individually to tag all resources, and by $N(T_i, T_j)$ the number of times two tags are used to tag the same resource. Then the similarity between any pair of tags i and j is defined as:

$$similarity(T_i, T_j) = \frac{N(T_i, T_j)}{\sqrt{N(T_i) * N(T_j)}} \tag{5.9}$$

We use the shorthand: sim_{ij} to denote $similarity(T_i, T_j)$. From these similarities we can construct a tag-tag correlation graph or network, where the nodes represent the tags themselves weighed by their absolute frequencies, while the edges are weighed with the cosine distance measure. We build a visualization of this weighed tag-tag correlation, by using a spring-embedder or spring relaxation type of algorithm. An analysis of the structural properties of such tag graphs may provide important insights into both how people tag and how structure emerges in collaborative tagging.

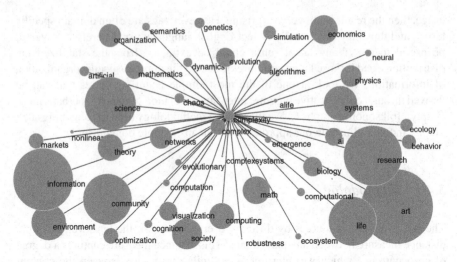

Fig. 5.11 Folksonomy graph, considering only correlations corresponding to central tag 'complexity'

5.4.2 Constructing the Tag Correlation (Folksonomy) Graphs

In order to exemplify our approach, we collected the data and constructed visualizations for a restricted class of 50 tags, all related to the tag 'complexity.' Our goal in this example was to examine which sciences the user community of del.icio.us expresses as most related to the problematic term 'complexity science.' The visualizations were made on Pajek (Batagelj and Mrvar 1998). The purpose of the visualization was to study whether the proposed method retrieves connection between a central tag 'complexity' and related disciplines. We considered two cases:

- Only the dependencies between the tag "complexity" and all other tags in the subset are taken into account when building the graph (Fig. 5.11).
- The weights of all the 1,175 possible edges between the 50 tags are considered (Fig. 5.12).

In both figures, the size of the nodes is proportional to the absolute frequencies of each tag, while the distances are, roughly speaking, inversely related to the distance measure as returned by the spring-embedder algorithm.[7] We tested two energy measures for the 'springs' attached to the edges in the visualization: Kamada-Kawai and Fruchterman-Reingold (Batagelj and Mrvar 1998). For lack of space, only the visualization returned by Kamada-Kawai is presented here, since we found it more faithful to the proportions in the data.

---

[7]For two of the tags, namely 'algorithms' and 'networks,' morphological stemming was employed. So both absolute frequencies and co-dependencies were summed over the singular form tag, i.e. 'network' and the plural 'networks,' since both forms occur with relatively high frequency.

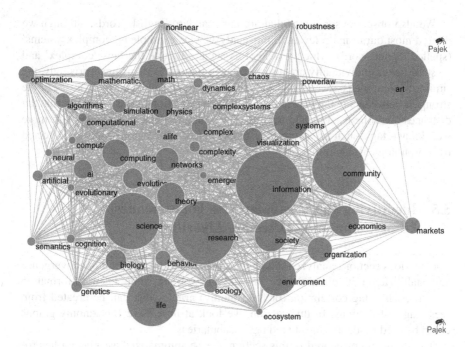

Fig. 5.12 Folksonomy graph, considering all relevant inter-tag correlations

The results from the visualization algorithm match relatively well with the intuitions of an expert in the organization of content in this field. Some nodes are much larger than others which again shows that taggers prefer to use general, heavily used tags (e.g. the tag 'art' was used 25 times more than 'chaos'). Tags such as 'chaos', 'alife', 'evolution', or 'networks' which correspond to topics generally seen as close to complexity science are close to it. At the other end, the tag 'art' is a large, distant node from 'complexity.' This is not so much due to the absence of sites discussing aspects of complexity in art as there are quite a few of such sites, but instead due to the fact that they represent only a small proportion of the total sites tagged with 'art,' leading to a large distance measure.

In Fig. 5.12, the distances to 'complexity' change significantly, due to the addition of the correlations to all other tags. However, one can observe several clusters emerging which match reasonably well with intuitions regarding the way these disciplines should be clustered. Thus, in the upper-left corner one can find tags such as 'mathematics', 'algorithmics', 'optimization', 'computation', while immediately below are the disciplines related to AI ('neural' [networks], 'evolutionary' [algorithms] and the like). The bottom left is occupied by tags with biology-related subjects, such as 'biology', 'life', 'genetics', 'ecology' etc, while the right-hand side consists of tags with more 'social' disciplines ('markets', 'economics', 'organization', 'society' etc.). Finally, some tags are both large and central, pertaining to all topics ('research', 'science', 'information').

We also observed some tags that are non-standard English words, although we filtered most out as not relevant to this analysis. One example is 'complexsystems' (spelled as one word), which was kept as such, although the tags 'complex' and 'system' taken individually are also present in the set. Perhaps unsurprisingly, the similarity computed between the tags 'complexsystems' and 'complex' is one of the strongest between any tag pair in this set. One implication of this finding is that tag distances could be used to find tags that have minor syntactic variance with more well-known tags, such as 'complexsystems,' but which cannot simply be detected by morphological stemming.

5.5   Identifying Tag Vocabularies in Folksonomies Using Community Detection Algorithms

The previous sections analyzed the temporal dynamics of distribution convergence and stabilization in collaborative tagging as well as some latent information structures, like tag correlation (or folksonomy) graphs, that can be created from these tag distributions. In this section, we look at how these folksonomy graphs could be used to identifying shared tag vocabularies.

The problem considered in this section can be summarized as: given a hetero-geneous set of tags (which can be represented as a folksonomy graph), how can we partition this set into subsets of related tags? We call this problem a *vocabulary identification* problem. It is important to note that we use the term 'vocabulary' only in a restricted sense, i.e. as a collection of related terms, relevant to a specific domain. For instance, a list of tropical diseases is a vocabulary, a list of electronic components in a given electronic device is a vocabulary, and a list of specialized terms connected to a given scientific subfield would all be vocabularies in our definition. We acknowledge that structural information is difficult to extract only from tags given the simple structure of folksonomies. Nevertheless, our approach could still prove useful in such applications: for example, one could construct the set of related terms as a first rough step and then a human expert (or, perhaps, another [semi]-automated method) could be used to add more detail to the extracted vocabulary set.

Note that the complexity-related disciplines data set (already introduced in Sect. 5.4) is a useful tool to examine this question, since the initial set of tags are heterogeneous (complexity science is, by its very nature, an interdisciplinary field), but there are natural divisions into sub-fields, based on different criteria. This allows easier intuitive interpretation of the obtained results (besides the mathematical modularity criteria described below). The technique we will use in our approach is based on the so-called 'community detection' algorithms, developed in the context of complex systems and network analysis theory (Newman 2004). Such techniques have been well studied at a formal level and have been used to study large-scale networks in a variety of fields from social analysis (e.g. analysis of co-citation networks, analysis of food chains) to gene interaction networks. Newman and Girvan (2004) provide an overview of existing applications of this theory, while Newman (2004) presents a formal analysis of the algorithm class used.

5.5.1 Using Community Detection Algorithms to Partition Tag Graphs

In network analysis theory, a community is defined as a subset of nodes that are connected more strongly to each other than to the rest of the network. In this interpretation, a community is related to clusters in the network. If the network analyzed is a social network (i.e. vertexes represent people), then 'community' has an intuitive interpretation. For example, in a social network where people who know each other are connected by edges, a group of friends are likely to be identified as a community, or people attending the same school may form a community. We should stress, however, that the network-theoretic notion of community is much broader, and is not exclusively applied to people. Some examples (Jin et al. 2007) include networks of items on Ebay, physics publications on arXiv, or even food webs in biology. We will use a community detection algorithm to identify 'vocabularies' within a folksonomy graph, identifying 'communities' as 'vocabularies.'

5.5.1.1 Community Detection: A Formal Discussion

Let the network considered be represented by a graph $G = (V,E)$, when $|V| = n$ and $|E| = m$. The community detection problem can be formalized as a partitioning problem, subject to a constraint. The partitioning algorithm will result in a finite number of explicit partitions, based on clusters in the network, that will be considered "communities." Each $v \in V$ must be assigned to exactly one cluster $C_1, C_2, ... C_{n_C}$, where all clusters are disjoint, i.e. $\forall v \in V, v \in C_i, v \in C_j \Rightarrow i = j$.

Generally speaking, determining the optimal partition with respect to a given metric is intractable, as the number of possible ways to partition a graph G is very large. Newman (2004) shows there are more than 2^{n-1} ways to form a partition, thus the problem is at least exponential in n. Furthermore, in many real life applications (including tagging), the optimal number of disjoint clusters n_C is generally not known in advance.

In order to compare which partition is optimal, the global metric used is *modularity*, henceforth denoted by Q. Intuitively, any edge that in a given partition has both ends in the same cluster contributes to increasing modularity, while any edge that "cuts across" clusters has a negative effect on modularity. Formally, let $e_{ij}, i, j = 1..n_C$ be the fraction of all edges in the graph that connect clusters i and j and let $a_i = \frac{1}{2}\sum_j e_{ij}$ be the fraction of the ends of edges in the graph that fall within cluster i (thus, we have $\sum_i a_i = \sum_{i,j} e_{ij} = m$).

The modularity Q of a graph $|G|$ with respect to a partition C is defined as:

$$Q(G,C) = \sum_i (e_{i,i} - a_i^2) \qquad (5.10)$$

Informally, so Q is defined as the fraction of edges in the network that fall within a partition, minus the expected value of the fraction of edges that would fall within the same partition if all edges would be assigned using a uniform, random distribution. These partitions are identified as communities by Newman and Girvan (2004). In tagging, all of these partitions are identified as a vocabulary.

As shown in Newman (2004), if $Q = 0$, then the chosen partition c shows the same modularity as a random division.[8] A value of Q closer to 1 is an indicator of stronger community structure – in real networks, however, the highest reported value is $Q = 0.75$. In practice, Newman (2004) found (based on a wide range of empirical studies) that values of Q above around 0.3 indicate a strong community structure for the given network. We will return shortly to define the algorithm by which this optimal partition can actually be computed, but first some additional steps are needed to link this formal definition to our tagging domain.

5.5.2 Edge Filtering Step

As shown in the tag graph construction step above, for our data set the initial inter-tag graph contains $\binom{50}{2} = 1225$ pairwise similarities (edges), one for each potential tag pair. So we make the choice to filter and use in further analysis only the top $m = k_d * n$ edges, corresponding to the strongest pairwise similarities. Here, k_d is a parameter that controls the density of the given graph (i.e. how many edges are there to be considered vs. the number of vertexes in the graph). In practice, we take values of $k_d = 1...10$, which for the tag graph we consider means a number of edges from 500 down to 50.

5.5.3 Normalized vs. Non-normalized Edge Weights

The graph community identification literature generally considers graphs consisting of discrete edges (for example, in a social network graph, people either know or do not know each other, edges do not usually encode a "degree" of friendship). In our graph, however, edges represent similarities between pairs of tags (c.f. (5.9)) (Newman and Girvan 2004). There are two ways to specify edge weights. The non-normalized case assigns each edge that is retained in the graph, after

---

[8]Note that Q can also take values smaller than 0, which would indicate that the chosen partition is worse than expected at random.

Algorithm 1 *GretedyQ Determination*: Given a graph $G = (V,E), |V| = n, |E| = m$
returns partition $< C_1,...C_{n_C} >$

---

1. $C_i = \{v_i\}, \forall i = \overline{1,n}$
2. $n_C = n$
3. $\forall i, j, e_{ij}$ initialized as in (5.11)
4. repeat
5. $< C_i, C_j >= \mathrm{argmax}_{c_i, c_j} (e_{ij} + e_{ji} - 2a_i a_j)$
6. $\Delta Q = \max_{c_i, c_j} (e_{ij} + e_{ji} - 2a_i a_j)$
7. $C_i = C_i \cup C_j, C_j = \emptyset$ //merge C_i and C_j
8. $n_C = n_C - 1$
9. until $\Delta Q \leq 0$
10. $maxQ = Q(C_1, .. C_{n_C})$

---

filtering, a weight of 1. Edges filtered out are implicitly assigned a weight of zero.
The normalized case assigns each edge a weight proportional to the similarity
between the tags corresponding to the ends. Formally, using the notations from (5.9)
to (5.10) from above, we initialize the values e_{ij} as:

$$e_{ij} = \frac{m}{\sum_{ij} sim_{ij}} sim_{ij} \tag{5.11}$$

Where $\frac{m}{\sum_{ij} sim_{ij}}$ is simply a normalization factor, which assures that $\sum_{ij} ei_{ij} = m$.

5.5.4 The Graph Partitioning Algorithm

Since we have established our framework, we can now formally define the graph
partitioning algorithm. As already shown, the number of possible partitions for this
problem is at least 2^{n-1} (e.g. for our 50 tag setting $2^{50} > 10^{15}$). Therefore, to explore
all these partitions exhaustively would be clearly unfeasible. The algorithm we use
to determine the optimal partition (Algorithm 1) is based on Newman (2004), and it
falls into the category of 'greedy' clustering heuristics.

Informally described, the algorithm runs as follows. Initially, each of the vertexes
(in our case, the tags) are assigned to their own individual cluster. Then, at each
iteration of the algorithm, two clusters are selected which, if merged, lead to the
highest increase in the modularity Q of the partition. As can be seen from lines 5–6
of Algorithm 1, because exactly two clusters are merged at each step, it is easy to
compute this increase in Q as: $\Delta Q = (e_{ij} + e_{ji} - 2a_i a_j)$ or $\Delta Q = 2 * (e_{ij} - a_i a_j)$ (the
value of e_{ij} being symmetric). The algorithm stops when no further increase in Q is
possible by further merging.

Note that it is possible to specify another stopping criteria in Algorithm 1, line
9, e.g. it is possible to ask the algorithm to return a minimum number of clusters
(subsets), by letting the algorithm run until n_C reaches this minimum value.

Cluster 1	Cluster 2	Cluster 3	Cluster 4	Cluster 5
computation	markets	semantics	powerlaw	genetics
optimization	economics	cognition	nonlinear	biology
visualization	society	neural	complexsystems	evolution
physics	community	ai	dynamics	evolutionary
mathematics	organization	alife	chaos	science
math	ecology	artificial	emergence	
computational	ecosystem	life	networks	
algorithms	environment	behavior	systems	
information		simulation	complex	
computing		research	complexity	
theory				

Fig. 5.13 Optimal partition in tag clusters (i.e. 'communities') of the folksonomy graph, when the *top* 200 edges are considered, two 1-tag clusters removed. This partition has a Q = 0.34. After eliminating the five tags mentioned at the *bottom*, Q can increase to 0.43

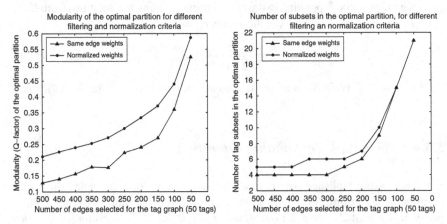

Fig. 5.14 Modularity (Q-factor) and number of partitions obtained from applying community detection algorithms to the scientific disciplines data set

5.5.5   Experimental Results

The experimental results from applying Algorithm 1 to our data set are shown in Fig. 5.14. In Fig. 5.13 we present a detailed snapshot of the partition obtained for one of the experimental configurations. There are several interesting results. First, it becomes clear that using normalized edge weights produces partitions with higher modularity than assigning all the top edges the same weight of 1. This was intuitively hypothesized by us, since edge weights represent additional information we can use, but it was confirmed experimentally. Second, we are clearly able to identify partitions with a modularity higher than around 0.3, which exhibit a strong community structure according to Newman and Girvan (2004). Yet perhaps the most noteworthy feature of the partitions is the rapid increase both in the modularity factor Q and in the number of partitions, as the number of edges filtered decreases (from left to right, in our figure). The filtering decision represents, in fact, a trade-off. Having too many edges in the graph may stop us from finding a partition with a reasonable modularity, due to the high volume of noise represented by weaker edges. However, keeping only a small proportion of the strongest edges (e.g. 100 or 50 for a 50-tag graph, in our example), may also have disadvantages, since we risk throwing away useful information. While a high modularity partition can be obtained this way, the graph may become too fragmented: arguably, dividing 50 tags into 10 or 15 vocabularies may not be a very useful.

Note that it is difficult to establish a general rule for what a 'good' or universally 'correct' partition should be in this setting. For example, even the trivial partition that assigns each tag to its own individual cluster cannot be rejected as "wrong" but such a trivial partition would not be considered a useful result for most purposes. In this paper we generally report the partitions found to have the highest modularity for the setting. However, for many applications, having a partition with a certain number of clusters, or some average cluster size, may be more desirable. The clustering algorithm proposed here (Algorithm 1) can be easily modified to account for such desiderata, by changing the stop criteria in line 9.

Figure 5.13 shows the solution with the highest modularity Q for a graph with 200 edges, in which seven clusters are identified. This partition assigns tags related to mathematics and computer science to Cluster 1, tags related to social science and phenomena to Cluster 2, complexity-related topics to Cluster 4 etc., while "art" is assigned to its own individual cluster. This matches quite well our intuition, and its modularity $Q = 0.34$ is above (albeit close) to the theoretical relevance threshold of 0.3.

5.5.5.1 Eliminating Tags from Resulting Partitions to Improve Modularity

The analysis in the previous section shows that community detection algorithms were able to produce useful partitions, with above-relevance modularity. Still, there are a few general-meaning tags that would fit well into any of the subsets resulting after the partition. These tags generally reduce the Q modularity measure significantly, since they increase the inter-cluster edges. Therefore, we hypothesized that the modularity of the resulting partitions could be greatly improved by removing just a few tags from the set under consideration. In order to test this hypothesis, we tested another greedy tag elimination algorithm, formally defined as Algorithm 2. Result graphs are shown in Fig. 5.15, while in Fig. 5.13 we show the top 5 tags that, if eliminated, would increase modularity Q from 0.34 to 0.43.

As seen in Fig. 5.2, for this data set only 5–6 tags need to be eliminated as eliminating more does not lead to a further increases in Q. In the example in Fig. 5.13, we see which these are, in order of elimination: theory, science, research, simulation, networks. In fact, these tags, that are marked for elimination automatically by Algorithm 2, are exactly those that are the most general in meaning and would fit well into any of the subsets.

Algorithm 2 *GreedyQ Elimination*: Given a partition $C_1, ...C_{n_C}$ of graph $G = (V, E)$ removes all vertexes $v_i \in V$ that increase Q

---

1. repeat
2. $v_i = \text{argmax}_{v_i}[Q(.., C_k \setminus \{v_i\}, ..) - Q(.., C_k, ..)]$
3. $\Delta Q = \text{max}_{v_i}[Q(.., C_k \setminus \{v_i\}, ..) - Q(.., C_k, ..)]$
     where $v_i \in C_k$ //C_k *is the partition of vertex i*
4. until $\Delta Q \leq 0$

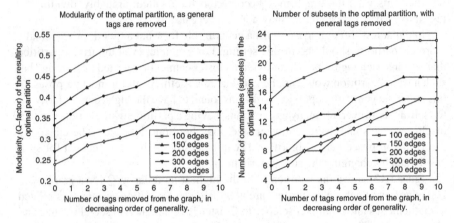

Fig. 5.15 Modularity (Q-factors) and number of partitions obtained after gradually eliminating tags from the data set, such as to increase the modularity. At each step, the tag that produced the highest increase in modularity between the initial and resulting partition was selected. In these results, all edge weights are normalized

Regarding scalability, it is relatively straightforward to show that both Algorithms 1 and 2 have a running time linear to the number of vertexes n, i.e. in this case, number of tags considered in the initial set. In the case of Algorithm 1, exactly two clusters of tags are merged at each step, so one cluster increases in size by a minimum of one, until the algorithm terminates. In case of Algorithm 2, one tag is eliminated per step, until termination. In practice, this scalability property means they are easily applicable to analyze much larger folksonomy systems.

We leave some aspects open to further work. For instance, in the current approach, similarity distances between pairs of tags are computed using all the tagging instances in the data set. In some applications, it might be useful to first partition the set of users that do the tagging, and then consider only the tags assigned by a certain class of users. For example, for tags related to a given scientific field, expert taggers may come up with a different vocabulary partition than novice users. This may require a twofold application of this algorithm: first to partition and select the set of users, and then the set of tags based on the most promising category of users.

5.6 Comparing Tags to Search Keywords

While these applications of tagging distributions have shown promise, one question that can be reasonably asked is how well these applications of tagging compare to some benchmark that does not use tagging distributions? In other words, is the notion of a Fregean sense inherently limited to only tags explicitly created in tagging systems? The most compelling other in which natural language terms are attached to URIs is that of search engines. One can consider the query terms of a user in a search engine as the implicit tagging of a resource, as is done in what has been termed 'query flow graphs' (Poblete and Baeza-Yates 2008). Thus, the main difference between search engine terms and tags is that in search engines natural language terms are used to discover a resource *pre-discovery*, while tagging are terms attached to a resource post-hoc. Regardless, this also means that the Fregean notion of a sense does not have to be confined to the collective tags attached to a resource, but can include search terms as well. However, as the data for the stabilization of search terms is not publically available like tagging systems, for the time being we will have to compare tagging to search terms using the more limited correlation graph techniques.

The idea of approximating semantics by using search engine data has, in fact, been proposed before, and is usually found in existing literature under the name of "Google distance." Cilibrasi and Vitanyi (2007) were the first to introduce the concept of "Google distance" from an information-theoretic standpoint, while other researchers (Gligorov et al. 2008) have recently proposed using it for tasks such as approximate ontology matching. It is fair to assume (although we have no way of knowing this with certainty), that current search engines and related applications, such as Google Sets also use text or query log mining techniques (as opposed to collaborative tagging) to solve similar problems.

There are two ways of comparing terms (in this case, keywords) using a search engine. One method would be to compare the number of resources that are retrieved using each of the keywords and their combinations. Another method is to use the query log data itself, where the co-occurrence of the terms in the same queries vs. their individual frequency is the indicator of semantic distance. We employ this latter method as it is more amendable to comparison with our work on tagging. In the latter method, the query terms are comparable to tags, where instead of basing our folksonomy graphs and vocabulary extraction on tags, we used query terms. In general, query log data is considered proprietary and much more difficult to obtain than tagging data. We were fortunate to have access to a large-scale data set of query log data, from two separate proposals awarded through Microsoft's "Beyond Search" awards. In the following we describe our methodology and empirical results.

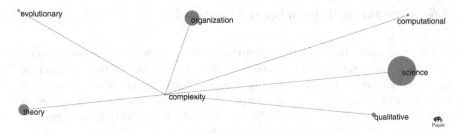

Fig. 5.16 Correlation graph from Microsoft queries, showing only correlations to the term "complexity"

5.6.1 Data Set and Methodology Employed

The data set we used consists of 101,000,000 organic search queries, produced from Microsoft search engine Live.com, during a 3-month interval in 2006. Based on this set of queries, we computed the bilateral correlation between all pairs from the set of complexity related terms considered in Sects. 5.4 and 5.5 above. The set of terms are, however, no longer treated as tags, but as search keywords.[9] The correlation between any two keywords T_i and T_j is computed using the cosine distance formula in (5.9) from Sect. 5.4 above. However, here $N(T_i, T_j)$ represents the number of queries in which the keywords T_i and T_j appear in together, while $N(T_i)$ and $N(T_j)$ are the numbers of queries in which T_i, respectively T_j appear in total (irrespective of other terms in the query), from the 101 million queries in the data set.

The rest of the analysis mirrors closely the steps described in Sects. 5.4 and 5.5, but optimizing the learning parameters which best fit this data set, in order to give both methods a fair chance in the comparison. More specifically, the Pajek visualization of the keyword graphs in Figs. 5.16 and 5.17 were also built by using a spring-embedder algorithm based on the Kamada-Kawai distance, while Fig. 5.18 shows the keyword vocabulary partition that maximizes the modularity coefficient Q in the new setting, considering the top 200 edges. For clarity, the graph pictures are depicted in a different color scheme, to clearly show they result from entirely different data sets: Figs. 5.11 and 5.12 from del.icio.us collaborative tagging data, and Figs. 5.16 and 5.17 from Microsoft's Live.com query logs.

---

[9]We acknowledge this method has some drawbacks, as a few terms in the complexity-related set, such as 'powerlaw' and 'complexsystems' (spelled as one word) or 'alife' (for 'artificial life') are natural to use as tags, but not very natural as search keywords. However, since there are only three such non-word tags, they do not significantly affect our analysis.

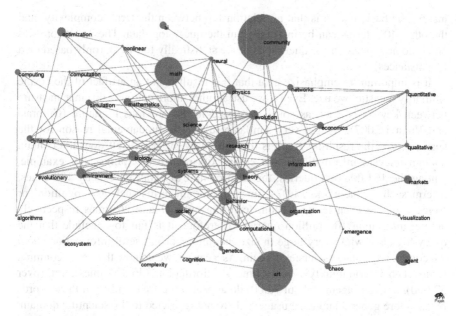

Fig. 5.17 Correlation graph obtained from Microsoft query logs, considering all relevant search terms

Cluster 1	Cluster 2	Cluster 3	Cluster 4	Cluster 5
complexity	systems	networks	algorithms	mathematics
evolution	visualization	ai	ecology	physics
evolutionary	organization	emergence	math	economics
chaos	information	neural	computing	art
cognition	community		optimization	science
biology			computation	simulation
theory			environment	dynamics
behavior				nonlinear
markets				computational
genetics				ecosystem
agent				

Fig. 5.18 Optimal partition into clusters, obtained from the Microsoft query data, when the *top* 200 edges are considered, smallest cluster not shown. The resulting partition has a $Q = 0.536$. However, nine terms were assigned to their own cluster, thus basically *left* unclassified

5.6.2   Discussion of the Results from the Query Log Data and Comparison

When comparing the graphs in Figs. 5.11 and 5.16 (i.e. the ones which only depict the relations to the central term 'complexity') an important difference can be observed. While the graph in Fig. 5.11, based on collaborative tagging data, shows 48 terms related to complexity, the one in Fig. 5.16, based on query log data, shows

just 6. The basic reason is that no relationship between the term 'complexity' and
the other 40+ terms can be inferred from the query log data. These relationships
either do not appear in the query logs or are statistically too weak (only based on a
few instances).

It is important to emphasize here that this result is not an artifact of the cosine
similarity measure we use. Even if we use another, more complex distance measure
between keywords, such as some suggested in the previous literature (Cilibrasi
and Vitanyi 2007), we get very similar results. The fundamental reason for the
sparseness of the resulting graph is that the query log data itself does not contain
enough relevant information about complexity-related disciplines. For example,
among the 101,000,000 queries, the term complexity appears exactly 138 times,
a term such as 'networks' 1,074 times. Important terms such as 'cognition' or
'semantics' are even less common, featuring only 47 and 26 times respectively
among more than 100 million queries. Therefore, it is fair to conclude that the
query log data, while very large in size, is quite poor in useful information about
the complexity-related sciences domain. As a caveat, we do note that more common
terms, such as 'community' (78,862 times), 'information' (36,520 times), 'art' (over
52,000), or even 'agent' (about 7,000) do appear more frequently, but these words
have a more general language usage and are not restricted to the scientific domain.
Therefore, these higher frequencies do not actually prove very useful for identifying
the relationship of these terms to complexity science, which was our initial target
question.

Turning our attention to the second graph in Fig. 5.17 and the partition in
Fig. 5.18, we can see that query logs can also produce good results in comparison
with tagging, although they are somewhat different from the ones obtained from
tagging. For example, if we compare the partitions obtained in Fig. 5.13 (resulting
from tagging data) and the one in Fig. 5.18 (from query log data), we see that
tagging produces a more precise partition of the disciplines into scientific sub-fields.
For instance, it is clear from Fig. 5.13 that cluster 1 corresponds to mathematics,
optimization and computation, cluster 2 to markets and economics, cluster 5 to
biology and genetics, cluster 4 to disciplines very related to complexity science
and so forth. The partition obtained from query log data in Fig. 5.18, while still
very reasonable, reflects perhaps how a general user would classify the disciplines,
rather than a specialist: organization is related to both information, systems and
community (cluster 2), research is either qualitative or quantitative (cluster 6), and
the like. There are also some counter-intuitive associations, such as putting biology
and markets in the same cluster (cluster 1). Note that the clustering (or modularity)
coefficient Q is higher in Fig. 5.18 than 5.13, but this is only because there are less
inter-connections between terms in general in the query log data, thus there are less
edges to 'cut' in the clustering algorithm.

5.7 Conclusions

To conclude, user-generated collaborative tags can serve as a *digital* neo-Fregean sense, a kind of sense more limited than the vaster notion of sense from Frege, but a notion with the distinct advantage of being *computational* and so tractable by machines. So we are interested in proving the existence of a **trace**, a *digital encoding of user behavior for a resource*. Using KL divergence, we can show that tagging distributions per resource do indeed stabilize the scale-free power law distribution, so that the 'tag cloud' of a resource after a certain point stabilizes into what is widely-accepted in a particular community to be a good description of the resource. Furthermore, this behavior of stabilization is a function of time and number of users, and does not simply reflect an artifact of the tag suggestion mechanism. Tagging can indeed be the foundation for a sense-based semantics on the Web.

Also, it seems tagging produces a richer notion of sense than search terms. This can probably be explained by the fact the del.icio.us users have more expertise and interest in complexity-related topics than general web searchers. Furthermore, they are probably more careful in selecting resources to tag and in selecting labels for them that would be useful to other users as well (general Web searchers are known to be 'lazy' in typing queries). As a caveat, we note that this target domain (i.e. complexity-related disciplines) is scientific and very specialized. If the target would be more general (for example, if we selected a set of terms related to pop-culture), the comparison might lead to different results. Also, people who sign up to use a collaborative tagging system are implicitly more willing to share their knowledge and expertise with a community of other users. By contrast, Web search is implicitly a private activity, where tracing an user's actual identity may not only be undesirable to the user, but also the user may not even be aware their activity is being tracked so their keywords can then be used by search engines or other programs to change the results for other users.

The question remains: while one can operationalize some notion of Fregean sense-based semantics on the Web in the form of collaborative tags, is this enough? After all, many URIs are not tagged at all! Superficially, the preliminary results from search engine keyword analysis seem to show that keywords are a much sparser source of sense than tags. However, these results only were shown on a tiny group of keywords gathered from a search engine on a particular topic. To think more broadly, perhaps *all* associated keywords with a particular resource could serve as a better sense-based semantics for a URI. This may include not only the keywords from tags explicitly given to that URI and from keywords used to reach a URI, but also from the terms accessible from the Web representations hosted at the URI, ranging from Semantic Web documents to hypertext web-pages. It is to this more comprehensive notion of computational sense that we turn next.

Chapter 6
The Semantics of Search

The solution to any problem in AI may be found in the writings of Wittgenstein, though the details of implementations are rather sketchy.

R.M. Duck-Lewis *(Hirst 2000)*

6.1 Introduction

What kinds of information should be used in the construction of the sense of a resource? Given our previous work, there appears to be a priori reason why we should confine ourselves to tags when constructing the sense of a resource. Up till now, we have been considering the sense-based semantics of a particular URI in the form (encoding) of a term frequency distribution. However, this seems limited. There is always the case of co-referential URIs, where a single resource is identified by multiple URIs. Should the semantics somehow combine the distributions of the various Web representations? If so, precisely how – and in particular if the Web representations are in multiple encodings? If one wanted the most thorough description of a resource, would it not make sense to define the semantics of these representations in terms of as many representations as possible, as it is well-known in statistical machine-learning that there's 'no data like more data,' such that simply adding more data under the right conditions can increase the likelihood of a stable and rich distributional semantics (Halevy et al. 2009).

Yet the intuition that simply adding more representations to the sense will increase its effectiveness needs to be operationalized and tested. A number of difficult questions immediately appear, such as how to identify possibly co-referential URIs for the same resource? Or to make matters worse, how to limit the kinds of encodings that the sense will be constructed with? These questions can be answered by attempting to fit the intuition within a well-understood experimental paradigm, which we believe can be the well-studied paradigm of information retrieval. To extend further, ***relevance feedback*** is the *use of explicit relevance judgments from* *users of a query in order to expand the query.* By 'expand the query,' we mean that the usually rather short query is expanded into a much larger query by adding words from known relevant documents. For example, a query on the hypertext Web for the Eiffel Tower given as 'eiffel' might be expanded into 'paris france eiffel tour.' If the relevant pages instead were about an Eiffel Tower replica in Texas, the same results query could be expanded into 'paris texas eiffel replica.' The same principle applies to the Semantic Web, except that the natural language terms may include Semantic Web URIs and terms resulting from inference or URI processing. The hypothesis of relevance feedback, as pioneered by Rocchio in the SMART retrieval system, is that the relevant documents will disambiguate and in general give a better description of the information need of the query than the query itself (Rocchio 1971). Relevance feedback has been shown in certain cases to improve retrieval performance significantly. Extending this classical work, *relevance models*, as formalized by Lavrenko (2008), create *language models directly from the indexed documents rather than explicitly waiting for the user to make a relevance judgment.* Relevance models are especially well-suited to our hypothesis that multiple kinds of encodings should be part of the same sense, as relevance models consider each source of data (query, documents, perhaps even tags and Semantic Web data) as 'snapshots' from some underlying generative model.

Since we will use representations from different sources of data, we cannot simply contain the notion of resource to a single URI, as currently – as content negotiation amongst various encodings is currently barely deployed on the Web – hypertext web-pages and Semantic Web documents encoded in RDF without exception almost always have different URIs. However, a web-page for the Eiffel Tower encoded in HTML and a Semantic Web document encoded in RDF can still share the same content of the Eiffel Tower, despite having differing URIs. So, the information pertaining to a resource will be spread amongst multiple co-referential URIs. Therefore, the best way to determine the set of URIs relevant to a particular resource is to attach the resource to the *information need* of an ordinary web user as expressed by a query in a search engine. Then the next step is to have humans judge a set of Web representations – either Semantic Web documents, hypertext web-pages, or both – and consider the set of these web representations and attendant URIs to be a partial snapshot of the relevant information pertaining to a sense.

This technique can be transformed into a testable hypothesis; the hypothesis put forward by Baeza-Yates that search on the Semantic Web can be used to improve traditional ad-hoc information retrieval for hypertext Web search engines and vice-versa (Baeza-Yates 2008). Currently, there exist several nascent Semantic Web search engines that specifically index and return ranked Linked Data in RDF in response to keyword queries. Yet their rankings are much less well-studied than hypertext Web rankings, and so are thought likely to be sub-optimal. While we realize the amount and sources of structured data on the Web are huge, to restrict and test the hypothesis of Baeza-Yates, from hereon we will assume that 'semantic search' refers to indexing and retrieving of Linked Data by search engines like Sindice and FALCON-S (Cheng et al. 2008), and hypertext search refers to the indexing and retrieval of hypertext documents on the World Wide Web by search engines like Google and Yahoo! Search. Our experimental hypothesis is that the statistical semantics of sense created from Semantic Web documents can help hypertext search and vice versa, and this can be empirically shown via the use of relevance feedback.

On an aside, we realize that our reduction of 'semantic search' to keyword-based information retrieval over the Semantic Web is very restrictive, as many people use 'semantic search' to mean simply search that relies on anything beyond surface syntax, including the categorization of complex queries (Baeza-Yates and Tiberi 2007) and entity-recognition using Semantic Web ontologies (Guha et al. 2003). We will not delve into an extended explanation of the diverse kinds of semantic search, as surveys of this kind already exist (Mangold 2007). Yet given the relative paucity of publicly accessible data-sets about the wider notion of semantics and the need to start with a simple rather than complex paradigm, we will restrict ourselves to the Semantic Web and assume a traditional, keyword-based ad-hoc information retrieval paradigm for both kinds of search, leaving issues like complex queries and natural language semantics for future research. Keyword search consisting of 1–2 terms should also be explored as it is the most common kind of query in today's Web search regardless of whether any results from this experiment can generalize to other kinds of semantic search (Silverstein et al. 1999). Until recently semantic search suffered from a lack of a thorough and neutral Cranfield-style evaluation, and so we carefully explain and employ the traditional information retrieval evaluation frameworks in our experiment to evaluate semantic search. At the time of the experiment, our evaluation was the first Cranfield-style evaluation for searching on the Semantic Web. This evaluation later generalized into the annual 'Semantic Search' competition,[1] which has since become a standard evaluation for search over RDF data (Blanco et al. 2011b). However, our particular evaluation presented here is still the only evaluation to determine relevance judgments over both hypertext and RDF using the same set of queries.

In Sect. 6.2 we first elucidate the general nature of search from hypertext documents to *semantic search* over Semantic Web documents. A general open-domain collection of user queries from a real hypertext query-log were run against the Semantic Web. Then human judges constructed a 'gold-standard' collection of queries and results judged for relevance, from both the Semantic and hypertext Web. Then in Sect. 6.3 we give a brief overview of information retrieval frameworks and ranking algorithms. While this section may be of interest to Semantic Web researchers unfamiliar with such techniques, information retrieval researchers may wish to proceed immediately past this section. Our system is described in Sect. 6.4. In Sect. 6.5, these techniques are applied to the 'gold standard' collection created in Sect. 6.2 so that the best parameters and algorithms for relevance feedback for both hypertext and semantic search can be determined. In Sects. 6.6 and 6.7 the effects of using pseudo-feedback and Semantic Web inference are evaluated. The system

---

[1]Sponsored by Yahoo! Research for both 2010 and 2011.

is evaluated against 'real-world' deployed systems in Sect. 6.8. Finally, in Sect. 6.9 future work on this particular system is detailed, and conclusions on the veracity of our method of sense-making are given in Sect. 6.9.1.

6.2   Is There Anything Worth Finding on the Semantic Web?

In this section we demonstrate that the Semantic Web does indeed contain information relevant to ordinary users by sampling the Semantic Web using real-world queries referring to entities and concepts from the query log of a major search engine. The main problem confronting any study of the Semantic Web is one of *sampling*. As almost any large-data database can easily be exported to RDF, statistics demonstrating the actual deployment of the Semantic Web can be biased by the automated release of large, if useless, data-sets, the equivalent of 'Semantic Web' spam. Also, large specialized databases like Bio2RDF can easily dwarf the rest of the Semantic Web in size. A more appropriate strategy would be to try to answer the question: What information is available on the Semantic Web that users are actually interested in? The first large-scale analysis of the Semantic Web was done via an inspection of the index of Swoogle by Ding and Finin (2006). The primary limitation of that study was that the large majority of the Semantic Web resources sampled did not contain rich information that many people would find interesting. For example, the vast majority of data on the Semantic Web in 2006 was Livejournal exporting every user's profile as FOAF and RSS 1.0 data that used Semantic Web techniques to structure the syntax of news feeds. Yet with information-rich and interlinked databases like Wikipedia being exported to the Semantic Web, today the Semantic Web may contain information needed by actual users. As there is no agreed-upon fashion to sample the Semantic Web (and the entire Web) in a fair manner, we will for our evaluation create a sample driven by queries from real-users using easily-accessible search engines that claim to have a Web-scale index, although independent verification of this is difficult if not impossible.

6.2.1   Inspecting the Semantic Web

In order to select real queries from users for our experiment, we used the query log of a popular hypertext search engine, the Web search query log of approximately 15 million distinct queries from Microsoft Live Search. This query log contained 6,623,635 unique queries corrected for capitalization. The main issue in using a query log is to get rid of navigational and transactional queries. A straightforward gazetteer-based and rule-based named entity recognizer was employed to discover the names of people and places (Mikheev et al. 1998), based off a list of names maintained by the Social Security Administration and a place name database provided by the Alexandria Digital Library Project. From the query log a total of

509,659 queries were identified as either (fundamentally analog) people or places by the named-entity recognizer, and we call these queries *entity queries*. Employing WordNet to represent abstract concepts, we chose queries recognized by WordNet that have *both* a hyponym and hypernym in WordNet. This resulted in a more restricted 16,698 queries that are supposed to be about abstract concepts realized by multiple entities, which we call *concept queries*.

A sample entity query from our list would be 'charles darwin,' while a sample concept query would be 'violin.' In our data-set using hypertext search, both queries return almost all relevant results. The query 'charles darwin' gives results that are entirely encyclopedia pages (Wikipedia, eHow, darwin-online.org.uk) and other factual sources of information, while 'violin' returns eight out of ten factual pages, with two results just being advertisements for violin makers. On the contrary for the Semantic Web, the query 'charles darwin' had six relevant results, with the rest being for places such as the city of Darwin and books or products mentioning Darwin. For 'violin,' only three contain relevant factual data, with the rest being the names of albums called 'Violin' and movies such as 'The Violin Maker.' From inspection of entities with relevant results, it appears the usual case for semantic search is that DBpedia and WordNet have a substantial amount of overlap in the concepts to which they give URIs. For example, they have distinct URIs for such concepts as 'violin' (http://dbpedia.org/resource/Violin vs. W3C WordNet's `synset-violin-noun-1`). Likewise, most repetition of entity URIs comes from WordNet and DBpedia, both of which have distinct URIs for famous people like Charles Darwin. In many cases, these URIs do not always appear at the top, but in the second or third position, with often an irrelevant URI at top. Lastly, much of the RDF that is retrieved seems to have little information in it, with DBPedia and WordNet being the most rich sources of information.

The results of running the selected queries against a Semantic Web search engine, FALCON-S's Object Search (Cheng et al. 2008), were surprisingly fruitful. For entity queries, there was an average of 1,339 URIs (S.D. 8,000) returned for each query. On the other hand, for concept queries, there were an average of 26,294 URIs (S.D. 14,1580) returned per query, with no queries returning zero documents. Such a high standard deviation in comparison to the average is a sure sign of a non-normal distribution such as a power-law distribution, and normal statistics such as average and standard deviation are not good characteristic measures of such distributions. As shown in Fig. 6.1, when plotted in logarithmic space, both entity queries and concept queries show a distribution that is heavily skewed towards a very large number of high-frequency results, with a steep drop-off to almost zero results instead of the characteristic long tail of a power law. For the vast majority of queries, far from having no information, the Semantic Web of Linked Data appears to have *too much data*, but for a minority of queries there is just *no data*. This is likely the result of the releasing of Linked Data in large 'chunks' from data-silos about specific topics rather than the more organic development of the hypertext Web that typically results in power-law distributions. Also, note that hypertext web-pages are updated as regards trends and current events much more quickly than the relatively slow-moving world of Linked Data.

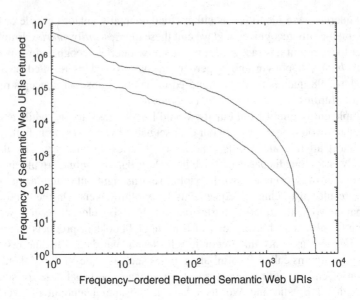

Fig. 6.1 The rank-ordered frequency distribution of the number of URIs returned from entity and concept queries, with the entity queries given on *bottom* and the concept queries on *top*

Another question is whether or not there is any correlation between the amount of URIs returned from the Semantic Web and the popularity of the query. As shown by Fig. 6.2, there is *no* correlation between the amount of URIs returned from the Semantic Web and the query popularity. For entity queries, the correlation coefficient was 0.0077, while for concept queries, the correlation coefficient was still insignificant, at 0.0125. The popularity of a query is not related to how much information the Semantic Web possesses on the information need expressed by the query: Popular queries may have little data, while infrequent queries may have a lot. This is likely due to the rapidly changing and event-dependent nature of hypertext Web queries versus the Semantic Web's preference for more permanent and less temporally-dependent data. For a more full exploration of the data-set used in this experiment, including types of URIs, see the paper on 'A Query-Driven Characterization of Linked Data' (Halpin 2009a). Since this data was collected in spring of 2009 it may not be currently accurate as a characterization of either FALCON-S or the state of Linked Data currently, but for evaluation purposes this sample should suffice, and using random selections from a real human query log is a definite advance, as randomly sampling all of Linked Data would result in an easily biased evaluation, away from what human users are interested in and towards what happens to be available as Linked Data.

Surprisingly, there is a large amount of information that may be of interest to ordinary hypertext users on the Semantic Web, although there is no correlation between the popularity of queries and the availability of that information on the

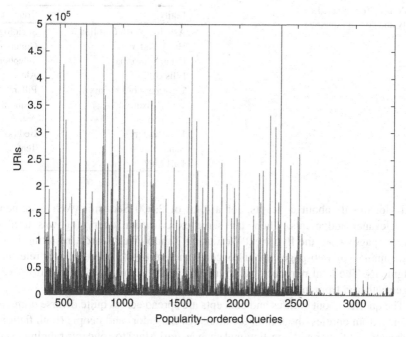

Fig. 6.2 The rank-ordered popularity of the queries is on the *x*-axis, with the *y* axis displaying the number of semantic web URIs returned, with the entity queries given on *bottom* and the concept queries on *top*

Semantic Web. The Semantic Web is not irrelevant to ordinary users as there is data on the Semantic Web ordinary users are interested in, even if it is distributed unevenly and does not correlate with the popularity of their queries.

6.2.2 Selecting Queries for Evaluation

In order to select a subset of informational queries for evaluation, we randomly selected 100 queries identified as abstract concepts by WordNet and then 100 queries identified as either people or places by the named entity recognizer, for a total of 200 queries to be used in evaluation. Constraints were placed on the URIs resulting from semantic search, such that at least 10 Semantic Web documents (a file containing a valid RDF graph) had to be retrieved from the URI returned by the Semantic Web search engine. This was necessary as some queries returned 0 or less than 10 URIs, as explained in Sect. 6.2.1. For each query, hypertext search always returned more than 10 URIs. So for each query, 10 Semantic Web documents were retrieved using the FALCON-S Object Search engine (Cheng et al. 2008), leading to a total of 1,000 Semantic Web documents about entities and 1,000 Semantic

Table 6.1 Ten selected
entity and concept queries

Entity	Concept
Ashville North Carolina	Sociology
Harry Potter	Clutch
Orlando Florida	Telephone
Ellis college	Ale
University of Phoenix	Pillar
Keith urban	Sequoia
Carolina	Aster
El Salvador	Bedroom
San Antonio	Tent
Earl May	Cinch

Web documents about concepts, for a total of 2,000 Semantic Web documents for relevance judgments. Then, the same experimental query log was used to retrieve pages from the hypertext Web using Yahoo! Web search, resulting in the same number of web-pages about concepts and entities (2,000 total) for relevance judgments. The total number of all Semantic Web documents and hypertext web-pages gathered from the queries is 4,000.

The queries about entities and concepts are spread across quite diverse domains, ranging from entities about both locations (El Salvador) and people (both fictional such as Harry Potter and non-fictional such as Earl May) to concepts ranging over a large degree of abstraction, from sociology to ale. A random selection of 10 queries from the entity and concept queries is given in Table 6.1. This set of 4,000 hypertext web-pages and Semantic Web documents are then used to evaluate our results in Sect. 6.5.

6.2.3 Relevance Judgments

For each of the 200 queries selected in Sect. 6.2.2, 10 hypertext web-pages and 10 Semantic Web documents need to be judged for relevance by three human judges, leading to a total of 12,000 judgments for relevance for our entire experiment, with the correct relevance determined by 'voting' amongst the three judges per document. Human judges each judged 25 queries presented in a randomized order, and were given a total of 3 h to judge the entire sample for relevancy. No researchers were part of the rating. The judges were each presented first with 10 hypertext web-pages and then with ten Semantic documents that could be about the same query. Before starting judging, the judges were given instructions and trained on 10 sample results (five web-pages and five Semantic Web documents). The human judges were forced to make binary judgments of relevance, so each result must be either relevant or irrelevant to the query. They were given the web-page selected by the human user from the query log as a 'gold standard' to determine the meaning of the keyword.

The standard TREC definition for relevance is "If you were writing a report on the subject of the topic and would use the information contained in the document in the report, then the document is relevant" (Hawking et al. 2000). As semantic search is supposed to be about entities and concepts rather than documents, semantic search needs a definition of relevance based around information about entities or concepts that is independent of particular terms in queries or documents. In one sense, this entity-centric relevance should have a wider remit than the document-centric relevance definition, as any information about the entity that could be relevant should be included. Yet in another sense, this definition is more restrictive, as if one considers the world (perhaps fuzzily) partitioned into distinct entities and concepts, then merely related information would not count. In the instructions, relevance was defined *as whether or not a result is about the same thing as the query, which can be determined by whether or not accurate information about the information need is expressed by the result.* The following example was given to the judges: "Given a query for 'Eiffel Tower,' a result entitled 'Monuments in Paris' would likely be relevant if there was information about the Eiffel Tower in the page, but a result entitled 'The Restaurant in the Eiffel Tower' containing only the address and menus of the restaurant would not be relevant."

Kinds of Web results that would ordinarily be considered relevant are therefore excluded. In particular, there is a restriction that the relevant information must be present in the result itself. This excludes possibly relevant information that is accessible via outbound links, even a single link. All manner of results that are collections of links are thus excluded from relevancy, including both 'link farms' purposely designed to be highly ranked by page-rank based search engines, as well as legitimate directories of high-quality links to relevant information. These hubs are excluded precisely because the information, even if it is only a link transversal away, is still not directly present in the retrieved result. By this same principle, results that merely redirect to another resource via some method besides the standardized HTTP methods are excluded, since a redirection can be considered a kind of link. They would be considered relevant only if additional information was included in the result besides the redirection itself.

In order to aid the judges, a Web-based interface was created to present the queries and results to the judges. Although an interface that presented the queries and the search interface in a manner similar to search engines was created, human judges preferred an interface that presented them the results for judgments one-at-a-time, forcing them to view a rendering of the web-page associated with each URI originally offered by the search engine. For each hypertext web-page, the web-page was rendered using the Firefox Web Browser and PageSaver Pro 2.0. For each Semantic Web document, the result was rendered (i.e. the triples and any associated text in the subject) by using the open-source Disco Hyperdata Browser with Firefox.[2] In both cases, the resulting rendering of the Web representation was

---

[2]The Disco Hyperdata Browser, a browser that renders Semantic Web data to HTML, is available at http://www4.wiwiss.fu-berlin.de/bizer/ng4j/disco/

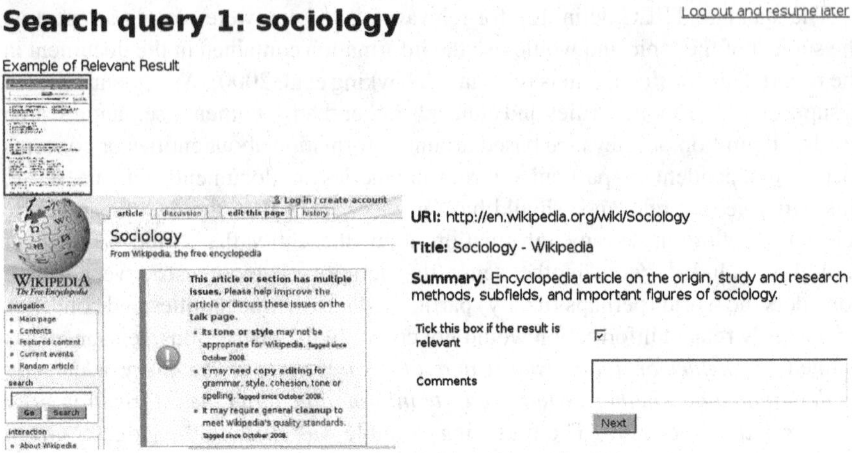

Search query 1: sociology

Example of Relevant Result

Fig. 6.3 The interface used to judge web-page results for relevancy

saved at 469 × 631 pixel resolution. The reason that the web-page was rendered instead of a link given directly to the URI is because of the unstable state of the Web, especially the hypertext Web. Even caching the HTML would have risked losing much of the graphic element of the hypertext Web. By creating 'snapshot' renderings, each judge at any given time was guaranteed to be presented with the result in the same visual form. One side-effect of this is that web-pages that heavily depend on non-standardized technologies or plug-ins would not render and were thus presented as blank screen shots to the user, but this formed a small minority of the data. The user-interface divided the evaluation into two steps:

- *Judging relevant results from a hypertext Web search:* The judge was given the search terms created by an actual human user for a query and an example relevant web-page whose full snapshot could be viewed by clicking on it. A full rendering of the retrieved web-page was presented to the user with its title and summary (as produced by Yahoo! Search) easily viewed by the judge as in Fig. 6.3. The judge clicked on the check-box if the result was considered relevant. Otherwise, the web-page was by default recorded as not relevant. The web-page results were presented to the judge one at a time, ten times for each query.
- *Judging relevant results from a Semantic Web search:* Next, the judge assessed all the Semantic Web results for relevancy. These results were retrieved from the Semantic Web using the same interface displayed to the judge in the first step as shown in Fig. 6.4, and a title was displayed by retrieving any literal values from `rdfs:label` properties and a summary by retrieving any literal values from `rdfs:comment` values. Using the same interface as in the first step, the judge had to determine whether or not the Semantic Web results were relevant.

After the ratings were completed, Fleiss' κ statistic was taken in order to test the reliability of inter-judge agreement on relevancy judgments (Fleiss 1971). Simple percentage agreement is not sufficient, as it does not take into account the

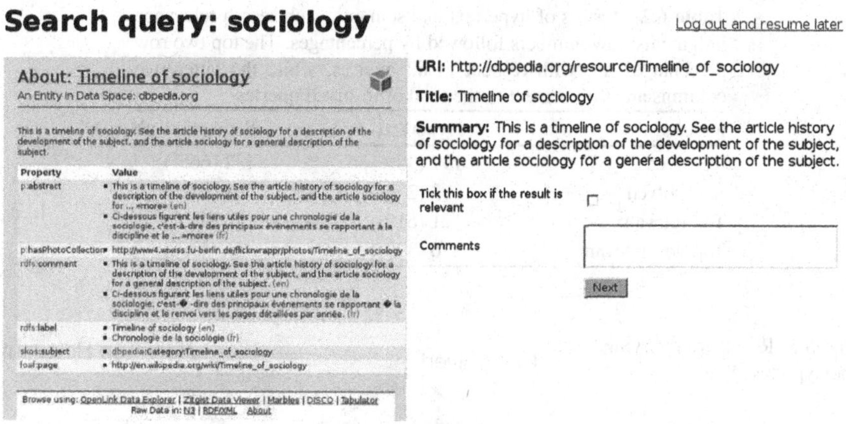

Search query: sociology

Log out and resume later

Fig. 6.4   The interface used to judge Semantic Web results for relevancy

likelihood of purely coincidental agreement by the judges. Fleiss' κ both corrects for chance agreement and can be used for more than two judges (Fleiss 1971). The null hypothesis is that the judges cannot distinguish relevant from irrelevant results, and so are judging results randomly. Overall, for both relevance judgments over Semantic Web results and web-page results, $\kappa = 0.5724$ ($p < 0.05$, 95% Confidence interval $[0.5678, 0.5771]$), indicating the rejection of the null hypothesis and 'moderate' agreement. For web-page results only, $\kappa = 0.5216$ ($p < 0.05$, 95% Confidence interval $[0.5150, 0.5282]$), also indicating the rejection of the null hypothesis and 'moderate' agreement. Lastly, for only Semantic Web results, $\kappa = 0.5925$ ($p < 0.05$, 95% Confidence interval $[0.5859, 0.5991]$), also indicating the null hypothesis is to be rejected and 'moderate' agreement. So, in all cases there is 'moderate' agreement, which is sufficient given the general difficulty of producing perfectly reliable relevancy judgments. Interestingly enough, the difference in κ between the web-page results and Semantic Web results show that the judges were actually *slightly* more reliable in their relevancy judgments of information from the Semantic Web rather than the hypertext Web. This is likely due to the more widely varying nature of the hypertext results, as compared to the more consistent informational nature of Semantic Web results.

Were judges more reliable with entities or concepts? Recalculating the κ for all results based on entity queries, $\kappa = 0.5989$ ($p < 0.05$, 95% Confidence interval $[0.5923, 0.6055]$), while for all results based on concept queries was $\kappa = 0.5447$ ($p < 0.05$, 95% Confidence interval $[0.5381, 0.5512]$). So it appears that judges are slightly more reliable discovering information about entities rather than concepts, backing the claim made by Hayes and Halpin that there is more agreement in general about 'less' abstract things like people and places rather than abstract concepts (Hayes and Halpin 2008). However, agreement is still very similar and 'moderate' for both information about entities and concepts. It is perhaps due to the entity-centric and concept-centric definition of relevance that the agreement was not higher.

Table 6.2 Results of hypertext and semantic web search relevance
judgments: raw numbers followed by percentages. The top two row
percentages are with respect to all queries, while the latter two
columns are with respect to the total of resolved queries

Results	Hypertext	Semantic web
Resolved	197 (98%)	132 (66%)
Unresolved	3 (2%)	68 (34%)
Top relevant	121 (61%)	76 (58%)
Top non-relevant	76 (39%)	56 (42%)

Fig. 6.5 Results of querying
the hypertext Web

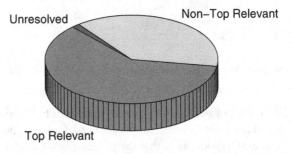

Fig. 6.6 Results of querying
the Semantic Web

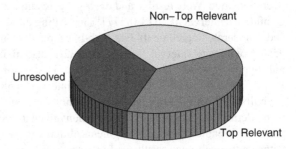

For the queries, much of the data is summarized in Table 6.2. **Resolved** queries
are *queries that return at least one relevant result* in the top 10 results, while
unresolved queries are *queries that return no relevant queries in the top 10 results*.
'Hypertext' means that the result was taken only over the hypertext Web results and
'Semantic Web' indicates the same for the Semantic Web results. The percentages
for resolved and unresolved for 'hypertext' and 'Semantic Web' were taken over
all the hypertext and Semantic Web relevancy corpora in order to allow direct
comparison. On the contrary, the percentages for 'Top Relevant' and 'Top Non-
Relevant' were computed as percentages over only resolved queries, and so exclude
unresolved queries. For ease of reference, a pie-chart for the hypertext relevancy is
given in Fig. 6.5 and for the Semantic Web relevancy in Fig. 6.6.

For both hypertext and Semantic search, there were 71 (18%) unresolved queries that did not have any results. For the hypertext Web search, only 3 (2%) queries were unresolved, while 68 (34%) of the queries were unresolved for the Semantic Web. This simply means that the hypertext search engines almost always returned at least one relevant result in the top 10, but that for the Semantic Web almost a third of all queries did not return any relevant result in the top 10. This only means there is much information that does not yet have a relevant form on the Semantic Web, unless it is hidden by the perhaps sub-optimal ranking by FALCON-S.

Another question is how many queries had a relevant result as their top result? In general, 197 queries (50%) had top-ranked relevant results over both Semantic Web and hypertext search. While the hypertext Web search had 121 (61%) top-ranked relevant results, the Semantic Web only had 76 (58%) top-ranked results. What is more compelling for relevance feedback is the number of relevant results that were *not* the top-ranked result. Again for both kinds of searches, there were 132 (33.0%) queries where a relevant result was *not* in the top position of the returned results. For the hypertext Web, there were 76 (39%) queries with a top non-relevant result. Yet for the Semantic Web there were 56 (42%) queries that had a top non-relevant result. So queries on the Semantic Web are more likely to turn up no relevant results in the top 10. When a relevant query is returned in the top 10 results it is quite likely that a non-relevant result will be in the top position for both the hypertext Web and the Semantic Web.

6.3 Information Retrieval for Web Search

In our evaluation we tested two general kinds of information retrieval frameworks: vector-space models and language models. In the *vector-space model*, document models are considered to be vectors of terms (usually called 'words' as they are usually, although not exclusively, from natural language, as we transform URIs into 'pseudo-words') where the weighing function and query expansion have no principled basis besides empirical results. Ranking is usually done via a comparison using the cosine distance, a natural comparison metric between vectors. The key to success with vector-space models tends to be the tuning of the parameters of their weighing function. While fine-turning these parameters has led to much practical success in information retrieval, the parameters have little formally-proven basis but are instead based on common-sense heuristics like document length and average document length.

Another approach, the *language model* approach, takes a formally principled and probabilistic approach to determining the ranking and weighting function. Instead of each document being considered some parametrized word-frequency vector, the documents are each considered to be samples from an underlying probabilistic language model M_D, of which D itself is only a single observation. In this manner, the query Q can itself also be considered a sample from a language model. In early language modeling efforts the probability that the language model of a document would generate the query is given by the ranking function of the document. A more sophisticated approach to language models considers that the query was a sample from an underlying *relevance model* of unknown relevant documents, but that the model could be estimated by computing the co-occurrence of the query terms with every term in the vocabulary. In this way, the query itself was just considered a limited sample that is automatically expanded before the search has even begun by re-sampling the underlying relevance model.

In detail, we will now inspect the various weighting and ranking functions of the two frameworks. A number of different options for the parameters of each weighting function and the appropriate ranking function will be considered.

6.3.1 Vector Space Models

6.3.1.1 Representation

Each vector-space model has as a parameter the factor m, the maximum *window size*, which is the number of words, ranked in descending order of frequency, that are used in the document models. In other words, the size of the vectors in the vector-space model is m. Words with a zero frequency are excluded from the document model.

6.3.1.2 Weighting Function: BM25

The current state of the art weighting function for vector-space models is *BM25*, one of a family of weighting functions explored by Robertson (1994) and a descendant of the *tf.idf* weighting scheme pioneered by Robertson and Spärck Jones (1976). In particular, we will use a version of *BM25* with the slight performance-enhancing modifications used in the InQuery system (Allan et al. 2000). This weighting scheme has been carefully optimized and routinely shows excellent performance in TREC competitions (Craswell et al. 2005). The InQuery BM25 function assigns the following weight to a word q occurring in a document D:

$$D_q = \frac{n(q,D)}{n(q,D) + 0.5 + 1.5 \frac{dl}{avg(dl)}} \frac{\log(0.5 + N/df(q))}{\log(1.0 + \log N)} \qquad (6.1)$$

The *BM25* weighting function is summed for every term $q \in Q$. For every q, *BM25* calculates the number of occurrences of a term q from the query in the document D, $n(q,D)$, and then weighs this by the length of document dl of document D in comparison to the average document length $avg(dl)$. This is in essence the equivalent of term frequency in $tf.idf$. The *BM25* weighting function then takes into account the total number of documents N and the document frequencies $df(q)$ of the query term. This second component is the idf component of classical $tf.idf$.

6.3.1.3 Ranking Function: Cosine and InQuery

The vector-space models have an intuitive ranking function in the form of cosine measurements. In particular, the cosine ranking function is given by (6.2), for a document D with query Q, where both D and Q contain q words, iterating over all words.

$$cos(D,Q) = \frac{D \cdot Q}{|D||Q|} = \frac{\Sigma_q Q_q D_q}{\sqrt{\Sigma_q Q_q^2}\sqrt{\Sigma_q D_q^2}} \tag{6.2}$$

The only question is whether or not the vectors should be normalized to have a Euclidean weight of 1, and whether or not the query terms themselves should be weighted. We investigate both options. The classical cosine is given as *cosine*, which normalizes the vector lengths and then proceeds to weight both the query terms and the vector terms by *BM25*. The version without normalization is called *inquery* after the *InQuery* system (Allan et al. 2000). The *inquery* ranking function is the same as *cosine* except without normalization each word in the query can be considered to have uniform weighing.

6.3.1.4 Relevance Feedback Algorithms: Okapi, LCA, and Ponte

There are quite a few options on how to expand queries in a vector-space model. One popular and straightforward method, first proposed by Rocchio (1971) and at one point used by the *Okapi* system (Robertson et al. 1994), is to expand the query by taking the average of the j total relevant document models R, with a document $D \in R$, and then simply replacing the query Q with the top m words from averaged relevant document models. This process is given by (6.3) and is referred to as *okapi*:

$$okapi(Q) = \frac{1}{j} \sum_{D \in R} D \tag{6.3}$$

Another state of the art query expansion technique is known as *Local Content Analysis* (*lca*) (Xu and Croft 1996). Given a query Q with query terms $q_1 \ldots q_k$ and a set of results D and a set of relevant documents R, then *lca* ranks every $w \in V$ by (6.4), where n is the size of the relevant documents R, idf_w is the inverse document frequency of word w, and D_q and D_w are the frequencies of the words w and $q \in Q$ in relevant document $D \in R$.

$$lca(w;Q) = \prod_{q \in Q} \left(0.1 + \frac{1/\log n}{1/idf_w} \log \sum_{r \in R} D_q D_w \right)^{idf_q} \tag{6.4}$$

After each word $w \in V$ has been ranked by *lca*, then the query expanded by LCA is just the top m words given by *lca*. Local Content Analysis attempts to select words from relevant documents to expand the query that have limited ambiguity, and so it does extra processing compared to the *okapi* method that simply averages the most frequent words in the relevant documents. In comparison, Local Content Analysis performs an operation similar in effect to $tf.idf$ on the possibly relevant terms, and so attempting by virtue of weighing to select only words w that both appear frequently with terms in query q but have a low overall frequency (idf_w) in all the results.

The final method we will use is the heuristic method developed by Ponte (1998), which we call *ponte*. Like *lca*, *ponte* ranks each word $w \in V$, but it does so differently. Instead of taking a heuristic-approach like *Okapi* or *LCA*, it takes a probabilistic approach. Given a set of relevant documents $R \in D$, Ponte's approach estimates the probability of each word $w \in V$ being in the relevant document, $P(w|D)$, divided by its overall probability of the word to occur in the results $P(w)$. Then the *Ponte* approach gives each $w \in V$ a score as given in (6.5) and then expands the query by using the m most relevant words as ranked by their scores.

$$Ponte(w;R) = \sum_{D \in R} log\left(\frac{P(w|D)}{P(w)}\right) \qquad (6.5)$$

6.3.2   Language Models

6.3.2.1   Representation

Language modeling frameworks in information retrieval represent each document as a language model given by an underlying multinomial probability distribution of word occurrences. Thus, for each word $w \in V$ there is a value that gives how likely an observation of word w is given D, i.e. $P(w|u_D(v))$. The document model distribution $u_D(v)$ is then estimated using the parameter ε_D, which allows a linear interpolation that takes into account the background probability of observing w in the entire collection C. This is given in (6.6).

$$u_D(w) = \varepsilon_D \frac{n(w,D)}{|D|} + (1 - \varepsilon_D)\frac{n(w,C)}{\sum_{v \in V} n(v,C)} \qquad (6.6)$$

The parameter ε_D just takes into account the relative likelihood of the word as observed in the given document D compared to the word given the entire collection of documents C. $|D|$ is the total number of words in document D, while $n(w,D)$ is the frequency of word d in document D. Further, $n(w,C)$ is the frequency of occurrence of the word w in the entire collection C divided by the occurrence of all words v in collection C.

6.3.2.2 Language Modeling Baseline

When no relevance judgments are available, the language modeling approach ranks documents D by the probability that the query Q could be observed during repeated random sampling from the distribution $u_D(\cdot)$. The typical sampling process assumes that words are drawn independently, with replacement, leading to the following retrieval score being assigned to document D:

$$P(Q|D) = \prod_{q \in Q} u_D(q) \tag{6.7}$$

The ranking function in (6.7) is called *query-likelihood* ranking and is used as a baseline for our language-modeling experiments.

6.3.2.3 Language Models and Relevance Feedback

The classical language-modeling approach to IR does not provide a natural mechanism to perform relevance feedback. However, a popular extension of the approach involves estimating a relevance-based model u_R in addition to the document-based model u_D, and comparing the resulting language models using information-theoretic measures. Estimation of u_D has been described above, so this section will describe two ways of estimating the relevance model u_R, and a way of measuring distance between u_Q and u_D for the purposes of document ranking.

Let $R = r_1 \ldots r_k$ be the set of k relevant documents, identified during the feedback process. One way of constructing a language model of R is to average the document models of each document in the set:

$$u_{R,avg}(w) = \frac{1}{k} \sum_{i=1}^{k} u_{r_i}(w) = \frac{1}{k} \sum_{i=1}^{k} \frac{n(w, r_i)}{|r_i|} \tag{6.8}$$

Here $n(w, r_i)$ is the number of times the word w occurs in the $i'th$ relevant document, and $|r_i|$ is the length of that document. Another way to estimate the same distribution would be to *concatenate* all relevant documents into one long string of text, and count word frequencies in that string:

$$u_{R,con}(w) = \frac{\sum_{i=1}^{k} n(w, r_i)}{\sum_{i=1}^{k} |r_i|} \tag{6.9}$$

Here the numerator $\sum_{i=1}^{k} n(w, r_i)$ represents the total number of times the word w occurs in the concatenated string, and the denominator is the length of the concatenated string. The difference between (6.8) and (6.9) is that the former treats every document equally, regardless of its length, whereas the latter favors longer documents (they are not individually penalized by dividing their contributing frequencies $n(w, r_i)$ by their length $|r_i|$).

6.3.2.4 Ranking Function: Cross Entropy

We now want to re-compute the retrieval score of document D based on the estimated language model of the relevant class u_R. What is needed is a principled way of comparing a relevance model u_R against a document language model u_D. One way of comparing probability that has shown the best performance in empirical information retrieval research (Lavrenko 2008) is cross entropy. Intuitively, cross entropy is an information-theoretic measure that measures the average number of bits needed to identify the probability of distribution p being generated if p was encoded using given probability distribution p rather than q itself. For the discrete case this is defined as:

$$H(p,q) = -\sum_x p(x) log(q(x)) \tag{6.10}$$

If one considers that the $u_R = p$ and that document model distribution $u_D = q$, then the two models can be compared directly using cross-entropy, as shown in (6.11). This use of cross entropy also fulfills the Probability Ranking Principle and so is directly comparable to vector-space ranking via cosine (Lavrenko 2008).

$$-H(u_R \| u_D) = \sum_{w \in V} u_R(w) \log u_D(w) \tag{6.11}$$

Note that either the *averaged* relevance model $u_{R,avg}$ or the *concatenated* relevance model $u_{R,con}$ can be used in (6.11). We refer to the former as *rm* and to the latter as *tf* in the following experiments.

6.4 System Description

We present a novel system that uses the same underlying information retrieval system on both hypertext and Semantic Web data so that relevance feedback can be done in a principled manner from both sources of data with language models. In our system, the query is run first against the hypertext Web and relevant hypertext results are then used to expand a Semantic Web search query with terms from resulting hypertext web-pages. The expanded query is then run against the Semantic Web, resulting in a different ranking of results than the non-expanded query. We can also then run the process backwards, using relevant Semantic Web data as relevance feedback to improve hypertext Web search.

This process is described using pseudo-code in Fig. 6.7 where the set of all queries to be run on the system is given by the *QuerySet* parameter. The two different kinds of relevance feedback are given by the *SearchType* parameter, with *SearchType=RDF* for searching over RDF data using HTML documents as data for relevance feedback-based query expansion, and *HTML* for searching over HTML documents with RDF as the data for relevance-feedback query expansion.

Fig. 6.7 Feedback-driven
semantic search

if $SearchType = RDF$
$\begin{cases} Data1 \in Representation(HTMLdata) \\ Data2 \in Representation(RDFdata) \end{cases}$
  else $SearchType = HTML$
$\begin{cases} Data1 \in Representation(RDFdata) \\ Data2 \in Representation(HTMLdata) \end{cases}$
for each $Query \in QuerySet$
$\begin{cases} FeedbackResults \leftarrow Feedback(Query, Data1) \\ ExpandedQuery \leftarrow Algorithm(FeedbackResults) \\ FinalResults \leftarrow Ranking(ExpandedQuery, Data2) \\ PresentResults(FinalResults) \end{cases}$

Representation is the internal data model used to represent the documents, either vector-space models or language models. The feedback used to expand the query is given by *Feedback* with the kind of relevance feedback algorithm used to expand the query given by *Algorithm*, which for relevance models are directly built into the representation. The ranking function (cross-entropy for language models, or some variation of cosine for vector-space models) is given by *Ranking*. The final results for each query are presented to the user in *PresentResults*.

We can compare both Semantic Web data and hypertext documents by considering both to be 'bags of words' and using relevance modelling techniques to expand the queries (Lavrenko and Croft 2001). We consider both to be 'bags of words.' Semantic Web data can be flattened, and URIs can be reduced to 'words' by the following steps:

- Reduce to the rightmost hierarchical component.
- If the rightmost component contains a fragment identifier (#), consider all characters right of the fragment identifier the rightmost hierarchical component.
- Tokenize the rightmost component on space, capitalization, and underscore.

So, http://www.example.org/hasArchitect would be reduced to two tokens, 'has' and 'architect.' Using this system, we evaluated both the vector-space and language models described in Sect. 6.3 on queries selected in Sect. 6.2.2 with relevance judgments on these queries selected in Sect. 6.2.3.

6.5 Feedback Evaluation

In this section we evaluate algorithms and parameters using relevance feedback against the same system without relevance feedback. In Sect. 6.8 we evaluate against deployed systems such as FALCON-S and Yahoo! Web Search. To preview our final results in Sect. 6.8, relevance feedback from the Semantic Web shows an impressive 25% gain in average precision over Yahoo! Web Search with a 16% gain in precision over FALCON-S without relevance feedback.

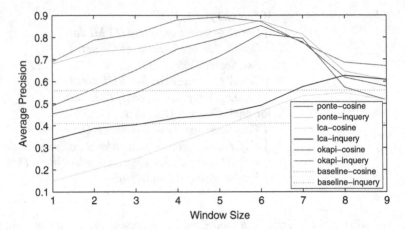

Fig. 6.8 Average precision scores for vector-space model parameters: relevance feedback from hypertext to Semantic Web

6.5.1   Hypertext to Semantic Web Feedback

6.5.1.1   Results

A number of parameters for our system were evaluated to determine which parameters provide the best results. For each of the parameter combinations, we compared the use of relevance feedback to a baseline system which did not use relevance feedback, yet used the same parameters with the exception of any relevance feedback-related parameters. The baseline system without feedback can also be considered an unsupervised algorithm, while a relevance feedback system can be thought of as a supervised algorithm. For example, the relevant hypertext web-pages R can be considered to be training data, while the Semantic Web documents D we wish to re-rank can be considered to be test data. The hypertext web-pages and Semantic Web documents are disjoint sets ($D \cap R = \emptyset$). For evaluation we used mean average precision (MAP) with the standard Wilcoxon sign-test, which we will often just call 'average precision.'

For vector-space models, the *okapi*, *lca*, and *ponte* relevance weighting functions were all run, each trying both the *inquery* and *cosine* ranking functions. The primary parameter to be varied was the *window size* (*m*), the number of top frequency words to be used in the vectors for both the query model and the document models. Baselines for both *cosine* and *inquery* were run with no relevance feedback. The parameter m was varied over $5, 10, 20, 50, 100, 300, 1,000, 3,000$. Mean average precision results are given in Fig. 6.8.

Interestingly enough, *okapi* relevance feedback weighting with a window size of 100 and an *inquery* comparison was the best, with a mean average precision of 0.8914 ($p < 0.05$). It outperformed the baseline of *inquery*, which has an average precision of 0.5595 ($p < 0.05$). Overall, *lca* did not perform as well, often

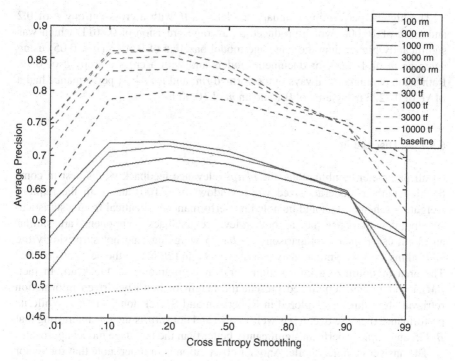

Fig. 6.9 Average precision scores for language model parameters: relevance feedback from hypertext to Semantic Web

performing below the baseline, although its performance increased as the window size increased, reaching an average precision of 0.6262 with $m = 3,000$ ($p < 0.05$). However, given that a window size of 10,000 covered most documents, increasing the window size will not likely result in better performance from *lca*. The *ponte* relevance feedback performed very well, reaching a maximum MAP 0.8756 with a window size of 300 using *inquery* weighing, and so was insignificantly different from *inquery* ($p > 0.05$). Lastly, both *ponte* and *okapi* experienced a significant decrease in performance as m was increased, so it appears that the window sizes of 300 and 100 are indeed optimal. Also, as regards comparing baselines, *inquery* outperformed *cosine* ($p < 0.05$).

For language models, both averaged relevance models *rm* and concatenated relevance models *tf* were investigated, with the primary parameter being m, the number of non-zero probability words used in the relevance model. The parameter m was varied between 100, 300, 1,000, 3,000, and 10,000. Remember that the query model *is* the relevance model for the language model-based frameworks. As is best practice in relevance modeling, the relevance models were not smoothed, but a number of different smoothing parameters for ε were investigated for the cross entropy ranking function, ranging from ε between 0.01, 0.1, 0.2, 0.5, 0.8, 0.9, and 0.99. The results are given in Fig. 6.9.

The highest performing language model was *tf* with a cross-entropy ε of 0.2 and an *m* of 10,000, which produced an average precision of 0.8611, which was significantly higher than the language model baseline of 0.5043 ($p < 0.05$) using again an *m* of 10,000 for document models and with a cross entropy ε of 0.99. Rather interestingly, *tf* always outperformed *rm*, and *rm*'s best performance had a MAP of 0.7223 using an ε of 0.1 and an *m* of 10,000.

6.5.1.2   Discussion

Of all parameter combinations, the *okapi* relevance feedback works best in combination with a moderate sized word-window ($m = 100$) and with the *inquery* weighting scheme. It should be noted its performance is identical from a statistical standpoint with *ponte*, but as both relevance feedback components are similar and both use *inquery* comparison and *BM*25 weighing, and not surprisingly the algorithms are very similar. Why would *inquery* and *BM*25 be the best performing? The area of optimizing information retrieval is infamously a black art. In fact, *BM*25 and *inquery* combined present the height of heuristic-driven information retrieval algorithms as explored in Robertson and Spärck Jones (1976). While its performance increase over *lca* is well-known and not surprising, it is interesting that *BM*25 and *inquery* perform significantly better than the language model approach.

The answer is rather subtle. Another observation is in order; note that for vector models, *inquery* always outperformed *cosine*, and that for language models *tf* always outperformed *rm*. Despite the differing frameworks of vector-space models and language models, both *cosine* and *rm* share the common characteristic of normalization. In essence, both *cosine* and *rm* normalize by documents: *cosine* normalizes term frequencies per vector before comparing vectors, while *rm* constructs a relevance model on a per-relevant document basis before creating the average relevance model. In contrast, *inquery* and *tf* do not normalize: *inquery* compares weighted term frequencies, and *tf* constructs a relevance model by combining all the relevance documents and then creating the relevance model from the *raw pool* of all relevant document models.

Thus it appears the answer is that any kind of normalization by length of the document hurts performance. The reason for this is likely because the text automatically extracted from hypertext documents is 'messy,' being of low quality and bursty, with highly varying document lengths. As observed informally earlier (Ding and Finin 2006) and more formally later (Halpin 2009a), the amount of triples in Semantic Web documents follow a power-law, so there are wildly varying document lengths of both the relevance model and the document models. Due to these factors, it is unwise to normalize the models, as that will almost certainly dampen the effect of valuable features like crucial keywords (such as 'Paris' and 'tourist' in disambiguating various 'eiffel'-related queries).

Then the reason *BM*25-based vector models in particular perform so well is that, due to its heuristics, it is able to effectively keep track of a term's document frequency and inverse document frequency accurately. Also, unlike most other algorithms, *BM*25 provides a slight amount of rather unprincipled non-linearity in the importance of the various variables (Robertson et al. 2004). This is important, as it provides a way of extenuating the effect of one particular parameter (in our case, likely term frequency and inverse term frequency) and then massively lowering the power of another parameter (in our case, likely the document length parameter). While *BM*25 can be outperformed normally by language models (Lavrenko 2008) in TREC competitions featuring high-quality samples of English, in the non-normal conditions of comparing natural language and pseudo-natural language terms extracted from structured data in RDF, it is not surprising that *okapi*, whose non-linearity allows certain highly relevant terms to have their frequency 'non-linearly' heightened, provides better results than more principled methods that derive their parameters by regarding the messy RDF and HTML-based corpus as a sample from a general underlying language model.

6.5.2 Semantic Web to Hypertext Feedback

In this section, we assume that the user or agent program has accessed or otherwise examined the Semantic Web documents from the URIs resulting from a Semantic Web search, and these Semantic Web documents are then used as relevance feedback to expand a query for the hypertext Web so that the feedback cycle has been reversed.

6.5.2.1 Results

The results for using Semantic Web documents as relevance feedback for hypertext Web search are surprisingly promising. The same parameters as explored in Sect. 6.5.1.1 were again explored. The average precision results for vector-space models are given in Fig. 6.10. The general trends from Sect. 6.5.1.1 were similar in this new data-set. In particular, *okapi* with a window size of 100 and the *inquery* comparison function again performed best with an average precision of 0.6423 ($p < 0.05$). Also *ponte* performed almost the same, again an insignificant difference from *okapi*, producing with the same window size of 100 an average precision of 0.6131 ($p > 0.05$). Utilizing again a large window of 3,000, *lca* had an average precision of 0.5359 ($p < 0.05$). Similarly, *inquery* consistently outperformed *cosine* in comparison, with *inquery* having a baseline average precision of 0.4643 ($p < 0.05$) in comparison with the average precision of *cosine* being 0.3470 ($p < 0.05$).

The results for language modeling were similar to the results in Sect. 6.5.1.1 and are given in Fig. 6.11, although a few differences are worth comment. The best performing language model was *tf* with an *m* of 10,000 and a cross entropy smoothing factor ε to 0.5, which produced an average precision of 0.6549 ($p < 0.05$). In contrast, the best-performing *rm*, with an *m* of 3,000 and $\varepsilon = 0.5$, only had an average precision of 0.4858 ($p < 0.05$). The *tf* relevance models consistently

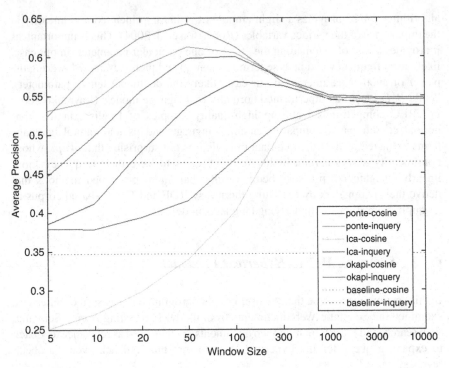

Fig. 6.10 Average precision scores for vector-space model parameters: relevance feedback from Semantic Web to hypertext

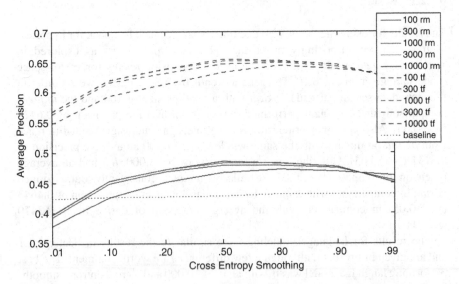

Fig. 6.11 Average precision scores for language model parameters: relevance feedback from hypertext to Semantic Web

performed better than *rm* relevance models ($p < 0.05$). The baseline for language modeling was also fairly poor with an average performance of 0.4284 ($p < 0.05$). This was the 'best' baseline using again an *m* of 10,000 for document models and cross entropy smoothing ε of 0.99. The general trends from the previous experiment then held, except the smoothing factor was more moderate and the difference between *tf* and *rm* was even more pronounced. However, the primary difference worth noting was that the best performing *tf* language model outperformed, if barely, the *okapi* (*BM*25 and *inquery*) vector model by a relatively small but still significant margin of 0.0126. Statistically, the difference was significant ($p < 0.05$).

6.5.2.2 Discussion

Why is *tf* relevance modeling better than *BM*25 and *inquery* vector-space models in using relevance feedback from the Semantic Web to hypertext? The high performance of *BM*25 and *inquery* has already been explained, and that explanation about why document-based normalization leads to worse performance still holds. Yet the rise in performance of *tf* language models seems odd. However, it makes sense if one considers the nature of the data involved. Recalling previous work (Halpin 2009a), there are two distinct conditions that separate this data-set from the more typical natural language samples as encountered in TREC (Hawking et al. 2000). In the case of using relevant hypertext results as feedback for the Semantic Web, the relevant document model was constructed from a very limited amount of messy hypertext data, which had many text fragments, with a large percentage coming from irrelevant textual data to deal with issues like web-page navigation. However, in using the Semantic Web for relevance feedback, these issues are reversed: the relevant document model is constructed out of relatively pristine Semantic Web documents and compared against noisy hypertext documents.

Rather shockingly, as the Semantic Web is mostly manually high-quality curated data from sources like DBpedia, the actual natural language fragments found on the Semantic Web, such as Wikipedia abstracts, are much better samples of natural language than the natural language samples found in hypertext. Furthermore, the distribution of 'natural' language terms extracted from RDF terms (such as 'sub class of' from `rdfs:subClassOf`), while often irregular, will either be repeated very heavily or fall into the sparse long tail. These two conditions can then be dealt with by the generative *tf* relevance models, since the long tail of automatically generated words from RDF will blend into the long tail of natural language terms, and the probabilistic model can properly 'dampen' without resorting to heuristic-driven non-linearities. Therefore, it is on some level not surprising that even hypertext Web search results can be improved by Semantic Web search results, because used in combination with the right relevance feedback parameters, in essence the hypertext search engine is being 'seeded' with high-quality structured and accurate descriptions of the information need of the query to be used for query expansion.

6.6   Pseudo-Feedback

In this section we explore a very easy-to-implement and feasible way to take advantage of relevance feedback without manual selection of relevant results by human users. One of the major problems of relevance feedback-based approaches is their dependence on manual selection of relevant results by human users. For example, in our experiments we used judges manually determining if web-pages were relevant using an experimental set-up that forced them to judge every result as relevant or not, which is not feasible for actual search engine use.

A well-known technique within relevance feedback is *pseudo-feedback*, namely simply assuming that the top x documents returned are relevant. Then, one can use this as a corpus of relevance documents to expand the queries in the same manner using language models as described in Sect. 6.3. However, in general pseudo-relevance feedback is a more feasible method, as human intervention is not required.

Using the same optimal parameters as discovered in Sect. 6.5.1.1, *tf* with $m = 10,000$ and $\varepsilon = 0.2$ was again deployed, but this time using pseudo-feedback. Can pseudo-feedback from hypertext Web search help improve the rankings of Semantic Web data? The answer is clearly positive. Employing all ten results as pseudo-relevance feedback and the same previously optimized parameters, the best pseudo-relevance feedback result had an average precision of 0.6240. This was considerably better than the baseline of just using relevance pseudo-feedback from the Semantic Web to itself, which only had an average precision of 0.5251 ($p < 0.05$), and also clearly above the 'best' baseline of 0.5043 ($p < 0.05$). However, as shown by Fig. 6.12, the results are still not nearly as good as using hypertext pages judged relevant by humans, which had an average precision of 0.8611 ($p < 0.05$). This is likely because, not surprisingly, the hypertext Web results contain many irrelevant text fragments that serve as noise, preventing the relevant feedback from boosting the results.

Can pseudo-feedback from the Semantic Web improve hypertext search? The answer is yes, but barely. The best result for average precision is 0.4321 ($p < 0.05$), which is better than the baseline of just using pseudo-feedback from hypertext Web results to themselves, which has an average precision of 0.3945 ($p < 0.05$) and the baseline without feedback at all of 0.4284 ($p < 0.05$). However, the pseudo-feedback results perform significantly worse by a large margin when compared to using Semantic Web documents judged relevant by humans as relevance feedback, which had an average precision of 0.6549 ($p < 0.05$). These results can be explained because, given the usual ambiguous and short one or two word queries, the Semantic Web tends to return structured data spread out of over multiple subjects even moreso than the hypertext Web. Therefore, adding pseudo-relevance feedback increases the amount of noise in the language model as opposed to using actual relevance feedback, hurting performance while still keeping it above baseline.

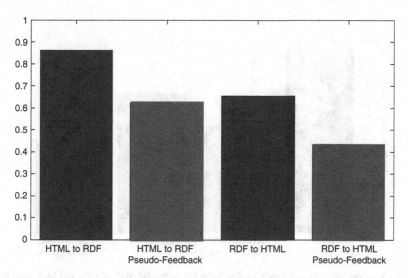

Fig. 6.12 Comparing relevance feedback to Pseudo-relevance feedback on the Semantic Web (*RDF*) and hypertext web (*HTML*)

6.7 Inference

In this section the effect of inference on relevance feedback is evaluated by considering inference to be document expansion. One of the characteristics of the Semantic Web is that the structure should allow one 'in theory' to discover more relevant data. The Semantic Web formalizes this in terms of type and sub-class hierarchies in RDF using RDF Schema (Brickley and Guha 2004). While inference routines are quite complicated as regards the various Semantic Web specifications, in practice the vast majority of inference that can be used on the Semantic Web is of two types (as shown by our survey of Linked Data (Halpin 2009a)), *rdf:subClassOf* that indicates a simple sub-class inheritance hierarchy and *rdf:type* that indicates a simple type. For our experiment, we followed all explicit *rdf:subClassOf* statements up one level in the sub-class hierarchy and explicit *rdf:type* links. The resulting retrieved Semantic Web data was all concatenated together, and then concatenated yet again with their source document from the Semantic Web. In this way, Semantic Web inference is considered as *document expansion*.

Inference was first tried using normal relevant feedback, again with the same best-performing parameters (*tf* with $m = 10,000$ and $\varepsilon = 0.2$). In the first case, the inference is used to expand Semantic Web documents in semantic search, and then the hypertext results are used as relevance feedback to improve the ranking. However, as shown in Fig. 6.13, deploying inference only causes a drop in performance. In particular, using hypertext Web results as relevance feedback to the Semantic Web, the system drops from a performance of 0.8611 to a performance of 0.4991 ($p < 0.05$). With pseudo-feedback over the top 10 documents, the performance

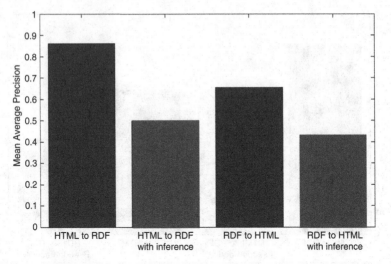

Fig. 6.13 Comparing the relevance feedback on the Semantic Web (*RDF*) and hypertext web (*HTML*) both without and with Semantic Web inference

drops even more, from 0.6240 to 0.4557 ($p < 0.05$). The use of inference actually makes the results worse than the baseline performance of language models of 0.5043 ($p < 0.05$) without either relevance feedback or inference.

The results of using inference to boost hypertext Web results using Semantic Web equally fail to materialize any performance gains. In this case, inference is used to expand Semantic Web documents, which are then used via relevance feedback to improve the ranking of hypertext search. Using the same parameters as above, the feedback from the expanded Semantic Web data to the hypertext Web results in an average precision of 0.4273, which is insignificantly different from the baseline of not using relevance feedback at all of 0.4284 ($p < 0.05$) and considerably worse than not using inference at all, which has a MAP of 0.6549 ($p < 0.05$). When pseudo-feedback is used, the results fall to the rather low score of 0.3861, which is clearly below the baseline of 0.4284 ($p < 0.05$). So, at least one obvious way of use of simple type and sub-class based Semantic Web inference seems to only lead to a decline in performance.

Why does inference hurt rather than help performance? One would naively assume that adding more knowledge in the form of the Semantic Web would help the results. However, this assumes the knowledge gained through inference would somehow lead to the discovery of new relevant terms. However, in the case of much inference with the Semantic Web, this is not the case. For example, simply consider the Semantic Web data about the query for the singer 'Britney Spears.' While the first Semantic Web document about Britney Spears gives a number of useful facts about her, such as the fact that she is a singer, determining that Britney Spears is a person via inference is of vastly less utility. For example, the Cycontology (Lenat 1990) declares that Britney Spears is a person, namely that "Something is an instance of Person if it is an individual Intelligent Agent with perceptual sensibility, capable of complex social relationships, and possessing a certain moral sophistication and an intrinsic moral value." In this regard, inference only serves as noise, adding irrelevant terms to the language models. For example, adding 'sophistication' to a query about 'Britney Spears' will likely not help discover relevant documents. Inference would be useful if it produced surprising information or reduced ambiguity. However, it appears that at least for simple RDF Schema vocabularies, information higher in the class hierarchy is usually knowledge that the user of the search engine already possesses (like Britney Spears is a person) and that the reduction of ambiguity is already done by the user in their selection of keywords. However, it is possible that more sophisticated inference techniques are needed, and that inference may help in specialized domains rather than open-ended Web search. Further experiments in parametrization of inference would be useful given that our exploration in this direction showed no performance increase, only performance decrease.

6.8 Deployed Systems

In this section we evaluate our system against 'real-world' deployed systems. One area we have not explored is how systems based on relevance feedback perform relative to systems that are actually deployed, as our previous work has always been evaluated against systems and parameters we created specifically for experimental evaluation. Our performance in Sects. 6.5.1.1 and 6.5.2.1 was only compared to baselines that were versions of our weighting function without a relevance feedback component. While that particular baseline is principled, the obvious needed comparison is against actual deployed commercial or academic systems where the precise parameters deployed may not be publicly available and so not easily simulated experimentally.

6.8.1 Results

The obvious baseline to choose to test against is the Semantic Web search engine, FALCON-S, from which we derived our original Semantic Web data in the experiment. The decision to use FALCON-S as opposed to any other Semantic Web search engine was based on the fact that FALCON-S returned more relevant results in the top 10 than other existing semantic search engines at the time using a random sample of 20 queries from the set of queries described in Sect. 6.2.2. Combined with the explosive growth of Linked Data over the last year and the changes in ranking algorithms of various semantic search engines, it is difficult to judge whether a given Semantic Web search engine is representative of semantic search. However, we would find it reasonable that if our proposed hypothesis works well on FALCON-S, it can be generalized to other Semantic Web search engines.

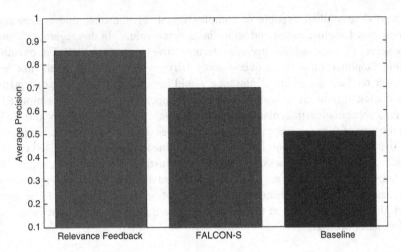

Fig. 6.14 Summary of best average precision scores: relevance feedback from hypertext to Semantic Web

We used the original ranking of the top 10 results given by FALCON-S to calculate its average precision, 0.6985. We then compared both the best baseline, *rm*, as well as the best system with feedback in Fig. 6.14. As shown, our system with feedback had significantly ($p < 0.05$) better average precision (0.8611) than FALCON-S (0.6985), as well better ($p < 0.05$) than the 'best' language model baseline without feedback (0.5043) as reported earlier as given in Sect. 6.5.1.1.

Average precision does not have an intuitive interpretation, besides the simple fact that a system with better average precision will in general deliver more accurate results closer to the top. In particular, one scenario we are interested in is having *only* the most relevant RDF data accessible from a single URI returned as the top result, so that this result is easily consumed by some program. For example, given the search 'amnesia nightclub,' a program should be able to consume RDF returned from the Semantic Web to produce with high reliability a single map and opening times for a particular nightclub in Ibiza in the limited screen space of the browser, instead of trying to display structured data for every nightclub called 'amnesia' in the entire world. In Table 6.2, we show that for a significant minority of URIs (42%), FALCON-S returned a non-relevant Semantic Web URI as the top result. Our feedback system achieves an average precision gain of 16% over FALCON-S. While a 16% gain in average precision may not seem huge, in reality the effect is quite dramatic, in particular as regards boosting relevant URIs to the top rank. So in Table 6.3, we present results of how our best parameters *tf* with $m = 10,000$ lead to the most relevant Semantic data in the top result. In particular, notice that 89% of resolved queries now have relevant data at the top position, as opposed to 58% without feedback. This would result in a noticeable gain in performance for users, which we would argue allows Semantic Web data to be retrieved with high-enough accuracy for actual deployment.

Table 6.3 Table comparing hypertext-based relevance feedback and FALCON-S

Results	Feedback	FALCON-S
Top relevant	118 (89%)	76 (58%)
Non-relevant top	14 (11%)	56 (42%)
Non-relevant top entity	9 (64%)	23 (41%)
Non-relevant concept	5 (36%)	33 (59%)

While performance is boosted for both entities and concepts, the main improvement comes from concept queries. Indeed, as concept queries are often one word and ambiguous, not to mention the case where the name of a concept has been taken over by some company, music band, or product, it should not be surprising that results for concept queries are considerably boosted by relevance feedback. Results for entity queries are also boosted. A quick inspection of the results reveals that the entity queries were the most troublesome, and that these entity queries gave both FALCON-S and our feedback system problems. These problematic queries were mainly very difficult queries where a number of Semantic Web documents all share similar natural language content. An example would be a query for 'sonny and cher,' which results in a number of distinct Semantic Web URIs: one for *Cher*, another one for *Sonny and Cher* the band, and another for 'The Sonny Side of Cher,' an album by Cher. For concepts, one difficult concept was the query 'rock.' Although the system was able to disambiguate the musical sense from the geological sense, there was a large cluster of Semantic Web URIs for rock music, ranging from *Hard Rock* to *Rock Music* to *Alternative Rock*. These types of queries seem to present the most difficulties for Semantic Web search engines.

Although less impressive than the results for using hypertext web-pages for relevance feedback for the Semantic Web, the feedback cycle from the Semantic Web to hypertext does improve significantly the results of even commercial hypertext web-engines, at least for our set of queries about concepts and entities. Given the unlimited API-based access offered by Yahoo! Web Search in comparison to Google and Microsoft web search, we used Yahoo! Web Search for hypertext searching in this experiment, and we expect that the results in a coarse-grained manner should generalize to other Web search engines. The hypertext results for our experiment were given by Yahoo! Web Search, and we calculated a mean average precision for Yahoo! Web Search to be 0.4039. This is slightly less than our baseline language model ranking, which had an average precision of 0.4284. As shown in Fig. 6.15, given that our feedback-based system had an average precision of 0.6549, our relevance feedback performs significantly ($p < 0.05$) better than Yahoo! Web Search and ($p < 0.05$) the baseline *rm* system.

6.8.2 Discussion

These results show our relevance feedback method works significantly better than various baselines, both internal baselines and state of the art commercial hypertext search engines and Semantic Web search engines. The parametrization of the precise

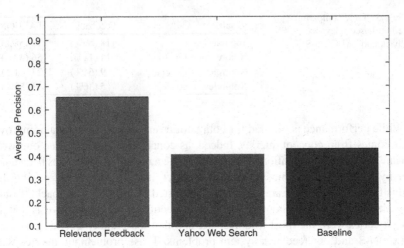

Fig. 6.15 Summary of best average precision scores: relevance feedback from Semantic Web to hypertext

information retrieval components used in our system is not entirely arbitrary, as argued above in Sects. 6.5.1.2 and 6.5.2.2. The gain of our relevance feedback system, a respectable 16% in average precision over the engine FALCON-S, intuitively makes the system's ability to place a relevant structured Semantic Web data in the top rank acceptable for most users.

More surprisingly, by incorporating human relevance judgments of Semantic Web documents, we make substantial gains over state of the art systems for hypertext Web search, a 25% gain in average precision over Yahoo! search. One important factor is the constant assault of hypertext search engines by spammers and others. Given the prevalence of a search engine optimization and spamming industry, it is not surprising that the average precision of even a commercial hypertext engine is not the best, and that it performs less well than Semantic Web search engines. Semantic Web search engines have a much smaller and cleaner world of data to deal with than the unruly hypertext Web, and hypertext Web search must be very fast and efficient. Even without feedback from the Semantic Web, an average precision of 40% is impressive, although far from the 65% precision using relevance feedback from the Semantic Web.

Interestingly enough, it seems that pseudo-feedback only helps marginally in improving hypertext Web search using Semantic Web data. Therefore, it is somewhat unrealistic to expect the Semantic Web to instantly improve hypertext Web search. Even with the help of the Semantic Web, hypertext search is unlikely to achieve near perfect results anytime soon. This should not be a surprise, as pseudo-feedback in general performs worse than relevance feedback. However, the loss of performance given by pseudo-feedback in comparison with traditional relevance feedback shows that for the Semantic Web using pseudo-feedback for concepts and entities is difficult, as many results that are about highly different things and subject matters may be returned. However, both pseudo-feedback and traditional relevance feedback help a fair amount in improving Semantic Web search using hypertext results, and as relevance judgments can be approximated by click-through logs of hypertext Web search engines, it is realistic and feasible to try to improve semantic search using relevance feedback from hypertext search. In fact, it is simple to implement pseudo-feedback from hypertext Web search using hypertext search engine APIs, as no manual relevance judgments must be made at all and the API simply can produce the top 10 results of any query quickly.

6.9 Future Work on Relevance Feedback

There are a number of areas where our project needs to be more thoroughly integrated with other approaches and improved. The expected criticism of this work is likely the choice of FALCON-S and Yahoo! Web search as a baseline, and that we should try this methodology over other Semantic Web search engines and hypertext Web search engines. Lastly, currently it is unknown how to combine traditional word-based techniques from information retrieval with structural techniques from the Semantic Web, and while our experiment with using inference as document expansion did not succeed, a more subtle approach may prove fruitful. At this point, we are currently pursuing this in context of creating a standardized evaluation framework for all Semantic search engines. The evaluation framework presented here has led to the first systematic evaluation of Semantic Web search at the Semantic Search 2010 workshop (Blanco et al. 2011a). Yet in our opinion the most exciting work is to be done as regards scaling our approach to work with live large-scale hypertext Web search engines.

While language models, particularly generative models like relevance models (Lavrenko 2008), should have theoretically higher performance than vector-space models, the reason why large-scale search engines do not in general implement language models for information retrieval is that the computational complexity of calculating distributions over billions of documents does not scale. However, there is reason to believe that relevance models could be scaled to work with Web search if they built their language sample from a suitably large 'clean' sample of natural language and also compressed the models by various means.

One of the looming deficits of our system is that for a substantial amount of our queries there are *no* relevant Semantic Web URIs with accessible RDF data. This amount is estimated to be 34% of all queries. However, these queries with no Semantic Web URIs in general *do* have relevant information on the hypertext Web, if not the Semantic Web. The automatic generation of Semantic Web triples from natural language text could be used in combination with our system to create automatically generated Semantic Web data, in response to user queries.

Another issue is how to determine judgments for relevance in a manner that scales to actual search engine use. Manual feedback, while providing the more accurate experimental set-up for testing relevance feedback, does not work in real search scenarios because users do not exhaustively select results based on relevance, but select on a small subset. However, pseudo-feedback does not take advantage of users selecting web-pages, but just assumes the top x are relevant. A better approach would be to consider click-through logs of search engines as incomplete approximations of manual relevance feedback (Cui et al. 2002). As we only had a small sample of the Microsoft Live Query log, this was unfeasible for our experiments, but would be compelling future work. There is a massive amount of human user click-through data available to commercial hypertext search engines, although Semantic Web data has little relevance feedback data itself. While it is easy enough to use query logs to determine relevant hypertext Web data, no such option exists for the Semantic Web. However, there are possible methodologies for determining the 'relevance' of Semantic Web data, even if machines rather than humans are consuming the data. For example, Semantic Web data that is consumed by applications like maps and calendar programs can be ascertained to be actually relevant.

Finally, while generic Semantic Web inference may not help in answering simple keyword-based queries for entities and concepts, further research needs to be done to determine if inference can help answer complex queries. While in most keyword-based searches the name of the information need is mentioned directly in the query, which in our experiment results from choosing the queries via a named entity recognizer, in complex queries only the type or attributes of the information need are mentioned directly. The name of particular answers is usually unknown. Therefore, some kind of inference may be crucial in determining what entities or concepts match the attributes or type mentioned in the query terms. For example, the SemSearch 2011 competition's 'complex query' task was very difficult for systems that did well on keyword search, and the winning system used a customized crawling of the Wikipedia type hierarchy (Blanco et al. 2011a).

6.9.1   Experimental Conclusions

This study features a number of results that impact the larger field of semantic search. First, it shows a rigorous information retrieval evaluation, the 'Cranfield paradigm', can be applied to semantic search despite the differences between the Semantic Web and hypertext. These differences are well-recorded in our sample of the Semantic Web as taken via FALCON-S using a query log, and reveals a number of large differences between the Semantic Web data and hypertext data, in particular that while relevant data for ordinary open-domain queries does appear on the Semantic Web, Semantic Web data is in general more sparse than hypertext data when given a keyword query from an ordinary user's hypertext Web search. However, when the Semantic Web does contain data relevant to a given query, that data is likely to be accurate information, a fact we exploit in our techniques.

Unlike previous work in semantic search that focuses usually on some form of PageRank or other link-based ranking, we concentrate on using techniques from information retrieval, including language models and vector-space models, over

Semantic Web data. Relevance feedback from hypertext Web data can improve Semantic Web search, and even vice versa, as we have rigorously and empirically shown. While relevance feedback is known to in general improve results, our use of wildly disparate sources of data such as the structured Semantic Web and the unstructured hypertext Web to serve as relevance feedback for each other is novel. Furthermore as regards relevance feedback, we show using vector-space models over hypertext data is optimal while language models are optimal when operating over Semantic Web. These techniques (as evidenced by the failure of relevance feedback to beat baseline results with incorrect parametrizations) must be parametrized correctly and use the correct weighting and ranking algorithm to be successful. It is shown by our results to be simply false to state that relevance feedback always improves performance over hypertext and Semantic Web search, but only under certain (although easily obtainable) parameters. We do this by treating both data sources as 'bags of words' and links in order to make them compatible and find from the Semantic Web high quality terms for use in language models. Also, untraditionally, we turn the URIs themselves into words. Our results demonstrate that our approach of using feedback from hypertext Web search helps users discover relevant Semantic Web data. The gain is significant over both baseline systems without feedback and the state of the art page-rank based mechanism used by FALCON-S and Yahoo! Web search. Furthermore, the finding of relevant structured Semantic Web data can even be improved by pseudo-feedback from hypertext search.

More exciting to the majority of users of the Web is the fact that apparently relevance feedback from the Semantic Web can improve hypertext Web search. However, pseudo-feedback also improves the quality of results of hypertext Web search engines, albeit to a lesser degree. Interestingly enough, using inference only hurt performance, due to the rather obscure terms from higher-level ontologies serving functionally as 'noise' in the feedback. Lastly, pseudo-feedback from the hypertext Web can help Semantic Web search today and can be easily implemented. Indeed, the key to high performance for search engines is the use of high quality data of any kind for query expansion, whether it is stored in a structured Semantic Web format or the hypertext Web. However, the Semantic Web, by its nature as a source of curated and formalized data, seems to be a better source of high quality data than the hypertext Web itself, albeit with less coverage. While it is trivial to observe that as the Semantic Web grows, semantic search will have more importance, it is surprising to demonstrate that as the Semantic Web grows, the Semantic Web can actually improve hypertext search.

6.9.2 The Equivalence of Sense and Content

The operative philosophical question is: Why does relevance feedback work between such diverse encodings? Although there appears to be a huge gulf between the Semantic Web and the hypertext Web, it is precisely because the same *content* is encoded in the unstructured hypertext and the structured Semantic Web representations that these two disparate sets of data can be used as relevance feedback for each other. This leads to an exciting conclusion, and one that complexifies the earlier picture of semantics considerably. If the Semantic Web is fundamentally about extending the Web to those things outside the Web, then we have to acknowledge that most of the current hypertext Web is already representational.

It is precisely the notion that sense – and therefore meaning as whole – is 'objective' that is crucial for our project of reconstructing meaning on the Web via computational traces of user behavior. The Fregean notion of sense is *identical* with our reconstructed notion of informational *content*. The content of information is precisely what is shared between the source and the receiver as a result of the conveyance of a particular message. By definition, this holding of content in common which is the result of the transmission of an information-bearing message *must* by definition involve at least *two* things: a source and a receiver. Furthermore, if the source and receiver are considered to be human agents capable of speaking natural language, then by the act of sharing sentences, which are just encodings shared over written letters or acoustic waves in natural language, the two speakers of language are sharing the content of those sentences. Since the content is possessed by two people, and is by definition of information the *same* content, insofar as *subjective* is defined to be that which is only possessed by a single agent and *objective* is defined to be that which is possessed by more than one agent (although not necessarily all agents), then *content is objective*.

The productive concepts from Web architecture map to the notion of a Fregean sense rather easily. Sentences and terms natural in a language have both a syntactic encoding and a semantic content (sense) that can realized over differing physical substrates. This is equivalent to how encodings like HTML and RDF enable a web-page author to share a particular sense with someone browsing the Web. A sentence is a fully-fledged information-carrying message that can have multiple realizations in the form of different utterances at different points in space and time, just as the selfsame web-page can be sent from different spatially-located servers at different times. The Gricean notion of a speaker's intentions then maps to the meaningful behavior a sentence is supposed to engender, which can be thought of as equivalent to the rendering and user behavior created as a result of interaction with the Web (Grice 1957). Yet this mapping creates new problems: the problem of sense disambiguation is now revealed to be much larger than previously supposed, as it now stretches into all sorts of non-natural languages, ranging from logical languages RDF to markup languages like HTML. Everything from messages in computer protocols (formal languages) to paintings (iconic languages) are now just encodings of information, and these too have senses and so possible ambiguities.

Representations are not just then 'in the head' but also present as an objective component of sentences as the *sense* of *names*. In particular, a name in natural language is no more than some encoding that has as its interpretation the sense of a (possibly and usually distal!) referent. The class of *proper names*, long a source of interest, is just a representation in natural language whose referent is an entity, such that the name 'TimBL' refers to the person Tim Berners-Lee, while the larger class of names such as 'towers' or 'integers' can refer to groups of entities and concepts. There may be some objection that a mere *name* in a sentence is a full-blooded representation. However, unlike some theories of representation such as those put forward by Cummins, we do not require that there be some "isomorphism" or other structured relationship between the representation and its referent (1996), we require the much less-demanding causal relationship with some impact upon the sense (content) and thus the meaningful behaviour of the agent. While it is obvious there is nothing inherent in the term 'Eiffel Tower' that leads the letters or phonemes in the name to correspond in any significant structural way with the Eiffel Tower itself, as long as the sense of the name is dependent on *there being a referent* that the name 'stands-in' for, so a name like the 'Eiffel Tower' is still a representation of the Eiffel Tower itself. The referent itself or some 'image' thereof does not have to be bundled along and carried with the sentence in any meaningful way. Our previous exposition of the representational cycle demonstrates that representation is primarily an historical chain with the first-mover of causal efficacy being the referent.

6.10   The Representational Nexus

The key insight of this experiment is that *Fregean sense is the same as informational content.* As sense walks hand-in-hand with our notion of reference, then it can also be said that multiple representations on the Web, both in hypertext and on the Semantic Web, can share the same sense. It is precisely this point that we so laboriously argued in Chap. 2, where we gave an account of the construction of a robust notion of content on top of information given in multiple and possibly non-natural language encodings. The convergence of informational content with linguistic sense is liberating for the philosophy of language, because while previously issues of sense and reference seem to have primarily been bound to natural languages, the move of identifying content with sense and sentences with encodings opens a whole new enterprise: the impact of sense and reference on non-natural languages, in particular the study of formal languages created by digital technology like the Web. Our interest in this is how these issues of meaning, sense, and reference can be analyzed in context with the World Wide Web. Surprisingly, classical problems of sense and reference re-emerge with a vengeance on the Web.

Representations can now be rethought as spread across multiple encodings. We call *the multitude of representations that share the same content* the **representational nexus** of the referent, a potentially large collection of representations in a variety of formal, natural, and even iconic languages that all share the same referent. For example, if one uses a search engine to look for the 'Eiffel Tower,' one gets a large number of web-pages that are to some extent all *about* the Eiffel Tower by virtue of having some meaningful relationship with it, ranging from pictures of the Eiffel Tower, maps to the Eiffel Tower and possibly even videos of the Eiffel Tower. These would all count as representations of the Eiffel Tower, and so would be part of the representational nexus of the Eiffel Tower. Therefore, the aggregate 'bag-of-words' of all these representations would be an even more adequate notion of sense than just the tags explicitly given to a resource. Yet imagine how large of a landscape this opens for sense, for it allows us to apply search terms, documents, queries, Semantic Web representations – almost anything! – as part of the creation of sense in aggregate.

This large aggregation has been phrased as the "database of intentions" by John Batelle, "the aggregate results of every search ever entered, every result list ever tendered, and every path taken as a result" (2003). This should remind us that behind all of these representations are the concrete needs of ordinary users of the Web. Our task is to now attempt to phrase a philosophical theory of meaning adequate to this enlarged position of sense on the Web.

Chapter 7
Social Semantics

Language is the body of the mind.

Anton Pannekoek *(1912)*

7.1 Introducing Social Semantics

As sense is objective, existing theories of representation must be reconstructed in order to create a theory of semantics that places this insight at its core. Yet is it really so odd to find in tag-clouds and search engine queries an objective notion of meaning? It should not be, as all of our examples so far have relied upon natural language, an everyday form of representation whose existence is objective by virtue of being public. It is precisely the social and thus public notion of language that has been strangely missing from the debates on reference and meaning on the Web so far. This is not a new philosophical insight: Wittgenstein points to a social and public notion of language when he says, "Do not ask yourself 'How does it work with me?' – ask 'What do I know about someone else?' " (Wittgenstein 1953). The use of language to co-ordinate action is public and inexorably social, involving more than one agent. So a third position, in contrast to both the logical and direct reference positions, can now be staked.

The **social semantics position** states that *meaning in language exists due to a form-of-life, and so names have a sense as a mechanism for the co-ordination of actions among multiple agents*. Importantly, social semantics enables us to advance an even more general theory of representation: namely that semantics as a clear and unambiguous mapping to a referent does not exist, but that representations are actually temporal-spatial extensions of things themselves, a kind of new collectivity that challenges any notion of a pre-given ontology.

The core of Wittgenstein's radical shift away from the logical atomism-as-metaphysics he espoused in *Tractatus* to his later work as exemplified by *Philosophical Investigations* was his own personal encounter with a form of embodied language that seemed to resist the straightjacket of logically-organized sense-data.

H. Halpin, *Social Semantics: The Search for Meaning on the Web*,
Semantic Web and Beyond 13, DOI 10.1007/978-1-4614-1885-6_7,
© Springer Science+Business Media New York 2013

When Wittgenstein was arguing with Piero Sraffa that everything in the world must be expressible by the grammar of logic, Sraffa made a flicking of his fingers underneath his chin, asking Wittgenstein, "What was the grammar of that?" (Monk 1991). Realizing that no logical grammar did justice to Sraffa's act, Wittgenstein abandoned his view of language as logic and rephrased it in terms of a "language game" (1953). The term **language-game** is "meant to bring into prominence the fact that the speaking of language is part of an activity, or of a form of life" (Wittgenstein 1953). So, languages are composed of *actions in the world*. Wittgenstein also points out that all the terms in a language derive their meaning from this interwoven web of action and words, so that the words compose a language in virtue of their relationships to other words and actions, for "these phenomena have no one thing in common which makes us use the same word for all – but that they are related to one another in many different ways. And it is because of this relationship, or these relationships, that we call them all 'language' ..." (Wittgenstein 1953). He illustrates language-games by reference to the Augustinian example of commanding a builder to stack building blocks in a certain order (1953), an example curiously computationalized by Terry Winograd in his famous SHRDLU program, where the point is not to refer to 'true' states-of-affairs but the creation of an actual building (1972).[1] Words are uttered with the extent intention of bringing into purpose a change of state of affairs of the world.[2]

To contrast this position with the direct reference position, the meaning of a URI is not determined by whatever referent is assigned to it by its owner, unless the owner and other agents actually can come to an agreement on its meaning. Social semantics does not give the owner of a URI any particular privilege, except for the obvious asymmetric technical privilege of having the ability to influence the use of the URI through hosting an accessible web-page or redirecting it to another URI. This radically undermines any 'special' knowledge of meaning given to experts by Putnam (1975), or any magical powers of naming thought to take place in a Kripkean

---

[1]"Let us imagine a language for which the description given by Augustine is right. The language is meant to serve for communication between a builder A and an assistant B. A is building with building-stones: there are blocks, pillars, slabs and beams. B has to pass the stones, and that in the order in which A needs them. For this purpose they use a language consisting of the words "block," "pillar," "slab," "beam." A calls them out; – B brings the stone which he has learnt to bring at such-and-such a call ..." (Wittgenstein 1953).

[2]We concur with Dummett that any account of meaning will have in essence three layers, where the outer layer has priority over the inner layers. First, the "core" would be the "theory of reference" while "surrounding the theory of reference will be a shell, forming the theory of sense" so that "the theory of reference and the theory of sense form together one part of the theory of meaning: the other, supplementary, part is the theory of force" (Dummett 1993b). Dummett calls *force*, the *intended use* of the sentence, as shown syntactically by mood (1993b). Wittgenstein also fails to be a strict behaviorist, for he also endorses a notion of purpose, by stating "It is in language that an expectation and its fulfillment make contact" (1953). We leave it to other theorists like Millikan to discuss a thorough exploration of intended purpose (1989), perhaps by deriving how the Darwinian notion of proper function can serve as an account for sense and intended purpose – and so contradicting Wittgenstein's statement that "Darwin's theory has no more to do with philosophy than any other hypothesis in natural science" (1921).

baptism (Kripke 1972). Baptizing is actually *social* and cannot function purely causally, since the naming convention requires communication between more than one person. The only way it could be purely causal would be if every person using the name had some form of direct acquaintance with the referent. The chain between the act of naming and the use of the name depends on reference. Ambiguities and errors can happen. For example, Gareth Evans pointed out famously that African natives may have used the word 'Madagascar' to refer to the African mainland but when Marco Polo heard it, he thought it referred to an island off of Africa. What should be clear is that the ambiguity remains, and even Kripke himself says "a name refers to an object if there exists a chain of communication, stretching back to baptism, at each stage of which there was a successful intention to preserve reference" (1972). The notion of success is undefined, but it is clear that the chain is not just one of causation, but of communication and so subject to ambiguity since communication often employs description, which by its nature is open to interpretation.

To contrast social semantics with descriptivist theories of reference, there is not a pre-given ontology (universe) of things that can even ambiguously serve as referents to representations by virtue of their satisfaction of descriptions. Instead of thinking of logic in terms of descriptions that have interpretation mappings to a world, logical semantics can be thought of as descriptions of an agent's public behavior. In terms of URIs, Wittgenstein does not equate the meaning of a sentence with truth or the satisfaction of a model unless these are accepted by all agents that use the URI. Wittgenstein retorts that only "in our language" can "we apply the calculus of truth" (Wittgenstein 1953). However, we would hold that Wittgenstein is being too curt, and that logical-based inference can approximate the shared meaning between agents, so logic (and logical ambiguity) becomes not a weakness but a strength.

Just as we found analogues of the descriptivist and causal theories of reference in the positions of Hayes and Berners-Lee, is there an existing computational analogue of this third position of social semantics? We believe so, and the answer lies in the theory of meaning implicit in information retrieval: the derivation of meaning via massive statistics that approximate the 'use' of a URI on the Web.

7.1.1 The Hidden History of Search Engines

The hidden lineage of social semantics comes, rather surprisingly, from existing Web search engines like Google. Information retrieval, and its data-driven methodology, *are* neo-Wittgensteinian philosophy of language given computational flesh, as held by Wilks (2008b). The discipline of information retrieval is directly descended from Wittgenstein himself via the under-appreciated philosopher and linguist Margaret Masterman. The secret history of how Wittgenstein influenced Web search engines is itself a fascinating trajectory. After all, Wittgenstein's infamous dictum that "meaning is use" seems often itself meaningless upon first glance; how can "meaning is use" possibly be operationalized into a basis for a science of language (Wittgenstein 1953)? The answer is obvious: in studying the structure of language empirically, which is to be done computationally by the statistical analysis of actual samples of human language. In other words, in the building of "language processing programs which had a sound philosophical basis" (Wilks 2005).

One of the six students of Wittgenstein's course that became *The Blue Book*, Masterman was exposed directly by Wittgenstein to the conceptual apparatus of the *Philosophical Investigations* (Sowa 2006). Twenty years later, she founded the Cambridge Language Research Unit, where the foundations for information retrieval were laid by a student of Masterman and Masterman's husband Richard Braithwaithe, Karen Spärck Jones (Wilks 2007). In her dissertation *Synonymy and Semantic Classification*, Spärck Jones stated that her dissertation proposed "a characterisation of, and a basis for deriving, semantic primitives, i.e. the general concepts under which natural language words and messages are categorized" (Spärck Jones 1986). She did this by applying the statistical 'Theory of Clumps' of Roger Needham – a theory that was itself one of the first to explicate what Wittgenstein called "family resemblances" – to words themselves, leading her to posit that words could be defined in terms of statistical clumps of other words (Needham 1962). Her technique prefigures much of the later work in the 'statistical turn' of natural language research and our own work in statistical notions of sense based on terms in the previous two chapters. Applying her work over larger and larger sources of natural language data, she later abandoned even the open-ended semantic primitives of Masterman. In her later critique of artificial intelligence, she argued that one of the key insights of information retrieval is that programs should take "words as they stand" and not as only adjuncts to some logical knowledge representation system (Spärck Jones 1999). The connection to search engines is clear: Altavista, the first modern Web search engine, was created after its inventor, Mike Burrows, e-mailed Spärck Jones and Needham over techniques in information retrieval.

Search engines work via analysis of existing web-pages, breaking them down into terms, and then mapping those terms and their frequencies in a given web-page into a large index. So, each URI can be thought of as collection of terms in this search engine index. As the collection of term frequencies gathered into this index grows, ranging over larger and larger sources of data like the Web, it approximates human language use, as has been shown by studies in computational linguistics (Keller and Lapata 2003). Users of a search engine then enter certain terms, the search query is mapped via certain algorithms against the index. This results in an unordered list of possibly relevant URIs, which for an index that covers the entire Web range from thousands to millions of URIs. In turn these URIs are then ranked and ordered using an algorithm such as Google's famous PageRanking algorithm, possibly with user feedback (Brin and Page 1998). To explicate how user-based relevance feedback works, search engines usually keep track of what URIs are actually clicked on by users. This stream of clicks by multiple users can be stored in a query log, and this query log can then be used to improve the discovery and ranking of URIs by search engines. By inspecting which terms lead to which URIs for multiple users, a set of terms that best describes a URI for users can be discovered. In this way, typing in terms into a search engine can be thought of as what Wittgenstein would term a 'language-game,' with success in this game being judged in terms of whether or not a given user can discover a relevant URI via the right keywords. The terms themselves may be ambiguous, but it does not matter if a relevant URI is discovered. In this way, the objective sense of a URI can be considered the search terms that can be used by multiple users to find a particular URI. What a URI means is precisely the set of search terms that leads multiple users to discover the URI in the context of satisfying a particular information need.

Tagging can then thought of as simply saving the keywords and even adding new terms to this game *after* the initial discovery of the URI to help the user find it again later, which would be particularly useful if the search engine changed its underlying algorithm or the terms used to discover the URI were counterintuitive. While the user may not be aware of it, as it *appears* that searching the Web using a search engine is a private experience, it is in fact mediated by a vast amount of web-pages stored in the search engine's index and the behavior of previous search users. So, in fact searching the web is both recordable and amendable to computational analysis, and is a prime example of the Fregean dictum that meaning is objective. Tagging is only easier for us to understand as *public* because the tags stored are usually publicly accessible on most systems (although they do not have to be). It is precisely this notion of meaning as public and objective that is the foundation for the later Wittgenstein's work, which in turn serves as the philosophical foundation for social semantics on the Web.

7.1.2   *Against Private Language*

One of the hidden presumptions of the descriptivist and causal theory of reference is the tradition that language can be a *private* phenomenon, that is possessed and used by a single agent to accurately describe and refer to the world. Wittgenstein, whose *Tractatus* was the original inspiration for this position, returned to refute this massive misinterpretation of his ideas by Russell, Carnap, and other logical positivists in his *Philosophical Investigations* (Wittgenstein 1953). Wittgenstein attacks the very idea of a private language, a language that is somehow only understood by a single person and hence untranslatable to other languages, where "the individual words of this language are to refer to what can only be known to the person speaking; to his immediate private sensations. So another person cannot understand the language" (Wittgenstein 1953). His primary example is the use of a language to describe sensations of pain. Wittgenstein argues that such a language is absurd, as there would be no "right" way to use the private word for the sensation, for "whatever is going to seem right to me is right" (1953). In his second famous attack on private language, Wittgenstein phrases an attack on private codes of behavior in the infamous example of rule-following in a game like chess, stating that: "It is not possible that there should have been only one occasion on which only one person obeyed a rule" (1953). Meaning in language is social, or it is not meaningful at all (as in a private language) and instances of language use must be objectively available as information in order for it to affect multiple agents. So ultimately meaning must involve *others*, where the meaning is precisely the effect of content upon behavior, is repeated in different circumstances and mediates the collective behavior of multiple agents.

Strangely enough, there is a deep metaphysical affinity between both the descriptivist and causal theories of reference as they both depend crucially on the notion of the undeniably *true* and yet *private* notion of direct acquaintance by individuals with sense-data. Kripkean baptism is just a sort of *ostentative* relationship between sense-data and a name, exemplified by the act of saying 'the name of that is the Eiffel Tower.' This supposedly 'causal' account of baptism is precisely the same as Russell's account of the use of names via direct acquaintance. A Russellian descriptivist would simply have some sense-data that they could label with 'that is an iron tower' and then generalize to other sets of 'sense data' to which one can apply the terms 'iron' and 'tower' via more complex logical statements involving towers and their descriptions. Likewise, the idea of direct acquaintance with sense-data equally underpins both Putnam and Berners-Lee, as both think that reference should be determined by expertise, for instead of just labeling a patch of sense-data with the term 'iron tower,' the scientists would label the sense-data with a name like 'iron tower' only after it successfully passed some authoritative test, such as a test for the chemical composition of iron.

The infamous example of the 'duck-rabbit' is Wittgenstein's attack on the notion of this true yet subjective sense data, and so undermines the very idea of establishing a referent via direct acquaintance and baptism (Wittgenstein 1953). If one cannot determine that a simple sketch is of a 'duck' or a 'rabbit,' then how can *anyone* objectively and without ambiguity attach a name to *any* patch of sense-data?[3] The indeterminacy of the infamous 'duck-rabbit' shows that, at least in some cases, there is no determinate nature of our phenomenological sense-data. Having disposed of the notion of ostentation somehow providing direct access to sense-data, Kripkean baptism is attacked next.

Wittgenstein holds that any act of baptism is incapable of assigning a name if the act is done by a private individual, "naming appears as a *queer* connection of a world with an object – and you really get such a queer connection of a word when a philosopher tries to bring out the relations between name and thing by staring at an object in front of him and repeating a name or even the word 'this' innumerable times" (Wittgenstein 1953). Indeed, such a relationship between a name and a thing must be social if it is not to descend into some sort of occultism. Only in a very rarefied imagination is this even possible because "naming is so far not a move in the language-game any more than putting a piece in its place on a board is a move in chess. We may say: *nothing* has so far been done, when a thing has been named. It has not even *got* a name except in the language game. This is what Frege meant too, when he said that a word has meaning only as part of a sentence" (Wittgenstein

---

[3]This point of Wittgenstein directly foreshadows the argument for the *indeterminacy of translation* of Quine (1960).

1953). Indeed, naming as a purely private convention serves no purpose. Names can only exist as part of a wider language. Even what appears to be the most private of sensory experiences is both determined and expressed by a public language.[4]

As championed by Searle's account of "social reality" in natural language, a name has meaning via the use and acceptance of speech acts in public language, so that a Kripkean baptism is only one kind of a wide array of possible speech acts (Searle 1995). To broaden our horizon, descriptions can be considered another kind of speech act in public language. Without this acknowledgment of a social semantics creating a shared objective social reality via its effects and usage by participating agents, we have no choice but to ascribe certain seemingly magical referential powers to baptism or mysteriously connect logical descriptions with sense-data via direct acquaintance. The magical connection between words and meaning, and between representations and referents, is revealed by social semantics to be founded on nothing other than the deployment of language for collective co-ordination.

7.2   Representations as Dynamic Ontology

We began with an investigation of representations not merely as explanatory factors in common-sense or scientific knowledge, but as matters of ontological fact.[5] Is there an objective criterion that can determine whether any thing *really* qualifies as a representation, regardless of the epistemological question of whether humans can know this is the case. This is a very distinct question from whether or not representations are inside the head – as is the focus of innumerable debates in artificial intelligence and cognitive science (Fodor 1975). One can accept not knowing whether or not there is an inner mental language but still accept that on some level the Mona Lisa is really – in other words, ontologically – a representation. This is also far beyond any arguments for representations being useful or not useful in terms of explanations in science (Bechtel 1998). One reason our investigation of representations has focused on the Web is precisely to take the anti-humanist position that whether or not something is a representation should be *independent* of any human observer – so that its sense can be thought of as objective.

---

[4]This is far from an exhaustive account of the many arguments against private language by Wittgenstein. The simple Cartesian example of dreaming would suffice to undermine any idea that sense-data is unquestionably a true given. However, while Descartes would have statements about 'sense data' made while dreaming be false, Wittgenstein would prefer those statements to simply be meaningless, neither strictly true or false. As he said in one of his last written statements towards the end of his life: "Someone who, dreaming, says 'I am dreaming,' even if he speaks audibly in doing so, is no more right than if he said in his dream 'it is raining,' while it was in fact raining. Even if his dream were actually connected with the noise of the rain" (Wittgenstein 1969).

[5]We use the term 'ontology' in its full philosophical meaning here rather than the more restrained engineering meaning of the term for the Semantic Web.

In Chap. 2, we carefully constructed in our theory of encoding-content duality what appears to be a thoroughly classical ontological framework for understanding semantics. This same framework is phrased by Wittgenstein when reading Augustine's "particular picture of the essence of human language" as the following: "The individual words in language name objects – sentences are combinations of such names. In this picture of language we find the roots of the following idea: Every word has a meaning. This meaning is correlated with the word. It is the object for which the word stands" (1953). Think of it in terms of this picture: there is a world where there are human agents, and *inside* their heads – inaccessible to others and so subjective – there is a shining aura, which is a manifestation of a magical meaning-making ability that connects referents to representations. When these humans encounter patches of sense-data via their sensory organs, the object impresses a representation into their heads, a sort of 'photocopy' or mental image with the selfsame content as the object. When the content is mentally encoded into an information-bearing message that transfers to another receiving agent, that agent's shining aura of intentionality shines in the same manner as the sender – i.e. they subjectively share the same true object as a referent of both their representations. This is the picture of meaning being 'inside the head,' and it is precisely this picture which is crumbling as a result of our study of the Web.

The objectivity of Fregean sense causes a profound shift in the metaphysical presuppositions of classical representational theory. Indeed, this is the source of Fregean's division of the subjective idea from the objective meaning, and his utter hostility to any thought of subjective ideas being the basis for mathematics and logic, as demonstrated in his review of Husserl's *Philosophy of Arithmetic* (Frege 1894). Frege does not completely discount the notion of referents as subjective ideas, but instead notices that sense determines the possible referents which various objects can satisfy (Frege 1892). So, instead of imagining the magical aura of meaning being a property of the agents, imagine that *any object* that encounters a human agent is bestowed a shining aura of meaning – which superficially appears to be the sort of explanation that we are advocating in our social 'meaning-as-use' position. However, this picture misrepresents our notion of the social as ridiculously human-centric, as any humanist notion of the social as a magic meaning-sauce is exceptionally ill-suited to understanding the notion of machine-driven semantics on the Web, where humans may be simply out of the loop entirely for a given interaction. Instead, a more adequate picture of Fregean meaning-as-objective would have all objects shining with meaning, with humans just being another object on par with blocks, trees, and so on. Meaning is literally a property of the world. Yet does this picture not simply descend into a sort of mysticism? Saying everything is meaningful is structurally the same as saying that nothing is meaningful since there is no difference that can make a difference.

Each generation must overcome its own subject-object contradiction, including the generation of the Web. The subject-object dichotomy reveals itself as a dichotomy between referent and representation, and reappears within the representation itself as a division between encoding and content. The point of social semantics is this: Meaning is not just a mapping between encoding (representation) and content (referent), but a reconciliation of this dichotomy; this is accomplished via the content (sense) being the objective and so governing the behavior of agents on a social level. So at long last ***meaning*** can be defined as *the causal effect of information as demonstrated by the collective social behavior of agents.*

There are also deeper ramifications not only on the agents, but the world. One of the central problems of both the descriptivist and causal theory of reference is that representation is imagined as attached to referents in an external, pre-given static world. The problem may not be representations per se, but the particular static ontology of the world of the classical theories of meaning, and so the mathematical models of the world in classical logic. Let's return to our representational cycle as given in Chap. 2, in which representations are held to be representations by virtue of a historical, causal chain spread out over time and space with their referents. There is a latent contradiction in the Web which we do not solve: namely, as representations are defined by *separation* over time and space, the inexorable trajectory of the Web is bent on eliminating this very division of time and space. The cycles of representation become ever more infinitesimal as the Web interconnects referents ever closer with their representational nexus. At a certain point, the operative question becomes whether or not the representational nexus simply becomes a new kind of first-class object?[6] In other words, the ontology of the world is dynamic, created as an enactment between a multiplicity of objects and representations that alter each of them in turn. A representation of an object is the *spreading out* of an object in time and space. It is not to say that the representational cycle and its vocabulary of referents disappear, but that they are mediated by objective sense and that the formation of a representation is just the first step of the unfolding of a new kind of object. In such a dialectic, the map becomes the territory.

Take the practical example of an ubiquitous Semantic Web; while today when we encounter commodities such as tomatoes on sale at the super-market we are unaware of their social history (they appear on the shelves as if by magic!), imagine a world where the Web made all that information public and immediately accessible. So when one saw a tomato, one would be informed of where it was picked and by whom, by what manner it arrived, the costs of this operation. Imagine this information being immediately available when one encountered the tomato, and imagine also that various information about yourself (such as your allergies, your previous meals, even aesthetic preferences) were available as well, and could even interact with the information about the tomato in real-time. Would not the entire *nature* of the tomato and your interaction with the world be altered, so that it would be correct to call the tomato and its extended nexus of representations a new kind of object? In this manner, we do not mean 'objective' to be defined in terms of a vision of the world from some God's eye vantage point independent of any subject, but

---

[6]This is distinctly opposed to the viewpoint of certain post-structuralist or postmodern theorists like Baudrillard who hold that representations are 'copies' that are just as real or true as their original referent (Baudrillard 1994). Instead, we challenge this belief in a singularly real or authentic (and so static) ontology by incorporating the referent and representation into a new ontological object.

that meaning is objective insofar as meaning *creates* objects. Representation returns as a *re*-presentation of a referent, which is nothing more than the *presence* of a new object being born.[7]

We can finally rephrase our picture of the world and representation to take into account this fundamental insight of social semantics. Instead of saying 'everything is interconnected,' we would preserve the scientific prerogative that 'some things are more or less connected than others' and it is the active reconfiguration of these objects that leads to a dynamic ontology that is far removed from the classical unchanging referents of our earlier picture. Instead of imagining everything shining with meaning, imagine a picture where the various objects in our ontology encounter each other, shining with greater or lesser intensity as they dynamically form new assemblages; these in turn transforming into new objects before our very eyes. There is no reason this process should be merely an immense ever-increasing agglomeration, as it should also feature the dimming and even dissolution of objects. The creation and destruction of these ontologies is social not in the sense of social as a property of interactions between agents (although that is surely how it begins), but social as seen as anything outside, over and above, the individual. The goal is not to drown ourselves in the social totality, but to emphasize how ontologies *pass through the world*. The social is not the inter-subjective individual sharing of information, but the objective coming-into-being of an object via ever-decreasing latency over time and space. This philosophical insight is at the present moment given form by a practical universalizing engineering project: URIs on the Web.

While this picture seems strange enough, we should not fault Augustine for missing it. The ultimate argument against sense-data is that we do not *perceive* 'greeness here now!' but instead we perceive a tree directly *as a tree*. We perceive this precisely because our meaningful ontology inherited from both our social interaction and the development of our bodies includes trees – but from another level the trees can be seen as just a component in a larger object, that of the forest. Yet in Augustine's time there was such an almost unchanging medieval world that featured such a high latency between referents and their representations that he cannot be faulted for missing the dynamic nature of ontology. As our social co-ordinations are increasingly externalized and ever-increasingly constitutive of both ourselves and our world in this era of the Web, the dynamic ontology of the world should be much more obvious. In this way, we can escape the ontological framework we are born into by embracing the cognitive scaffolding necessary to continually re-invent the ontological lens through which we constitute ourselves and the world.

---

[7]The fact that on the Web these new objects are digital means that what we may be seeing now is the digitalization of the world, a notion that should be more widely explicated on its own.

7.3 A Statistical Semantic Web

If there is anything to be learned from this encounter of philosophy and the Web, it is that one can never escape philosophical problems, even on the Web. They cannot simply be ignored. The philosophy of language has had a large influence on knowledge representation languages in general, in particular the influence of logical theories of reference on artificial intelligence that has continued to influence the Web via Pat Hayes. Yet strangely enough, it is the philosophically untrained Berners-Lee that ends up arguing what has been accepted in philosophical circles as the causal theory of reference, a theory of reference that is widely accepted in some circles to be correct. Even more surprisingly, it appears that search engines like Google embody an alternative theory of meaning, one based on an objective notion of sense implicitly given by Wittgenstein. So how does social semantics play out for the Semantic Web?

The Semantic Web has yet to be widely deployed, and it could be precisely due to the persistence of these very problems of the philosophy of language regarding meaning and reference. We have argued that the debates over the meaning and reference of URIs can be seen as a return of the debate between the causal and descriptivist theories of reference in the philosophy language, with this time the subject being URIs rather than natural language names. In this way, it has been shown that in the course of the practice of computer science, even in such a new undertheorized and undisciplined frontier like the Web, robustly philosophical problems arise. In stumbling on the difficult philosophical problem of reference and meaning, it appears that the success of the Semantic Web, one of the most ambitious projects of knowledge representation so far, has been stymied. Unfortunately due to the hold of the descriptivist and causal theories of reference on the minds behind the Semantic Web, the 'Semantic' Web has no meaning for most users, but is a meaningless jumble of URIs threaded to together by a hard-to-understand knowledge representation language.

Wittgenstein says "to invent a language could mean to invent an instrument for a particular purpose" (Wittgenstein 1953). The purposes of evolved natural languages are incredibly varied, but new formal languages are invented for a purpose as well. What is the purpose of the Semantic Web? Why would anyone participate in this particular language game rather than the language game of the hypertext Web, or some other language game altogether? On this point, the Semantic Web is positively schizophrenic, vacillating between a *first-generation* vision of classical artificial intelligence replete with inference-driven agents, and a *second-generation* vision of opening databases according to the principles of Web architecture for applications that cannot yet be imagined. Obviously, these purposes have mostly been successful at attracting artificial intelligence researchers to the fold. The purpose of the Semantic Web is to find and incorporate new information into our form-of-life, into our very ontology.

The social semantics position on the Web can now answer our original question: What is the meaning of a URI? *Since the Web, including the Semantic Web, is a form of language, as a language exists as a mechanism for co-ordination among multiple* *agents, then the meaning of an URI is the use of the URI by a community of agents,* *a use that can be traced by the computational sense of the URI ranging across* *tags, queries, and whatever representations are hosted at the URI.* As information retrieval is only one kind of interaction with the Web, attaching the Semantic Web to more rich Web-mediated social interaction is exactly what is necessary to create a *third-generation* Semantic Web based on lived social interactions and dynamic ontologies. The use of a robust computational notion of sense should be able to automatically identify resources across multiple URIs in order to deliver timely information to users as needed, and so eventually create dynamic ontologies that respond in real-time to new information needs. Tagging systems show how this is already organically happening, and our initial results with search show how this process can be extended.

In contrast to Wilk's interpretation of Wittgenstein and computational linguistics (Wilks 2008b), we do not hold that either sense or a wider notion of meaning can be accounted for by some 'mental' lexicon or even massive statistics on word-use on the Web, although the latter would certainly play a role as a computational trace of a sense. Taking the role of embodiment and the world seriously, it would be a mistake to separate language from the world and the actions of agents therein. Therefore, natural language processing itself is not a firm foundation for semantics on the Web. On the contrary, it is crucial to attach the use of words and meaning to particular embodied language-games, like the use of search engines. After all, to use words to retrieve web-pages is vastly different than using words in dialogue with another human. Many of the characteristics of terms typed into search engines or tagging systems, such as their extreme brevity, will have no clear analogue to natural language use. The open-ended innovative use of language on the Web makes the creation of finite lexicons difficult if not impossible.

The most revolutionary concept of Wittgenstein is the *form-of-life*, and everything else in his philosophy flows from this. The key to understanding the form-of-life is that the meaning of a word is *not* just in other words, but in the entire activity of the agents that share the language that uses the word. If the Semantic Web is to succeed, it must take into account not only natural language, but the real activity of users on the Web, in order to base a new language-game upon this form of life. Currently, the primary approach is to build Semantic Web ontologies direct from the text in web-pages in natural language (Brewster et al. 2007). We should notice that there is a *particular* use of natural language on the Web that is hegemonic: the searching for information by using brief natural language keywords. While this is far from the only use of the Web, it is by far the most dominant, as shown by various studies of user behavior on the Web (Batelle 2003). This constant and near obsessive use of Web search engines *is* the de-facto cybernetic form of life on the Web. So, any attempt to 'boot-strap' a new language-game for the Semantic Web will have to take into account that the search for information via keywords and social networks is *fundamental* for the Web, a point routinely ignored by both the direct reference and the logicist positions.

While firmly based on Wittgenstein, the position that the Semantic Web is an attempt to create a new kind of language goes against a certain quietism of Wittgenstein, namely that "philosophy may in no way interfere with the actual use of language; it can in the end only describe it" (Wittgenstein 1953). This would lend credence to Wilk's position of the primacy of the lexicon (Wilks 1975) Social semantics on the Web is not a mere application of Wittgenstein's insights, but a profound transformation of them. Berners-Lee responds to such quietism with a radical riposte, that on the Web "we are not analyzing a world, we are building it" (Berners-Lee 2003a). This radical outlook that engineering systems *are* philosophy given a digital embodiment is best summarized by Berners-Lee himself in the statement that "we are not experimental philosophers, we are philosophical engineers" (2003a). So our approach is neo-Wittgensteinian rather than Wittgensteinian. In contrast to any purely descriptive science, the primary difference of what has been termed the "science of the Web" is that not only can engineered systems be constructed to test theories, as done in traditional modeling in almost all scientific fields, but these models can be released upon the world at large through the Web (Berners-Lee et al. 2006). We hope by integrating the Semantic Web with the work of information retrieval as pioneered by Karen Spärck Jones, the Semantic Web can have a second lease on life and be tested on a large scale as a truly universal space of data. The initial results as given so far are promising.

Furthermore, just because we find the descriptivist theory of reference insufficient does not mean logic should be neglected for the future of the Web: to do such a thing is throwing the impressive computational baby out with the muddled metaphysical bathwater. Inference could be useful for the Semantic Web. The question that bedeviled the causal theory of reference was that of ambiguity. Does ambiguity result from a failed use of language? Ambiguity is built into social semantics, and the kind of ambiguity that Wittgenstein is concerned with is not the kind of ambiguity resulting from entailments failing to constrain interpretations. For Wittgenstein, ambiguity is naturally constrained by the conventions of the language, which are restricted in turn by the external world. While neo-Wittgensteinian social semantics would note that there is always some ambiguity in language, worrying about this ambiguity misses the point, as the point of a language game is not to pin down names to referents exactly, but instead to share enough of a convention to accomplish some task or solve some problem. Ambiguity is usually solved by the embodied or implicit context given in the language. The role of descriptions and inference is not in determining referents, but rather only when the various agents in a language-game are not clear about the role of a name in a language game, so that "an explanation may indeed rest on another one that has been given, but none in need of another – unless *we* require it to prevent a misunderstanding" (Wittgenstein 1953). In this manner, inference and entailments that restrict interpretations, as defended by Hayes, are a logical analogue to the real-world context that both constrain ambiguity in a language game, while usually never dispelling it. While some inferential mechanisms can be useful when errors are made in a language game, in general inference cannot express all the constraints given by the contextual use of a name in a language game. However, it is a beginning, and an important one. As a methodology for formally specifying the behavior of machines, formal logic has barely begun.

Searching and tagging the large hypertext Web leads to a 'statistical semantic web,' where the meaning of a resource is given by the combined activity of users with that of massive statistically-driven algorithms that are based on the computational trace of the sense of a resource. In this way, the bet of using URIs as a universal naming scheme for things can just as easily be tied to statistical methods from information retrieval as to logic-based knowledge representations. Obviously, the use of URIs should be tied to both. To apply Wittgenstein to the Semantic Web, the first observation is that the Semantic Web *is* a *new* language-game. There is no reason why language-games in a Wittgensteinian sense have to be restricted to natural languages, for Wittgenstein himself notes that "new types of language, new language-games, as we may say, come into existence, and others become obsolete and get forgotten" (Wittgenstein 1953). The struggle over the Identity Crisis within the Semantic Web is precisely the struggle over the conventions of meaning needed for a new language. Remember that for social semantics the terms 'language' and 'sense' can be *neutral* between formal languages for computers and natural languages for humans. Formal languages are often mistakenly thought to be meaningless due to their not taking into account the concrete activity that occurs as a result of their use, instead mischaracterized as pure "syntax churning" (Harnad 1990). Given that agents can be computers just like humans, and computers have their own norms for behavior in terms of protocols, then there seems to be no reason why computers cannot create meaningful new language-games. So from the perspective of social semantics, when a new URI comes into play on the Semantic Web, the agents do not have to specify the referents of the URI to use it meaningfully. If the referent of a name has to be specified for the name to be used, it only has to be specified to the minimal conditions necessary to co-ordinate actions between agents. Contra Berners-Lee's direct reference position, only in very rare language games does the referent of some representation have to be specified in an 'unambiguous' manner. In fact, acknowledging the kinds of complex social-technical interactions of language and the world exemplified by the feedback loop between humans and search on the Web may indeed be more likely to do justice to the potential of the Web. There is much work to be done, for all we have presented so far is an informal sketch of social semantics, and a computationally operationalized and testable science of social computation is clearly the next step. In fact, there is no reason to believe that we will even understand the worlds we are bringing into being without the collective intelligence of the Web.

7.4   Towards Collective Intelligence

To explain collective intelligence, we should lean upon the Extended Mind thesis (Clark and Chalmers 1998). Clark and Chalmers introduce us to Otto, a man with an impaired memory who navigates about his life via the use of his notebook, in particular to the Museum of Modern Art (1998). Let us assume Otto has a serious memory impairment. Otto is trying to navigate to the Museum of Modern Art and uses his notebook as a surrogate memory in order to discover the location. Otto has a map in his notebook to the Eiffel Tower made for the precise purpose of navigating individuals to the monument. Otto can get to the museum with the map, but without the map he would be lost. In this regard, the map qualifies as an 'external' representation that can drive the cognitive processes of an agent in a similar fashion to the way that classical artificial intelligence assumed internal representations did. Interestingly enough, Clark points out that if external factors are driving the process, then they deserve some of the credit, for "if, as we confront some task, a part of the world functions as a process which, were it done in the head, we would have no hesitation in recognizing as part of the cognitive process, then that part of the world is (so we claim) part of the cognitive process" (1998). The map and other external representations have been dubbed "cognitive technology" (Clark 2000).

The Web then presents an interesting twist on the Extended Mind Hypothesis. Again, Otto is using a web-page on his mobile phone to find his way to the Museum of Modern Art. While we could have had Otto using the Web as ordinary Web users did years ago, simply downloading some directions and following them, we now add a twist. Imagine that Otto and Otto's friend Inga are using a map-producing web-page that allows users to add annotations and corrections, a sort of wiki of maps. Inga, noticing that the main entrance to the Museum of Modern Art is closed temporarily due to construction and so the entrance has moved over a block, adds this annotation to the map, correcting an error as regards where the entrance to the Museum of Modern Art should be. This correction is propagated at speeds very close to real-time back to the central database behind the Web site. Otto is running a few minutes behind Inga, and because this correction to the map is being propagated to his map on his personal digital assistant, Otto can successfully navigate to the new entrance a block away. This (near) real-time updating of the representation was crucial for Otto's success. Given his memory issues, Otto would have otherwise walked right into the closed construction area around the old entrance to the Museum and been rather confused. This active manipulation with updating of an external representation lets Inga and Otto possess some form of dynamically-changing collective cognitive state. Furthermore, they can use their ability to update this shared external representation to influence each other for their greater collective success. In this manner, the external representation is clearly social, and the cognitive credit must be spread across not only multiple people, but the representation they use in common to successfully accomplish their behavior. Clark and Chalmers agree that cognition can be socially extended: "what about socially extended cognition? Could my mental states be partly constituted by the states of other thinkers? We see no reason why not, in principle" (1998). We could extend their story by arguing that socially extended cognition is now mediated by external representations, in particular by digital representations and other information on the Web.

One of the obvious requirements for any process to be part of an extended mind is that it is accessible when needed to solve some problem. The obvious requirement is that the representation needed by the subject be within its effective reach, not separated from the subject in space or time. So if Otto's notebook with the map to the museum has been left at home in Boston when he is in New York, the notebook cannot count as part of his extended mind. Furthermore, if his notebook exists only in the past, having been was destroyed in a fire before Otto could use it, then the notebook also could not count as part of Otto's extended mind. The point here is that at least a minimal condition for anything to be cognitive technology is that it must be accessible over the bounds of space and time when needed with a reasonable latency – in other words, have "reliable coupling," (Clark and Chalmers 1998). The technical trajectory of Licklider's "Man-Machine Symbiosis" project, which could be considered the engineering twin of the philosophical Extended Mind thesis, is precisely to overcome the barriers of time and space that separate representations and their users and so allow the formation of not only new objects, but also new collective and digitally mediated *subjects*. The Web is just the latest incarnation of this trend.

One of the strange repercussions that follows straightforwardly from our neo-Wittgensteinian approach is that as more and more of language – and thus our shared sense that guides our behavior – gets encoded in external representations with the possibility of low-latency Web access, it becomes equally increasingly unclear where the precise boundary between the individual and their external representation lies. If the cycle of connection and disconnection happens constantly, over many individuals, the very boundaries of agents become difficult to detect. If we become dependent on the Web, defining intelligence in terms of a fully autonomous agent then becomes not even an accurate portrayal of human intelligence, but "a certain conception of the human individual that may have applied, at best, to that faction of humanity who had the wealth, power, and leisure to conceptualize themselves as autonomous beings exercising their will through individual agency and choice" (Hayles 1999). By jettisoning this conception, yet reconstructing the commitment to a certain kind or degree of embodiment, a new kind of philosophy that takes the Web seriously can do justice to complex phenomena such as the advent of the Web and the increasing recognition of what Engelbart termed "collective intelligence" (Engelbart and Ruilifson 1999). Pierre Levy notes that cognitive science "has been limited to human intelligence in general, independent of time, place, or culture, while intelligence has always been artificial, outfitted with signs and technologies, in the process of becoming, collective" (1994). The vast technological changes humanity has engendered across the world are now reshaping the boundaries of not only the world but ourselves. This process has been ongoing since the dawn of humanity, whose most momentous event was the evolution of natural language, but it has been happening on time-scales that we could not grasp within a single lifetime. Only now due to the incredible progress of the Web do changes in our language and ontology become self-evident within the scope of a single life. Social semantics makes this clear in terms of representation, but we have only begun to theorize this fundamental change on the level of the individual subject, which is rapidly being transformed by a world of representations into a collective intelligence. The task of the future is to both understand and bring into being this collective intelligence.

References

Allan J, Connell M, Croft WB, Feng FF, Fisher D, Li X (2000) INQUERY and TREC-9. In: Proceedings of the ninth text retrieval conference (TREC-9), Gaithersburg, pp 551–562

Althusser L (1912) Marxism And Darwinism. Verso, http://www.marxists.org/archive/pannekoe/1912/marxism-darwinism.htm. Accessed 9 Jan 2008 (trans: Weiser N)

Althusser L (1963) In: Marxism and humanism. For Marx, Verso, republished in 2005 by Verso (trans: Brewster B), Verso, London

Anderson C (2006) The long tail. Random House Business Books, London

Andrews K, Kappe F, Maurer H (1995) The Hyper-G network information system. J Univers Comput Sci 1(4):206–220

Anklesaria F, McCahill M, Linder P, Johnson D, Torrey D, Alberti B (1993) IETF RFC 1436 the Internet Gopher protocol. Category: informational. http://www.ietf.org/rfc/rfc1436.txt. Accessed 5 Oct 2008

van Assem M, Gangemi A, Brickley D (2006) RDF/OWL representation of WordNet. Editor's draft, W3C. http://www.w3.org/2001/sw/BestPractices/WNET/wn-conversion. Accessed 20 Nov 2008

Auer S, Bizer C, Lehmann J, Kobilarov G, Cyganiak R, Ives Z (2007) DBpedia: a nucleus for a web of open data. In: Proceedings of the international and Asian Semantic Web conference (ISWC/ASWC2007), Busan, pp 718–728

Baeza-Yates R (2008) From capturing semantics to semantic search: a virtuous cycle. In: Proceedings of the 5th European Semantic Web conference, Tenerife, pp 1–2

Baeza-Yates RA, Tiberi A (2007) Extracting semantic relations from query logs. In: Proceedings of the conference on knowledge discovery and data-mining (KDD), San Jose, pp 76–85

Bar-Yam Y (2003) Dynamics of complex systems (Studies in Nonlinearity). Westview Press, Boulder

Batagelj V, Mrvar A (1998) Pajek – a program for large network analysis. Connections 21:47–57

Batelle J (2003) The database of intentions. http://battellemedia.com/archives/000063.php. Accessed 11 Dec 2008

Bateson G (2001) Steps to an ecology of mind. University of Chicago Press, Chicago

Baudrillard J (1994) Simulacra and simulation. University of Michigan Press, Ann Arbor

Bechtel W (1998) Representations and cognitive explanations: assessing the dynamicist's challenge in cognitive science. Cogn Sci 22:295–318

Berners-Lee T (1989) Information management: a proposal. Technical report, CERN. http://www.w3.org/History/1989/proposal.html. Accessed 12 July 2008

Berners-Lee T (1991) Document naming. Informal draft. http://www.w3.org/DesignIssues/Naming. Accessed 28 July 2008

H. Halpin, *Social Semantics: The Search for Meaning on the Web*,
Semantic Web and Beyond 13, DOI 10.1007/978-1-4614-1885-6,
© Springer Science+Business Media New York 2013

Berners-Lee T (1994a) IETF RFC 1630 Universal Resource Identifiers (URI). http://www.ietf.org/
    rfc/rfc1630.txt. Accessed 3 May 2008
Berners-Lee T (1994b) World wide web future directions. Plenary talk. http://www.w3.org/Talks/
    WWW94Tim/. Accessed 5 Oct 2008
Berners-Lee T (1996a) Generic resources. Informal draft. http://www.w3.org/DesignIssues/
    Generic.html. Accessed 4 Dec 2008
Berners-Lee T (1996b) Universal Resource Identifiers: axioms of web architecture. Informal draft.
    http://www.w3.org/DesignIssues/Axioms.html. Accessed 5 Sept 2008
Berners-Lee T (1998a) Cool URIs don't change. http://www.w3.org/Provider/Style/URI. Accessed
    19 Nov 2008
Berners-Lee T (1998b) Semantic Web road map. Informal draft. http://www.w3.org/DesignIssues/
    Semantic.html. Accessed 12 Apr 2008
Berners-Lee T (1998c) What the Semantic Web can represent. Informal draft. http://www.w3.org/
    DesignIssues/rdfnot.html. Accessed 12 Sept 2008
Berners-Lee T (2000) Weaving the web. Texere Publishing, London
Berners-Lee T (2003a) Message on www-tag@w3.org list. http://lists.w3.org/Archives/Public/
    www-tag/2003Jul/0158.html. Accessed 15 Nov 2008
Berners-Lee T (2003b) Message to www-tag@w3.org. http://lists.w3.org/Archives/Public/www-
    tag/2003Jul/0127.html. Accessed 15 Nov 2008
Berners-Lee T (2003c) Message to www-tag@w3.org. http://lists.w3.org/Archives/Public/www-
    tag/2003Jul/0022.html. Accessed 15 Nov 2008
Berners-Lee T, Connolly D (1993) IETF working draft HyperText Markup Language (HTML):
    a representation of textual information and metainformation for retrieval and interchange.
    http://www.w3.org/MarkUp/draft-ietf-iiir-html-01.txt
Berners-Lee T, Cailliau R, Groff JF, Pollermann B (1992) World-Wide Web: the information
    universe. In: Electronic Networking: Research, Applications, Policy. 1(2):74–82
Berners-Lee T, Fielding R, McCahill M (1994) IETF RFC 1738 Uniform Resource Locators
    (URL). Proposed standard. http://www.ietf.org/rfc/rfc1738.txt. Accessed 3 Sept 2008
Berners-Lee T, Fielding R, Frystyk H (1996) IETF RFC 1945 HyperText Transfer Protocol
    (HTTP/1.0). http://www.ietf.org/rfc/rfc1945.txt. Accessed 5 Oct 2008
Berners-Lee T, Fielding R, Masinter L (1998) IETF RFC 2396 Uniform Resource Identifiers
    (URI): generic syntax. http://www.ietf.org/rfc/rfc2396.txt. Accessed 15 Sept 2008
Berners-Lee T, Hendler J, Lassila O (2001) The Semantic Web. Sci Am 284(5):35–43
Berners-Lee T, Hall W, Hendler J, Shadbolt N, Weitzner DJ (2006) Creating a science of the web.
    Science 313(5788):769–771
Berners-Lee T, Fielding R, Masinter L (2005) IETF RFC 3986 Uniform Resource Identifiers
    (URI): generic syntax. http://www.ietf.org/rfc/rfc3986.txt. Accessed 2 Apr 2008
Bizer C, Cygniak R, Heath T (2007) How to publish linked data on the web. http://www4.wiwiss.
    fu-berlin.de/bizer/pub/LinkedDataTutorial/. Accessed 28 May 2008
Bizer C, Heath T, Idehen K, Berners-Lee T (2008) Linked data on the web. In: Proceedings of the
    WWW2008 workshop on linked data on the web, Beijing. URL http://CEUR-WS.org/Vol-369/
    paper00.pdf
Blanco R, Halpin H, Herzig D, Mika P, Pound J, Thompson H, Duc TT (2011a) Entity search
    evaluation over structured web data. In: Proceedings of the 1st international workshop on entity-
    oriented search workshop (SIGIR 2011), ACM, New York
Blanco R, Halpin H, Herzig D, Mika P, Pound J, Thompson H, Duc TT (2011b) Repeatable and
    reliable search system evaluation using crowd-sourcing. In: Proceedings of the 34th annual
    international ACM-SIGIR conference on research and development in information retrieval,
    ACM Press, Beijing
Boley H, Kifer M (2008) RIF Basic Logic Dialect. Working draft, W3C. http://www.w3.org/TR/
    rif-bld/. Accessed 8 Aug 2008
Bollen D, Halpin H (2009) An experimental analysis of suggestions in collaborative tagging. In:
    Web intelligence, Milan, pp 108–115
Borden J, Bray T (2002) Resource Directory Discovery Language (RDDL). http://www.rddl.org/

Bornholdt S, Ebel H (2001) World Wide Web scaling exponent from Simon's 1955 model. Phys Rev E 64(3):(R)–1 035104–4

Bouquet P, Stoermer H, Tummarello G, Halpin H (eds) (2007) Proceedings of the WWW2007 workshop I^3: Identity, Identifiers, Identification, entity-centric approaches to information and knowledge management on the web, Banff, 8 May 2007, CEUR Workshop Proceedings, CEUR-WS.org

Bouquet P, Stoermer H, Tummarello G, Halpin H (eds) (2008) Proceedings of the ESWC2008 workshop on identity, reference, and the web, Tenerife, 1st June 2008, CEUR Workshop Proceedings

Box D, Ehnebuske D, Kakivaya G, Layman A, Mendelsohn N, Nielsen H, Thatte S, Winer D (2000) Simple Object Access Protocol (SOAP) 1.1. http://www.w3.org/TR/2000/NOTE-SOAP-20000508/

Brachman R (1983) What IS-A is and isn't: an analysis of taxonomic links in semantic networks. IEEE Comput 16(10):30–36

Brachman R, Smith B (1980) Special issue on knowledge representation. SIGART Newsl 70:1–38

Brachman R, Schmolze J (1985) An overview of the KL-ONE knowledge representation system. Cogn Sci 9(2):171–216

Bray T, Paoli J, Sperberg-McQueen C (1998) Extensible Markup Language (XML). Recommendation, W3C. http://www.w3.org/TR/1998/REC-xml-19980210. Accessed 10 Mar 2008

Brewster C, Iria J, Zhang Z, Ciravegna F, Guthrie L, Wilks Y (2007) Dynamic iterative ontology learning. In: Proceedings of the recent advances in natural language processing conference (RANLP), Borovets

Brickley D, Guha RV (2004) RDF Vocubulary Description Language 1.0: RDF Schema. Recommendation, W3C. http://www.w3.org/TR/rdf-schema/. Accessed 15 Nov 2008

Brin S, Page L (1998) The anatomy of a large-scale hypertextual web search engine. In: Proceedings of the international conference on World Wide Web (WWW), Brisbane, pp 107–117

Brooks R (1991) Intelligence without representation. Artif Intell 47(1–3):139–159

Bush V (1945) As we may think. Atl Mon 1(176):101–108

Butterfield S (2004) Folksonomy. http://www.sylloge.com/personal/2004/08/folksonomy-social-classification-great.html. Accessed 15 Nov 2008

Carnap R (1928) The logical structure of the world. University of California Press, Berkeley. Republished in 1967

Carnap R (1947) Meaning and necessity: a study in semantics and modal logic. University of Chicago Press, Chicago

Carnap R (1950) Empiricism, semantics, and ontology. Rev Int Philos 4:20–40

Carnap R, Bar-Hillel Y (1952) An outline of a theory of semantic information. Technical Report, RLE-TR-247-03150899, Research Laboratory of Electronics, Massachusetts Institute of Technology

Carpenter B (1996) IETF RFC 1958 architectural principles of the Internet. http://www.ietf.org/rfc/rfc1958.txt. Accessed 12 Mar 2008

Cattuto C (2006) Semiotic dyanmics in online social communities. Eur. Physc. J. C 46(2):33–37

Cerf V, Kahn R (1974) A protocol for packet network intercommunication. IEEE Trans Commun 22(4):637–648

Chalmers D (1995) Facing up to the problem of consciousness. J Conscious Stud 2(3):200–219

Chalmers DJ (2006) Two-dimensional semantics. In: Lepore E, Smith BC (eds) Oxford handbook of the philosophy of language. Oxford University Press, New York

Cheng G, Ge W, Qu Y (2008) FALCONS: searching and browsing entities on the Semantic Web. In: Proceedings of the the World Wide Web conference, Beijing

Chomsky N (1957) Syntactic structures. Mouton, Paris

Cilibrasi R, Vitanyi P (2007) The Google similarity distance. IEEE Trans Knowl Data Eng 19(3):370–382

Clark K (1978) Negation as failure. In: Gallaire H, Minker J, Nicolas J (eds) Logic and databases. Plenum, New York

Clark A (1997) Being there: putting brain, body, and world together again. MIT Press, Cambridge

Clark A (2000) Mindware: an introduction to the philosophy of cognitive science. Oxford University Press, Oxford

Clark A, Chalmers D (1998) The extended mind. Analysis 58(1):7–19

Clauset A, Shalizi C, Newman M (2007) Power-law distributions in empirical data. http://arxiv.org/abs/0706.1062v1. Accessed 13 Oct 2008

Connolly D (1998) The XML revolution. Nature. http://www.nature.com/nature/webmatters/xml/xml.html. Accessed 3 Apr 2008

Connolly D (2002) An evaluation of the World Wide Web with respect to Engelbart's requirements. Informal Draft. http://www.w3.org/Architecture/NOTE-ioh-arch. Accessed 4 Dec 2008

Connolly D (2006) A pragmatic theory of reference for the web. In: Proceedings of identity, reference, and the web workshop at the WWW conference. http://www.ibiblio.org/hhalpin/irw2006/dconnolly2006.pdf. Accessed 22 Nov 2008

Connolly D (2007) Gleaning Resource Descriptions from Dialects of Languages (GRDDL). Technical report, W3C recommendation. URL http://www.w3.org/TR/grddl/

Craswell N, Zaragoza H, Robertson S (2005) Microsoft Cambridge at TREC-14: enterprise track. In: Proceedings of the seventh text retrieval conference (TREC-7), Gaithersburg, p http://research.microsoft.com/apps/pubs/default.aspx?id=65241. Accessed 10 Jan 2009

Cui H, Wen JR, Nie JY, Ma WY (2002) Probabilistic query expansion using query logs. In: Proceedings of the 11th international conference on World Wide Web (WWW 2002). ACM, New York, pp 325–332

Cummins R (1996) Representations, targets, and attitudes. MIT, Cambridge

Dellschaft K, Staab S (2008) An epistemic dynamic model for tagging systems. In: Proceedings of the 19th ACM conference on hypertext and hypermedia (HYPERTEXT'08). ACM Press, New York, pp 71–80

Delugach H (2007) ISO Common logic. Standard, ISO. http://cl.tamu.edu/. Accessed 8 Mar 2008

Dennett D (1981) Brainstorms: philosophical essays on mind and psychology. MIT Press, Cambridge

DeRose S, Maler E, Orchard D (2001) XML Linking (XLink) version 1.0. Technical report, W3C Recommendation. http://www.w3.org/TR/xlink/. Accessed 12 Nov 2008

Detlefsen M (1990) Brouwerian intuitionism. Mind 99(396):501–534

Ding L, Finin T (2006) Characterizing the semantic web on the web. In: Proceedings of the international Semantic Web conference (ISWC), Athens, pp 242–257

Dowty D (2007) Compositionality as an empirical problem. In: Barker C, Jacobson P (eds) Direct compositionality. Oxford University Press, Oxford, pp 23–101

Dretske F (1981) Knowledge and the flow of information. MIT, Cambridge

Dreyfus H (1979) What computers still can't do: a critique of artificial reason. MIT, Cambridge

Dummett M (1973) Frege: philosophy of language. Duckworth, London

Dummett M (1993a) What is a theory of meaning. In: The seas of language. Oxford University Press, Oxford, pp 1–33. (Originally published in Truth and meaning: essays in semantics in 1976)

Dummett M (1993b) What is a theory of meaning. In: The Seas of Language. Oxford University Press, Oxford, pp 1–33. (Originally published in Mind and language in 1975)

Engelbart D (1962) Augmenting human intellect: a conceptual framework. Technical report, Stanford Research Institute, aFOSR-3233 summary report

Engelbart D (1990) Knowledge-domain interoperability and an open hyperdocument system. In: Proceedings of the conference on computer-supported collaborative work, Los Angeles, pp 143–156

Engelbart D, Ruilifson J (1999) Bootstrapping our collective intelligence. ACM Comput Surv 31(4):38. URL http://portal.acm.org/citation.cfm?id=346040

Ferraiolo J (2002) Scalar Vector Graphics (SVG) 1.0 specification. Recommendation, W3C. http://www.w3.org/TR/2001/REC-SVG-20010904/. Accessed 22 Apr 2008

Fielding R (2010) Architectural styles and the design of network-based software architectures. Ph.D. thesis, University of California, Irvine

Fielding R, Gettys J, Mogul J, Frystyk H, Berners-Lee T (1999) IETF RFC 2616 HyperText Transfer Protocol – HTTP 1.1. http://www.ietf.org/rfc/rfc2616.txt. Accessed 2 Apr 2008

Fleiss J (1971) Measuring nominal scale agreement among many raters. Psychol Bull 76:378–382

Floridi L (2004) Open problems in the philosophy of information. Metaphilosophy 35(4):554–582

Fodor J (1975) The language of thought. MIT, Cambridge

Foucault M (1970) The order of things: an archaeology of the human sciences. Pantheon Books, New York

Fountain A, Hall W, Heath I, Davis H (1990) Microcosm: an open model for hypermedia with dynamic linking. In: Proceedings of hypertext: concepts, systems and applications (ECHT), Paris, pp 298–311

Frege G (1892) Uber sinn und bedeutung. Zeitshrift fur Philosophie and philosophie Kritic 100:25–50. Reprinted in Frege G (1956) The philosophical writings of Gottlieb Frege (trans: Black M). Blackwell, Oxford

Frege G (1894) Rezension von E. Husserl: Philosophie der arithmetic. Zeitschrift fur Philosophie und Philosophische 103:313–332

Galloway A (2004) Protocol: how control exists after decentralization. MIT Press, Boston

Gangemi A (2008) Norms and plans as unification criteria for social collectives. J Auton Agents Multi-Agent Syst 16(3):70–112

Gangemi A, Presutti V (2009) Ontology design patterns. In: Staab S, Studer R (eds) Handbook on ontologies, 2nd edn. Springer, Berlin

Gerber A, van der Merwe A, Barnard A (2008) A functional semantic web architecture. In: Proceedings of the 5th European Semantic Web conference, Tenerife, pp 273–287

Gligorov R, Aleksovski Z, ten Cate W, van Harmelen F (2008) Using Google distance to weight approximate ontology matches. In: Proceedings of 16th international World Wide Web conference (WWW'07), Banff, Alberta. ACM Press, pp 767–775

Golder S, Huberman B (2006) Usage patterns of collaborative tagging systems. J Inf Sci 32(2):198–208

Goodman N (1968) Languages of art: an approach to a theory of symbols. Bobbs-Merrill, Indianapolis

Grice P (1957) Meaning. Philos Rev 66:377–388

Guha RV (1996) Meta Content Framework: a whitepaper. http://www.guha.com/mcf/wp.html. Accessed 11 Aug 2008

Guha RV, Lenat D (1993) Language, representation and contexts. J Inf Process 15(3):149–174

Guha R, McCool R, Miller E (2003) Semantic search. In: Proceedings of the international conference on World Wide Web (WWW). ACM, New York, pp 700–709

Hafner K, Lyons M (1996) Where wizards stay up late: the origins of the internet. Simon and Schuster, New York

Halasz F, Schwartz M (1994) The Dexter hypertext reference model. Commun ACM 37(2):30–39

Halevy AY, Norvig P, Pereira F (2009) The unreasonable effectiveness of data. IEEE Intell Syst 24(2):8–12

Halpin H (2004) The Semantic Web: the origins of artificial intelligence redux. In: Proceedings of third international workshop on the history and philosophy of logic, mathematics, and computation (HPLMC-04 2005), Donostia San Sebastian. Republished in 2007 by Icfai University Press in The Semantic Web. http://www.ibiblio.org/hhalpin/homepage/publications/airedux.pdf. Accessed 2 Apr 2008

Halpin H (2006) Representationalism: the hard problem for artificial life. In: Proceedings of artificial life X, Bloomington, pp 527–534

Halpin H (2008a) Foundations of a philosophy of collective intelligence. In: Proceedings of convention for the society for the study of artificial intelligence and simulation of behavior, Aberdeen

Halpin H (2008b) Philosophical engineering: towards a philosophy of the web. APA Newsl Philos Comput 7(2):5–11

Halpin H (2009a) A query-driven characterization of linked data. In: Proceedings of the linked data workshop at the World Wide Web conference, CEUM-WS, Madrid

Halpin H (2009b) Sense and reference on the web. Ph.D. thesis, University of Edinburgh, School of Informatics, Institute for Communicating and Collaborative Systems, Edinburgh

Halpin H (2011) Sense and reference on the web. Minds Mach 21(2):153–178

Halpin H, Presutti V (2009) An ontology of resources: solving the identity crisis. In: Proceedings of the 6th European semantic web conference on the semantic web: research and applications. ESWC 2009 Heraklion. Springer, Berlin/Heidelberg, pp 521–534

Halpin H, Thompson HS (2009) Social meaning on the web: from Wittgenstein to search engines. IEEE Intell Syst 24(6):27–31

Halpin H, Presutti V (2011) The identity of resources on the web: an ontology for web architecture. Appl Ontol 6(3):263–293

Halpin H, Lavrenko V (2011a) Relevance feedback between hypertext and semantic web search: frameworks and evaluation. J Web Semant 9(4):474–489

Halpin H, Lavrenko V (2011b) Relevance feedback between web search and the semantic web. In: Proceedings of the international joint conference on artificial intelligence (IJCAI), Barcelona, pp 2250–2255

Halpin H, Hayes P, Thompson HS (eds) (2006) Proceedings of the WWW2006 workshop on identity, reference, and the web, CEUR Workshop Proceedings, Edinburgh, 23 May 2008

Halpin H, Robu V, Shepherd H (2007) The complex dynamics of collaborative tagging. In: Proceedings of the 16th international World Wide Web conference (WWW'07), Banff, pp 211–220

Halpin H, Clark A, Wheeler M (2010) Towards a philosophy of the web: representation, enaction, collective intelligence. In: Proceedings of the web science conference: extending the Frontiers of society on-line (WebSci 2010), Raleigh, pp 1–5

Halvey M, Keane MT (2007) An assesment of tag presentation techniques. In: Proceedings of the 16th international World Wide Web conference (WWW 2007). ACM Press, New York, pp 1313–1314

Harnad S (1990) The symbol grounding problem. Physica D 42:335–346

Haugeland J (1981) Analog and analog. In: Biro J, Shahan R (eds) Mind, brain, and function. Harvester Press, ACM, New York, pp 213–226

Haugeland J (1991) Representational genera. In: Ramsey WM, Stich SP, Rumelhart DE (eds) Philosophy and connectionist theory. Erlbaum, Mahwah, pp 61–89

Hawking D, Voorhees E, Craswell N, Bailey P (2000) Overview of the trec-8 web track. In: Proceedings of the text retrieval conference (TREC), ACM, pp 131–150

Hayes P (1977) In defense of logic. In: Proceedings of international joint conference on artificial intelligence, Massachusetts Institute of Technology, Cambridge, pp 559–565

Hayes P (1979) The naive physics manifesto. In: Michie D (ed) Expert systems in the micro-electronic age. Edinburgh University Press, Edinburgh, pp 242–270

Hayes P (2002) Catching the dream. http://www.aifb.uni-karlsruhe.de/~sst/is/WebOntologyLanguage/hayes.htm. Accessed 17 Oct 2008

Hayes P (2003a) Message to www-rdf-comments@w3.org. http://lists.w3.org/Archives/Public/www-tag/2003Jul/0147.html. Accessed 15 Nov 2008

Hayes P (2003b) Message to www-rdf-comments@w3.org. http://lists.w3.org/Archives/Public/www-tag/2003Jul/0198.html. Accessed 15 Nov 2008

Hayes P (2004) RDF Semantics. Recommendation, W3C. http://www.w3.org/TR/rdf-mt/. Accessed 21 Sept 2008

Hayes P (2006) In defense of ambiguity. In: Invited talk at the identity, reference, and the web workshop at the WWW conference, Edinburgh. http://www.ibiblio.org/hhalpin/irw2006/hayes.pdf

Hayes P, Halpin H (2008) In defense of ambiguity. Int J Semant Web Inf Syst 4(3):1–18

Hayles NK (1999) How we became posthuman: virtual bodies in cybernetics, literature and informatics. University of Chicago Press, Chicago

Hayles NK (2005) My mother was a computer: digital subjects and literary texts. University of Chicago Press, Chicago

Hegel G (1959) Säammtliche Werke. Fromann, Stuttgart

Hendler J, Golbeck J (2008) Metcalfe's law, Web 2.0, and Semantic Web. Web Semant 6(1): 14–20. http://dx.doi.org/10.1016/j.websem.2007.11.008

Hirst G (2000) Context as a spurious concept. In: Proceedings of context in knowledge representation and natural language, AAAI Fall Symposium, North Falmouth, pp 273–287

Israel D, Perry J (1990) What is information? In: Hanson P (ed) Information, language, and cognition. University of British Columbia Press, Vancouver, pp 1–19

Jacobs I (1999) W3C mission statement. Technical report, W3C. http://www.w3.org/Consortium/

Jacob E (2004) Classification and categorization: a difference that makes a difference. Libr Trends 52(3):515–540

Jacobs I, Walsh N (2004) Architecture of the World Wide Web. Technical report, W3C. http://www.w3.org/TR/webarch/. Accessed 12 Oct 2008

Jameson F (1981) The political unconscious. Cornell University Press, Ithaca, Vancouver

Jin RKX, Parkes DC, Wolfe PJ (2007) Analysis of bidding networks in eBay: aggregate preference identification through community detection. In: Proceedings of AAAI workshop on plan, activity and intent recognition (PAIR)

Keller F, Lapata M (2003) Using the web to obtain frequencies for unseen bigrams. Comput Linguist 29(3):459–484

Klyne G, Carroll J (2004) Resource Description Framework (RDF): concepts and abstract syntax. Recommendation, W3C. http://www.w3.org/TR/rdf-concepts/

Koller D, Pfeffer A (1998) Probabilistic frame-based systems. In: Proceedings of the 15th national conference on artificial intelligence, Madison, pp 580–587

Kripke S (1972) Naming and necessity. Harvard University Press, Cambridge

Lavrenko V (2008) A generative theory of relevance. Springer, Berlin

Lavrenko V, Croft WB (2001) Relevance-based language models. In: Proceedings of the twenty-fourth annual international ACM-SIGIR conference on research and development in information retrieval. ACM Press, New Orleans, pp 120–127

Leiner B, Cerf V, Clark D, Kahn R, Kleinrock L, Lynch D, Postel J, Roberts L, Wolff S (2003) A brief history of the internet. http://www.isoc.org/internet/history/brief.shtml. Accessed 20 Mar 2008

Lenat D (1990) Cyc: towards programs with common sense. Commun ACM 8(33):30–49

Levensque H, Brachman R (1987) Expressiveness and tractability in knowledge representation and reasoning. Comput Intell 3(1):78–103

Levy P (1994) Collective intelligence: mankind's emerging world in cyberspace. Plenum Press, New York

Lewis D (1971) Analog and digital. Nous 1(5):321–327

Licklider J (1960) Man-computer symbiosis. IRE Trans Hum Factors Electron 1:4–11

Luntley M (1999) Contemporary philosophy of thought. Blackwell, London

Lyotard JF (1988) The inhuman: reflections on time. Editions Galilee, Paris, France, republished 1998 by Blackwell (Trans: Bennington and Rachel Bowlby), London

Mandelbrot B (1953) An informational theory of the statistical structure of languages. In: Jackson W (ed) Communication theory. Academic, New York

Mangold C (2007) A survey and classification of semantic search approaches. Int J Metadata Semant Ontol 2(1):23–34

Manning C, Schutze H (2002) Foundations of statistical natural language processing. MIT, London

Marlow C, Naaman M, Boyd D, Davis M (2006) Position paper, tagging, taxonomy, flickr, article, toread. In: Collaborative web tagging workshop at WWW'06, Edinburgh

Masterman M (1961) Semantic message detection for machine translation, using an interlingua. In: Proceedings of international conference on machine translation of languages and applied language analysis, London

Mathes A (2004) Folksonomies: cooperative classification and communication through shared metadata. http://www.adammathes.com/academic/computer-mediated-communication/folksonomies.html

McCarthy J (1959) Programs with common-sense. Nature 188:77–91. http://www-formal.stanford.edu/jmc/mcc59.html

McCarthy J (1980) Circumspection – a form of nonmonotonic reasoning. Artif Intell 1(13):27–39

McCarthy J (1992) 1959 memorandum. IEEE Ann Hist Comput 14(1):20–23. Reprint of original memo made in 1952

McCarthy J, Hayes P (1969) Some philosophical problems from the standpoint of artificial intelligence. In: Meltzer B, Michie D (eds) Machine intelligence, vol 4. Edinburgh University Press, Edinburgh, pp 463–502

McCarthy J, Minksy M, Rochester N, Shannon C (1955) A proposal for the Dartmouth summer research project on artificial intelligence. Technical report, Dartmouth College. http://www-formal.stanford.edu/jmc/history/dartmouth/dartmouth.html. Accessed 12 Mar 2008

McDermott D (1987) A critique of pure reason. Comput Intell 33(3):151–160

McKay D (1955) The place of meaning in the theory of information. In: Cherry E (ed) Information theory. Basic Books, New York, pp 215–225

Mealling M, Daniel R (1999) IETFRFC 2483 URI resolution services necessary for URN resolution. Experimental. http://www.ietf.org/rfc/rfc2483.txt. Accessed 13 Apr 2008

Mendelsohn N (2006) The self-describing web. Draft TAG finding, W3C. http://www.w3.org/2001/tag/doc/namespaceState-2006-01-09.html. Accessed 7 Mar 2008

Mika P (2005) Ontologies are us: a unified model of social networks and semantics. In: Proceedings of the 4th international Semantic Web conference (ISWC'05). LNCS, vol 3729. Springer, Berlin/Heidelberg

Mikheev A, Grover C, Moens M (1998) Description of the LTG system used for MUC. In: Seventh message understanding conference: Proceedings of the Message Understanding Conference, Fairfax

Millikan R (1984) Language, thought and other biological categories: new foundations for realism. MIT, Cambridge

Millikan R (1989) Biosemantics. J Philos 86:281–297

Millikan R (2004) Varieties of meaning. MIT, Cambridge

Minsky M (1975) A framework for representing knowledge. In: Winston P (ed) The psychology of computer vision. McGraw Hill, Columbus, pp 211–277

Moats R (1997) IETF RFC 2141 URN syntax. http://www.ietf.org/rfc/rfc2141.txt

Mockapetris P (1983) IETF RFC 882 domain names – concpets and facilities. http://www.ietf.org/rfc/rfc882.txt. Accessed 12 Mar 2008

Mogul J (2002) Clarifying the fundamentals of HTTP. In: Proceedings of the 11th international World Wide Web conference(WWW), Honolulu, pp 444–457

Monk R (1991) Ludwig Wittgenstein: the duty of genius. Penguin, New York

Monnin A, Limpens F, Gandon F, Laniado D (2010) Speech acts meet tagging: nicetag ontology. In: Proceedings of the 6th international conference on semantic systems. I-SEMANTICS '10. ACM, New York, pp 31:1–31:10. http://doi.acm.org/10.1145/1839707.1839746, URL http://doi.acm.org/10.1145/1839707.1839746

Mueller V (2008) Representation in digital systems. In: Proceedings of Current Issues in Computing and Philosophy. Amsterdam http://www.interdisciplines.org/adaptation/papers/7. Accessed 8 Mar 2008

Needham R (1962) A method for using computers in information classification. In: Proceedings of the IFIP congress, Vienna, pp 284–287

Nelson T (1965) Complex information processing: a file structure for the complex, the changing and the indeterminate. In: Proceedings of 20th national conference of the association for computing machinery, Cleveland, pp 84–100

Newell A (1980) Physical symbol systems. Cogn Sci 1(4):135–183

Newman MEJ (2004) Fast algorithm for detecting community structure in networks. Phys Rev E 69:066133

Newman M (2005) Power laws, pareto distributions and Zipf's law. Contemp Phys 46:323–351

Newman MEJ, Girvan M (2004) Finding and evaluating community structure in networks. Phys Rev E 69: 026113

Parsia B (2003) Message to www-rdf-comments@w3.org. http://lists.w3.org/Archives/Public/www-rdf-comments/2003JanMar/0366.html. Accessed 15 Nov 2008

Pennebaker W, Mitchell J (1992) Joint photographic still image data compression standard (Standard, ISO). Van Nostrand Reinhold, New York

Poblete B, Baeza-Yates R (2008) Query-sets: using implicit feedback and query patterns to organize web documents. In: WWW '08: Proceeding of the 17th international conference on World Wide Web. ACM, New York, pp 41–50

Ponte JM (1998) A language modeling approach to information retrieval. Ph.d. dissertation, University of Massachusets

Postel J (1982) IETF RFC 821 simple mail transfer protocol. http://www.ietf.org/rfc/rfc821.txt

Postel J (1994) IETF RFC 1590 media type registration procedure. Category: informational. http://www.ietf.org/rfc/rfc1590.txt

Postel J, Reynolds J (1985) IETF RFC 959 File Transfer Protocol: FTP. http://www.ietf.org/rfc/rfc959txt

Presutti V, Gangemi A (2008) Identity of resources and entities on the web. Int J Semant Web Inf Syst 4(2):49–72

Prud'hommeaux E, Seaborne A (2008) SPARQL Query Language for RDF. Recommendation, W3C. http://www.w3.org/TR/rdf-sparql-query/

Putnam H (1975) The meaning of meaning. In: Gunderson K (ed) Language, mind, and knowledge. University of Minnesota Press, Minneapolis

Quillian MR (1968) Semantic memory. In: Minsky M (ed) Semantic information processing. MIT, Cambridge, pp 216–270

Quine WVO (1951) Two dogmas of empiricism. Philos Rev 60:20–43

Quine W (1960) Word and object. MIT, Boston

Raggett D, LeHors A, Jacobs I (1999) HTML 4.01 specification. Recommendation, W3C. http://www.w3.org/TR/REC-html40/

Rattenbury T, Good N, Naaman M (2007) Towards automatic extraction of event and place semantics from Flickr tags. In: Press A (ed) Proceedings of SIGIR'07, Amsterdam, pp 103–110

Reiter R (1978) On closed world data bases. In: Gallaire H, Minker J (eds) Logic and data bases. Plenum Publishing, New York

Robertson SE, Spärck Jones K (1976) Relevance weighting of search terms. J Am Soc Inf Sci 27:129–146

Robertson SE, Walker S, Jones S, Hancock-Beaulieu MM, Gatford M (1994) Okapi at TREC-3. In: Proceedings of the third text retrieval conference (TREC-3), Gaithersburg, pp 109–126

Robertson S, Zaragoza H, Taylor M (2004) Simple BM25 extension to multiple weighted fields. In: Proceedings of the ACM international conference on information and knowledge management (CIKM). ACM, Washington, pp 42–49

Robu V, Poutré JAL (2006) Retrieving utility graphs used in multi-item negotiation through collaborative filtering. In: Proceedings of RRS'06, Hakodate (Springer LNCI, to appear)

Robu V, Halpin H, Shepherd H (2009) Emergence of consensus and shared vocabularies in collaborative tagging systems. ACM Trans Web 3:14:1–14:34

Rocchio J (1971) Relevance feedback in information retrieval. In: Salton G (ed) The SMART retrieval system: experiments in automatic document processing. Prentice-Hall Inc., Uppder Saddle River, pp 313–32

Russell B (1905) On denoting. Mind 14:479–493

Sarwar B, Karypis G, Konstan J, Riedl J (2001) Item-based collaborative filtering recommendation algorithms. In: Tenth international World Wide Web conference (WWW10), Hong Kong

Schank R (1972) Conceptual dependency: a theory of natural language understanding. Cogn Psychol 3(4):532–631

Schmidt-Schauss M (1989) Subsumption in KL-ONE is undecidable. In: Proceedings of the 1st international conference on principles of knowledge representation and reasoning, M. Kaufmann, San Mateo, pp 421–431

Searle J (1995) The construction of social reality. The Free Press, New York

Shannon C, Weaver W (1963) The mathematical theory of communication. University of Illinois Press, Urbana. Republished 1963

Shen K, Wu L (2005) Folksonomy as a complex network. http://arxiv.org/abs/cs.IR/0509072

Silverstein C, Marais H, Henzinger M, Moricz M (1999) Analysis of a very large web search engine query log. SIGIR Forum 33(1):6–12

Simon H (1955) On a class of skew distribution functions. Biometrika 42(3/4):425–440

Simondon G (1958) Du mode d'existence des objets techniques. Aubier, Paris, France, english Translation accessed on the web at http://accursedshare.blogspot.com/2007/11/gilbert-simondon-on-mode-of-existence.html. Accessed 7 Sept 2008

Smith BC (1984) Reflection and semantics in LISP. In: Proceedings of 11th ACM SIGACT-SIGPLAN symposium on principles of programming languages. ACM, New York, pp 23–35

Smith BC (1986) The correspondence continuum. In: Proceedings of the sixth Canadian conference on artificial intelligence, Montreal

Smith BC (1991) The owl and the electric encyclopedia. Artif Intell 47:251–288

Smith BC (1996) On the origin of objects. MIT, Cambridge

Smith BC (1997) One hundred billion lines of C++. LeHigh Cog Sci News 1(10). http://www.ageofsignificance.org/people/bcsmith/papers/smith-billion.html

Smith BC (2002) The foundations of computing. In: Scheutze M (ed) Computationalism: new directions. MIT, Cambridge

Sollins K, Masinter L (1994) IETF RFC 1737 functional requirements for Uniform Resource Names. http://www.ietf.org/rfc/rfc1737.txt. Accessed 20 Apr 2008

Sowa J (1976) Conceptual graphs for a data base interface. IBM J Res Dev 20(4):336–357

Sowa J (1987) Semantic networks. In: Shapiro S (ed) Encyclopedia of artificial intelligence. Wiley and Sons, New York, pp 1011–1024

Sowa J (2006) Review of language, cohesion, and form by Margaret Masterman. Comput Linguist 4(32):551–553

Spärck Jones K (1986) Synonymy and semantic classification. Edinburgh University Press, Edinburgh

Spärck Jones K (1999) Information retrieval and artificial intelligence. Artif Intell J 114:257–281

Spärck Jones K (2004) What's new about the Semantic Web?: Some questions. SIGIR Forum 38(2):18–23

Suchanek FM, Vojnovic M, Gunawardena D (2008) Social tags: meaning and suggestions. In: 17th ACM conference on information and knowledge management (CIKM 2008), Napa Valley

Tarski A (1935) The concept of truth in formalized languages. Studia Philosophia 1:261–405. Reprinted in Tarski A (1956) Logic, semantics and metamathematics (trans: Woodger JH). Oxford University Press, Oxford

Tarski A (1944) The semantic conception of truth and the foundations of semantics. Philos Phenomenol Res 4:341–375

Thompson H, Beech D, Maloney M, Mendelsohn N (2004) XML Schema part 1: structures. Recommendation, W3C. http://www.w3.org/TR/xmlschema-1/

Togia T, McNeill F, Bundy A (2010) Harnessing the power of folksonomies for formal ontology matching on the fly. In: Proceedings of the ISWC 2010 workshop on ontology matching, Shanghai

Turing AM (1950) Computing machinery and intelligence. Mind 59:433–460

Wadler P (2001) The Girard-Reynolds isomorphism. In: International symposium of theoretical aspects of computer software, Sendai

Waldrop MM (2001) The dream machine: J.C.R. Licklider and the revolution that made computing personal. Penguin, New York

Walsh N, Thompson H (2007) Associating resources with namespaces. TAG finding. http://www.w3.org/2001/tag/doc/nsDocuments/

Watts D, Strogatz S (1998) Collective dynamics of 'small-world' networks. Nature 393(6684): 440–442

Wheeler M (2005) Reconstructing the cognitive world: the next step. MIT, Cambridge

Wheeler M (2008) The Fourth Way: a comment on Halpin's 'Philosophical Engineering'. APA Newsl Philos Comput 8(1):9–12

Wiener N (1948) Cybernetics or control and communication in the animal and the machine. MIT, Cambridge

Wilks Y (1975) A preferential, pattern-seeking, semantics for natural language inference. Artif Intell 6(1):53–74

Wilks Y (2005) A personal memoir: Margaret Masterman (1910–1986). In: Masterman M (ed) Language cohesion and form. Cambridge University Press, Cambridge

Wilks Y (2007) Karen Spärck Jones (1935–2007). IEEE Intell Syst 22(3):8–9

Wilks Y (2008a) The Semantic Web: apotheosis of annotation, but what are its semantics? IEEE Intell Syst 23(3):41–49

Wilks Y (2008b) What would a Wittgensteinian computational linguistics be like? In: Proceedings of convention for the society for the study of artificial intelligence and simulation of behavior, Aberdeen

Winograd T (1972) Procedures as a representation for data in a computer program for understanding natural language. Cogn Psychol 3(1):1–191

Winograd T (1976) Towards a procedural understanding of semantics. Stanford artificial intelligence laboratory memo AIM-292. Computer Science Department, Stanford University, Stanford

Wittgenstein L (1921) Tractatus logico-philosophicus. Routledge, New York. Republished 2001

Wittgenstein L (1953) Philosophical investigations. Blackwell Publishers, London. Republished 2001

Wittgenstein L (1969) On certainty. Harper and Row, New York

Woods W (1975) What's in a link: foundations for semantic networks. In: Representation and understanding: studies in cognitive science. Academic, Orlando, pp 35–82

Xu J, Croft WB (1996) Query expansion using local and global document analysis. In: Proceedings of the nineteenth annual international ACM-SIGIR conference on research and development in information retrieval, Zurich, pp 4–11

Yule G (1925) A mathematical theory of evolution, based on the conclusions of Dr. J.C. Willis, F.R.S. Philos Trans R Soc London Ser B 213:21–87

Zimmerman H (1980) The ISO model of architecture for Open Systems Interconnection. IEEE Trans Commun 28(4):425–432

Index

A

Access, 4, 12, 14, 17, 21, 26–28, 30, 35, 37, 43–47, 49, 50, 52, 58, 60, 61, 65–68, 71, 77–80, 85, 87, 88, 92, 100, 101, 105, 123, 143, 179, 192, 202

Agent, 6, 17–20, 24, 27–35, 37–42, 44–50, 60–63, 67, 68, 71, 77, 78, 83, 85–88, 90, 91, 102, 105, 132, 146, 171, 176, 184, 185, 187–189, 191–202

Analog, 35, 153

Artificial intelligence (AI), 1–3, 5, 10, 11, 17, 49, 52, 53, 55–57, 61, 64, 81-83, 88, 190, 193, 197, 201

Authority, 21, 27, 29, 44, 103

B

Baptism, 102–104, 189, 192, 193

Berners-Lee, T., 2, 3, 5, 12, 14–17, 19, 21, 26–31, 36, 37, 42–44, 46, 47, 49, 51, 52, 56, 58, 59, 62, 64, 66, 71, 75, 76, 80–82, 86–89, 98, 101, 103–107, 184, 189, 192, 197, 199, 200

C

Carnap, R., 23, 89, 93–96, 191

Causal theory of reference, 89, 101–105, 191, 195, 197, 199

Channel, 12, 21, 22

Clark, A., 3, 6, 49, 200–202

Client, 18, 19, 21, 22, 27, 28, 37, 68, 74, 77, 78

Client-server architecture, 18, 68

Collective intelligence, 6, 82, 112, 200–203

Complete, 4, 44, 48, 61, 65, 93, 112, 118

Compositionality, 26, 97, 98

Concept queries, 153–156, 159, 179

Connected, 14, 37, 39, 40, 54, 58, 90, 110, 136, 137, 193, 196

Consistent, 50, 61, 62, 93, 96, 108, 115, 116, 159

Content
negotiation, 31–34, 74, 75, 150
type, 19, 20, 32, 77, 79

Convention, 7, 18, 27, 68, 80, 85, 97, 189, 193, 199, 200

Coreferential URIs, 30, 149, 150

D

Depiction, 32, 37, 60, 72, 76

Description, 17, 32, 33, 37, 42, 54, 55, 60–62, 64, 66, 68, 72, 80, 82, 86, 91–95, 97–103, 108, 147, 149, 150, 166–167, 173, 188, 189, 192, 193, 199

Descriptivist theory of reference, 89, 91–102, 189, 191, 195, 197, 199

Digital, 2, 10, 11, 35–37, 39, 43, 44, 51, 52, 65, 66, 147, 152, 185, 196, 199, 201

Direct acquaintance, 41, 95, 96, 98, 100, 102, 189, 192, 193

Direct reference position, 5, 85, 89, 101–106, 187, 188, 200

Disconnected, 37, 38, 40, 43, 71

Domain name, 13, 27, 29, 30, 44, 46, 104

Dretske, F., 23, 24, 34

Dummett, M., 89–91, 106, 188

E

Encoding, 17–26, 30–37, 40, 41, 49, 51, 52, 56, 58, 65, 66, 74, 75, 79, 82, 91, 98, 147, 149, 150, 183–185, 194

Engelbart, D., 9, 11–14, 44–46, 66, 82, 202

H. Halpin, *Social Semantics: The Search for Meaning on the Web*, Semantic Web and Beyond 13, DOI 10.1007/978-1-4614-1885-6, © Springer Science+Business Media New York 2013